Contents at a Glar

D0128828

Table of Contents

Introduction

Welcome to *Public Speaking Skills For Dummies!*

If you're thumbing through this book, you've probably seen a speech or two in your life that had a message that really affected you. Maybe it made you think on the way home in a way that made your brain feel good, as if it were exercising. The speaker gave you the feeling that you were involved.

The next day you woke up depressed. How could someone be so darn convincing with nothing on the lectern but a glass of water?

Most people think of public speaking as just that: a well-dressed person under a spotlight with one of those headset microphones that are reserved for someone who is speaking to hundreds or thousands. These people are the elite of the public speaking world — they're the pros. But when you think of baseball, do you think only about the major leagues? Or do you have memories of playing as a youngster?

That's more like how this book treats public speaking. In my view, *public speaking* happens anytime anyone is speaking publicly. For some, that fancy mic is the goal. For others, maybe the goal is getting the confidence to speak to a stranger at a party. Maybe the goal is to carry a long story to a group of friends all the way to what you know is a beautiful payoff at the end. Maybe you want to nail that interview. Or maybe you want to tell your boss what you really think about how things are being run — without falling over or sweating from your palms. I'm here to tell you, even if you *do* want to get under that spotlight, the problems you'll face are the same whether you're speaking to 2 people or 2,000.

This book is intended to help you *find your voice.* As a *vocal pedagogue* (a fancy name for *speech coach*), I've seen just about every problem a speaker can have. I've worked with mumblers. I've helped fidgeters. I've dealt with those who have no problem delivering speeches that are written for them, but can hardly speak when it's their own words. And of course, I see many people who are just scared to death of public speaking.

I can help you with those things and more. The first thing this book will do is help you figure out what your problems are in order to solve them. Being an effective public speaker takes time, patience, and practice. You may never get the opportunity to speak to a rapt crowd through a microphone headset. But if you're diligent enough, you will be able to if you ever get the call.

How This Book Is Organized

This book is laid out the same way that I teach my voice and speech classes. My workshops are 3–6 hours long. For individual one-on-one coaching, each session lasts an hour. The progression of learning is different for everyone. That's why this book offers solutions for every problem that I commonly work with.

Do you lack confidence? Do negative thoughts manifest themselves and hinder your performance? What can you do to stop them?

For some, the problem is physical. Breath is a vitally important part of the process. We'll dive into common breathing habits and issues and find out how to address them. Something else we'll look at is how that stubborn old evolutionary fight, flight, or freeze response factors into performance anxiety. How can we get over such a natural function of our bodies?

We're going to get into particulars, too. Reading a speech is more than just speaking: First you have put on your writer hat. Before my clients walk in the door, I ask them to have a speech ready to practice with. For many people, even if they're pretty good at writing, their writing doesn't sound like *them*. It should. We'll delve into crafting your speech before you have to give it.

Once that speech is written, how do you lift it from the page? You can use devices like punctuation and all kind of markups to show how you want to say it, but not everything can be indicated on paper. We'll work on tone and pitch, when to get quiet, what raising your voice does, and how to do it effectively.

Then we'll try to put it all together. We'll talk about the resonance of your voice and how that affects your message. We'll go into what *articulators* are and how to use them so even people in the back of the room can understand you. Breathing is once again important in making sure all your words are heard.

We'll go through which style of public speaking might pertain to you and your needs. How can you have more impact with a slide show presentation — or do you really even need to bother with that? What to do for a job interview? How do the rules change when you're having a conversation and there's no script? What do you do when things don't go as planned?

There are exercises sprinkled all over this book. And I want to point out that you can read this entire book and learn absorb everything in it, but I can't take you the rest of the way. You must practice regularly to become the type of speaker that you want to be.

Foolish Assumptions

Because you are reading this book, I've made a few assumptions about you:

>> You don't have a degree in public speaking and have not been formally trained.

>> You may be required to speak publicly. Maybe it's part of your job. Or maybe you've been asked to speak at your brother's wedding. Or maybe you're tired of missing out on conversations at parties. In some way, you're looking to enhance your presentation skills.

>> You're tired of freaking out every time you have to speak in front of people.

>> You think your presentations are boring.

>> You feel that you're often not understood by those you're talking to.

>> You want to rock a presentation.

Maybe you know which problems with speaking you have, and they're very specific. Chances are, you'll find them addressed in this book. They say the definition of insanity is doing the same thing over and over and expecting different results. If you've already gone insane and grabbed this book as a remedy, congrats on the first step. You're already on your way.

If you don't know what's wrong with your presentation style, or if you even have a style, how do you know how to fix it? We'll talk a lot about that too.

Most people don't know what makes a great speaker, but they know what makes a bad one. I work with clients who stop me when I'm giving them feedback after they've presented and say that they thought they were pretty good. That may be true, but you don't want to be just pretty good. You want to be fabulous. That's what we're going for.

Icons

Throughout the book you'll see little graphics that flag certain paragraphs. Here's what those mean:

TIP

This one indicates something helpful that you would do well to pay attention to or try yourself. These are often the result of hard-won experience that you can take and use for yourself.

REMEMBER

This icon points out information you're advised to tuck in your mind somewhere for later use.

TECHNICAL STUFF

This rarely used icon pops up when it's time to get into some nitty-gritty details that may go beyond what you really need. Feel free to skip these if you're in a hurry.

WARNING

This icon points out potential trouble or other things you should avoid, usually giving at least one good reason you should avoid it.

Beyond the Book

To view this book's Cheat Sheet, simply go to www.dummies.com and search for "Public Speaking Skills Cheat Sheet" for a handy reference guide that covers common questions and insights about public speaking.

Where to Go from Here

You can read this book from beginning to end if you want, or you can jump straight to chapters that especially pertain to you or your situation. The book is divided into separate parts and chapters. The table of contents and the index are there to help you easily find topics and dive right in to those.

For example, do you sound like bacon frying in a pan? Do you end sentences with a question even though they should be a statement? Do people always comment that they can't hear you? These and other specific situations are listed in the index and table of contents.

Of course, if you just want to start learning how to improve your public speaking skills, you can always tackle this book the old-school way. You know, by finding a comfortable chair, pouring a cup of tea or coffee, and turning to Chapter 1. However you use this book, I hope you find it helpful on your journey to being a great public speaker.

1
Laying the Groundwork

Find out all the different skills involved in becoming an effective and well-rounded public speaker — and what you'll gain from this book.

Reprogram engrained habits of negative thinking, understand the fight, flight, or freeze response, and start thinking Yes Let's when confronted with the challenges of public speaking.

» Writing your script

» Learning to practice

Chapter **1**

Getting Started with Public Speaking

You may have picked up this book because you've been told you need to give a speech. And, if like the vast majority of people, you're really scared. And maybe you have good reason. Maybe you saw a video of yourself and can't believe you move around so much.

Time for a reality check. When you give a speech or presentation, it's all about your message to the audience. It is not really about *you*. Some of the smartest and the most accomplished people tend to forget about the message and focus all their anxiety on themselves as speakers. "Should I have cut my hair? What if I forget the most important point?"

TIP

First things first: Live in the present. And when you're speaking, the present means delivering your message to the audience.

You may have no idea what you're going to do before you read this book. And there may times when you feel out of your comfort zone. I get it — it's my specialty. But isn't being out of your comfort zone supposed to be a good thing? It's a big part of how you grow as a person.

TIP

Something else you need to be prepared for to really get what I'll be teaching you: You need to learn to feel comfortable with discomfort.

Dealing with Issues That Stand in Your Way

Whether or not you have a good idea of what your specific problem with public speaking may be, many issues can arise while preparing for and during your speech. It's important to have a good sense of them. You may be afraid, your body language may be making you feel less than confident, you could have a vocal problem, you could be running out of breath and not getting to the ends of your sentences. There are many possible reasons for these things.

REMEMBER

Here are a few things to remember:

>> Performing requires effort — but you don't want the audience to see that effort.

>> A powerful speaker is relaxed and comfortable.

>> Your public speaking voice should be the same one you use when talking to your family, friends, and colleagues. (I have a client who is a politician, who told a friend that he was working with me. "Whatever you do," his friend said, "don't turn into one of those fake-sounding politicians." You need to have your own style and sound like yourself.)

You may just need little tweaks — or you may need more work.

Fighting the fight, flight, or freeze response

You've probably heard the statistics. People rate public speaking up there with *dying* on the all-time fears list. It should be no surprise then that during public speaking, the automatic response that we usually see when facing a life-threatening situation kicks in: It's sometimes called the *fight, flight, or freeze* response. This was first described by physiologist Walter Bradford Cannon in his book *The Wisdom of the Body* in 1932. It's a physiological response to fear that traces back to prehistoric days. A Cro-Magnon was always on guard, looking out for danger — because danger was real back then, and it came from everywhere. We aren't cavepersons anymore, despite how you may feel some days behind the lectern, *but we still feel the fear*. It's built in to us.

Let's get something straight right off the bat: It's okay to be nervous, because that shows that you care. When you're presenting, adrenaline (often triggered by fear) courses through your body. That's a good thing. That adrenaline is doing you good — it's giving you an extra boost during an extraordinary time. When your body is stressed for a long time, as when a prehistoric ancestor was fighting off a herd of saber-toothed cats, the stress hormone cortisol is also secreted. And that's when we have problems. When you're scared, your voice reflects it. You may sound shaky, or you speed up, or you speak so quietly that you can't be heard, or you blank and can't think of what to say next.

TIP

Here's something you're going to hear a lot about in this book. The best solution to conquering fear and anxiety is proper breathing technique. Breathing slowly — as opposed to the short little breaths you take when anxious — stimulates your brain to activate the calming rest and digest parasympathetic nervous system. Basically, proper slow breathing shuts off the tap that's supplying you with stress. As I argue in future chapters, by adopting a positive attitude, changing your body language, and saying yes instead of no, you can actually change the way you feel about yourself. And that translates into better public speaking. I talk more about this in Chapters 2, 5, and 15.

Affirming your worth with affirmations

Do you say no before you say yes? People are hard-wired to say *no* first, thanks to our ancestors the aforementioned cave dwellers. Is your own mind getting in the way of success? You can get positive about presenting by adopting a better attitude.

That all starts with affirmations. *Affirmations* help to kick-start belief in yourself. "I am a great speaker," "My message rocks!" and "I am the expert!" Say these things to yourself and before you know it you'll start believing them — and believing in yourself.

One of Stephen Covey's Habits for Highly Effective People is to begin with the end in mind. What do you want to happen *after* the speech? What do you want the audience to *do?* Put your focus on the audience and the message you want to impart on them. I discuss more about this in Chapter 11.

Creating reality with visualization

Most people are very good at imagining themselves doing something negative. Why not turn that around and visualize a great presentation? Picture the audience nodding in approval. Your mind plays tricks on you all the time through negative thinking. Well, two can play at that game. The brain is plastic. You can consciously change it to think more positively.

I talk about two kinds of visualization: *External* visualization is where you're looking at yourself as if you're in a movie, and *internal visualization* is where you see yourself actually performing the task from your point of view. Elite athletes use both kinds and find them very beneficial.

If you're using external imagery, you can watch yourself sitting in the audience, rising when the host calls your name, calmly striding up to the lectern, taking three breaths, and beginning your speech — which will be great. The audience is giving you appreciative nonverbal reactions. Your visual aids are all in place. You end your speech to genuine applause.

With internal imagery, you simulate giving the speech in your own body. When you go through your speech, how are you feeling? What are you seeing and hearing? More about this can be found in Chapters 2 and 20.

Getting rid of tension

We all need some amount tension in our bodies. If we didn't have tension, we wouldn't be able to sit or stand. So, it's not tension in general that we need to think about and get rid of, but rather, *misplaced* tension.

Proper alignment is the first step in relieving unnecessary tension. The spine, as you know, is crucial to alignment. It's the mast of your ship. If you have unnecessary tension, it starts with your spine. And that makes it harder on your muscles to just keep you standing. Then everything else gets out of whack. Your breath will be impeded, your shoulders and neck may be tight, and your vocal energy may be low. The audience mirrors you, so if you're feeling tense, they will too. Chapter 4 describes vocal problems and exercises that can help.

So what can you do about it? You have to get physical. Working out relieves tension. Go for a walk or run, dust off your bike, hit the pool, or practice some yoga. I talk more about this in Chapter 10.

Progressive relaxation is a tension and release exercise that was developed by American physician Edmond Jacobson in 1908 to help patients overcome their anxiety. This is an exercise where you tense all body parts individually and then release to feel the difference. You start by lying on the floor in a quiet place. You learn to tense and release all parts of your body. Then if you feel tense before or during a presentation, you can tense a part of your body, like your toes, and release. See Chapter 3 for a full description of this exercise.

Improving Your Body Language

Body language can be even more important than your voice in delivering your message to the audience. Body language is crucial in exuding confidence in yourself and showing trust in your audience.

TIP

Believe it or not, changing your posture can actually change your mood and, ultimately, how you perform.

First things first. You need to stand up straight — not like you're waiting for the sergeant to inspect your barracks, but in what I call an *up and out* position. You feel your bones stacked up on top of each other, your head is directly over your shoulders and on top of your neck, your chin is neither tucked in nor jutting forward, your chest is out, your feet are planted, and you have energy surging through your body past the crown of your head and up into the sky.

The opposite is the *down and in* position. When you slouch and gaze at the floor, it doesn't show confidence in you or your audience. Averting your eyes and looking down send the message to the audience that you'd rather be anywhere else. If you're not properly aligned, down and in also impedes your breath. You won't be able to drop your breath deep into your body like you should. In Chapter 15 I discuss this in more detail.

Here are some other body language tips:

>> Handshakes are part of body language too. Give a firm one if you want to make a good impression. Don't be a limp rag, but don't squeeze and hang on for dear life. That may make a lasting impression, but not a good one.

>> If you'll be presenting sitting down, such as in a boardroom, have both feet firmly planted on the floor and don't slouch into your chair.

>> Crossing your arms while talking to colleagues at the water cooler may feel natural for you, but what impression does it give to your listeners? Defensiveness, that's what. Crossing your legs may feel comfortable, but to some it looks like you are in a closed-off position. Crossing your arms and your legs doesn't make you look very approachable.

Gesturing

You don't know what to do with your hands? Try moving them. Practice doing that and see how comfortable it becomes and how it activates your parasympathetic nervous system.

The autonomic nervous system consists of three parts:

>> The *enteric* system controls the stomach and intestines.

>> The *sympathetic* nervous system activates the "fight or flight" response.

>> The *parasympathetic nervous system,* or the "rest and digest" system.

In Mark Bowden's book *Winning Body Language* (McGraw-Hill Education, 2010), the author states that moving your hands in a horizontal plane extending out from your navel has a calming effect and activates the parasympathetic nervous system. He calls this the *truth plane* because you look and feel more genuine when your hands are in this position.

TIP

When you're giving your presentation seated at a boardroom table, gesture away. Just make sure to keep your hands up where everyone can see them. If you drop them under the table, no one knows what is going on down there. Chapter 15 talks more about this.

Moving

Some speakers just want to stay put and stand motionless behind the lectern. That may be fine (unless they're gripping the thing with white knuckles). Others feel the need to move constantly. Both are individual choices and are up to you.

TIP

When you do move, make sure you move with a purpose. Choreograph where you want to move and when. The movement should make sense in combination with what you're talking about. Through practice, movement will soon become second nature.

WARNING

Swaying side to side or back and forth is fine for rocking a baby. When you're speaking, though, you want the focus to be on what you have to say. Plant those feet and imagine roots growing down from them into the earth. Chapter 15 goes into more detail about this.

Making eye contact

The audience is your friend, and they want you to succeed. Believe it or not, they're not planning to throw rotten fruit at you the moment you falter.

TIP

Find someone in the audience who is giving you nonverbal cues that she's listening and is interested in what you're saying. Look her directly in the eye for about five or six seconds. Then move on to someone else. Look at the same person for too long, and she'll start to feel uncomfortable. And the rest of the audience may start wondering why that one person is getting a solo performance.

If you're really that scared when you speak, find that friendly face and look at that person. Sometimes you may feel that it's easier to look above and over the audience's heads. That way, you don't have to connect with them. But the audience can tell that you're not looking at them. If your eyes are the windows to your soul, the audience is never going to get to know you if they can't engage with you and your message. Practice when the stakes are low — look your colleagues in the eye, the delivery guy, your kid's basketball coach.

You'll can read more about this stuff in Chapter 15.

Adjusting Your Pace

One of the most common problems I see is speakers speeding up their speeches as they progress through them. It's obvious they want to get their speech over with as soon as possible.

If you find yourself speeding up, but you don't feel particularly scared, maybe you've practiced it so much that you're just going through the motions. Think of the way you absentmindedly murmured the Pledge of Allegiance as a kid, or the Lord's Prayer. Congrats on being prepared — but you're doing it wrong.

When you deliver your speech, that's the first time the audience will hear it. A speech is a performance. When you watch a play, the actors don't do everything faster than they did on opening night just because they know their lines better. Be clear and slow down so that the audience has time to register what you just said. Practice saying one sentence slowly. Then take a breath.

I talk more about this in Chapter 9.

Perfecting the pause

What is that little dot at the end of a sentence? Right, it's a period and it represents the end of a thought. Use it to pause and take a breath. When speakers pause, it shows that they are confident and that they have control of their presentation.

A pause can also create suspense for the audience. What is the speaker going to say next? As a speaker, you may feel as if your pause is soooo long. Actually, you're really just taking a breath. The audience doesn't see it as taking a long time.

When you pause to take a breath or allow a thought to land and take hold of them, it shows the audience you're confident. You've got this under control.

Often, people use *filler words* in place of breath pauses, like *um* and *ah*. Some people feel as if they must constantly keep talking. Don't do this. Yes, it may give you time to gather your thoughts for your next sentence, but you're taking away the opportunity for the audience to do the same.

When you tell a joke or a humorous story or even say a line that the audience laughs at, pause and wait for the laugh to subside. Otherwise, they'll miss what you say next.

I talk more about all of this in Chapter 9.

Supporting Your Breath

If you take away only one thing from this book, let it be *the importance of breath.* Breath is your fuel. It's the stuff that runs your speech. Breathing deep and slow helps you relax, and when you feel relaxed, you're less stressed. It's a perfect feedback loop.

Your *diaphragm* is a cone-shaped muscle attached to the lower edges of your ribcage. When you breathe in, the abdominal and pelvic muscles relax, the diaphragm flattens, the ribs expand up and out, and the breath enters the lungs. When you breathe, I want you to visualize your breath dropping deep into your lower abdomen. Chapter 14 covers breathing in detail.

To find out if you're breathing correctly, put one hand on your upper chest and the other on your lower abdomen and inhale. Pay attention to which hand moves first. If it's your hand on your upper chest, then you are not taking full breaths. Imagine filling your lungs up like a balloon. Balloons fill up starting at the bottom. When you exhale, your balloon deflates, and your navel is pressed toward your spine.

Taking the time to breathe deeply will help you sustain your breath to the end of your sentence. If you run out of breath before the sentence is over, you tend to drop your volume and mumble your way through the end of the sentence. When you do that, the audience can't hear what you said. You lose your impact, and your message is lost.

If you hold your breath because you missed something in your speech or you look out at that audience gripped with fear, your brain won't get the oxygen it needs — and you may blank. So keep breathing! I discuss this in further detail in Chapters 9 and 14.

EXERCISE: SAYING DIFFERENT SENTENCES, TAKING DIFFERENT BREATHS

This exercise can improve your lung capacity and how much breath you need for each sentence.

Different sentences require different amounts of breath. Speak each of the following lines on one breath:

- I read *For Dummies* books. (breathe)

- I read *For Dummies* books because they give me so much information. (breathe)

- I read *For Dummies* books because they give me so much information that I can use every day. (breathe)

Each sentence requires more breath. Your breath should sound as free and easy on the last sentence as on the first. For each, try to take in only as much breath as you need. Try not to lift your shoulders when you breathe in.

Boosting Confidence through Preparation and Training

You've been asked to present and you're thinking, *Why me? I'm not worthy!* Sure, you may look snazzy and dressed up, but inside you're screaming, *I'm an imposter!*

TIP

Get rid of self-defeating thoughts. Let them go. You *are* good or you wouldn't have been asked to speak.

Perfection doesn't exist. And if it did, it would be boring. You don't want to strive to be perfect. How about striving for excellence instead? Be the best you can be. That is what the audience wants — to see your authentic self, flaws and all.

Think of your presentation as a learning experience. I know, your dad told you that all the time through school. You didn't listen? Well, listen now. Analyze how you did afterward. Have a checklist of things you did that you felt good about and things that you could improve. The more you present, the more your list of improvements will shrink.

Do you try to wing a speech? How did that go? Winging an important presentation doesn't work for most people. Even if you manage to fill up the allotted time, you may have missed important facts. You probably rambled on because you had no idea where your speech was going. You were grasping for what to say next, what you wanted to remember, what you were forgetting. Recall that the audience mimics what they see — if you look and feel befuddled, so will they.

TIP

It all comes down to practice, practice, practice. It takes years to go from amateur to master in any field of endeavor. The thing about learning a new skill is that you just don't learn it and forget about it. What makes people great at anything is that they always learn it more from doing it over and over. Even if you give the same presentation 20 times, each time will be different. So take the mistakes and learn from them to get better.

TIP

Never look in the mirror when practicing your presentation. You look in a mirror to make sure that your shirt is tucked in, that your hair is parted correctly, or that the piece of spinach is off your teeth. And these are the things you're doing when you look in the mirror while practicing. You're not in the moment. It's much better to record yourself on video — or record your voice on your phone or other device to hear how you sound. Chapter 9 talks more about this.

Breathing (your own) life into speeches

For writers, it's all about finding your voice. It's the first step to becoming confident in your work. The same can be said for writing a speech. I don't care if your speech is about fractions or septic systems or deodorant sales. Get some personality into your speech.

A speech is a great opportunity to give the audience a real treat. You want to show the world that you're an intelligent human being when you present. You're not writing a technical manual — you're allowing your audience to look deep into you.

TIP

After you've written your speech, practice it out loud. Did you write it in your own voice? You'll discover what words fit for you and the audience. More on this in Chapter 6.

Planning out your speech

As you write your speech, ask yourself:

>> What do you want to say?

>> What does the audience need to hear?

>> Why are you speaking to them?

In the public speaking world, speeches have three main purposes:

>> **To entertain:** That's the speech you give at a wedding.

>> **To persuade:** That's when you're selling something, an idea, service, or tangible object.

>> **To inform:** You're giving information. Think of a college lecture.

I believe you need *all three components* in your speech. Doing that will make your speech a lot more interesting.

How should you begin your presentation? With a rhetorical question that the audience doesn't have to answer but that gets them thinking? A statistic or cool fact? A provocative or inspiring quote? A comment about an event that happened locally, a compliment to the audience, or a personal story?

All of those have the same objective: to get the audience engaged right off the bat. There's more about this in Chapter 6.

Getting ready for the big day

It's the night before your speech. You've gone over your presentation enough times to feel really comfortable with it. What now? Make a list of things you need to be a success. For example, do you have your speech printed out or your cue cards? Do you have your USB stick or any visuals handy? Where's your water bottle? Will the hotel supply you with a water glass? Will they give you some food beforehand? Practice in the clothes you plan to wear, because you never know if that tie is too tight or those heels too high.

On the day of the event, get to the venue early and meet your organizer or the person you've been in contact with. Talk to the technician or the person responsible for your visuals. Walk on the stage if you can — it will help you feel more comfortable when you do it for real. Meet the early birds and have a good chat. That's another good way to feel more comfortable. It's also a good way to feel out the tone of the conference or meeting. Did they just listen to a speaker who told them that they will need two million dollars in the bank to retire? That would be good to know.

TIP

Don't take yourself too seriously. Yes, you need to do well when you present. You want to get your message across. But there's no need to put undue pressure on yourself. I talk about this in detail in Chapter 16.

Eating right to feel good

Think you can run off to your early morning presentation after skipping breakfast? Maybe you're experiencing butterflies in your stomach and can't keep anything down but coffee. Unless you've been living under a rock, you must've heard that breakfast is the most important meal of the day.

Any meal is important before giving a speech. You need something in your stomach — and I'm not talking about a donut and coffee. That will make you jittery and you'll crash and burn. Eat some protein and complex carbs.

Turn to Chapter 10 for more detail.

Honing Your Delivery

Warming up is vital if you want to give a great speech. You're a *speech athlete*, and all athletes warm up before they compete. Remember, you are using your body. Speakers, just like athletic competitors, need to warm up physically and vocally. There are samples of warmups in Chapters 10, 20, and 22.

Articulating

What's that you say? You might be passionate about your speech, but if you don't open your mouth and pronounce your words clearly, know one will care. *Articulation* helps you communicate your ideas to your audience. That starts with your mouth.

You need to open your mouth to be understood clearly. Many speakers hardly open their mouths. Perhaps they're mirroring other people around them who have shut their traps. Or mumbling is a habit. Or they're scared. Your *articulators* include the tongue, lips, jaw, and the soft palate.

You may feel self-conscious about your accent. By the way, we all have accents — we all sound different depending on region of origin and other factors. If you're from New York, your *accent* or how you pronounce words is probably very different from a Texan's. All you Canadians out there, don't be thinking that the only people with accents are from Quebec and Newfoundland. Every community says words differently. So embrace your accent. You don't need to get rid of it — in fact, you can't. You just need to be clear in your pronunciation.

If you're told constantly to speak up, you don't have to push your voice. Just make sure you pronounce the endings of the words. Don't think your microphone will be your savior. Yes, a mic will amplify your sound so the audience will hear you at the back of the room. But they'll also hear your vocal problems, too.

Resonating

Your whole body resonates and amplifies your sound. The most important parts are the head, throat, mouth, and chest. Think of yourself as an amplifier. If you hold tension in your body, you won't be able to resonate fully, and your sound won't be as rich and vibrant.

Using the right tone

You express meaning through tone. Yes, *express*. Speakers often have trouble with this because they don't want to exaggerate and look foolish. But if you feel excited that the stocks have grown in the company portfolio, shouldn't you show it? Yes — make sure you show it.

When you speak, you need to use vocal variety. The speaker who sits on one note is boring and loses the audience's attention.

Be mindful of what you're saying and how you're saying it. If you're selling a group of seniors a new retirement package, don't be condescending. Remember your message and what you want the seniors to do. You don't want them to write you off as some young whipper snapper who just wants his money.

You can find more about all of this in Chapters 12 through 14.

Adding visuals

Visuals like slide shows *can* help enhance your message. But make sure they really add to your presentation and don't just give you something you think you can hide behind.

You definitely don't need to put a whole bunch of words on slides and proceed to read them. Boring! Your slides or other visuals should only relate to main points or provide context for what you're saying.

Answer this question: Do your slides truly complement your speech or did you just stick them in because you felt your words weren't enough? If you took the slides away (which could happen — machinery has a tendency to fail at the worst possible moments), could you still give your speech with full confidence? Your answer should be yes.

TIP

Try using pictures. When we look at a picture, it evokes feelings in us and carries us into our imagination. That's usually more than words on a slide could ever do. Words on a slide just give the audience a visual version of what you're saying already.

Make sure you're consistent with your message. If you are talking about, say, plumbers and their right to make a choice about striking, and your slides are all about stats on how many plumbers are in the union, the audience doesn't know which to focus on. If they read the stats, they miss what you have said. If they listen to you, they miss the stats. If they read the stats fast and you're still talking they may just zone out completely.

TIP

Be creative. Think outside the box. Try to incorporate other kinds of visuals, such as props. Props can create more impact have more impact than a PowerPoint slide. Just make sure to use a prop that's big enough for the whole audience to see.

Chapter 7 discusses visual aids in detail.

Getting laughs

Getting the audience laughing can be a fantastic technique. But comedy can be tricky to pull off. The audience will smell a phony, so be authentic. Even if you aren't a naturally born jokester, you can tell a joke or a humorous story. You don't need to be a comedian to be funny. The trick is to find your funny bone and add humor to your speech without alienating the audience.

Start by writing what you know. Write about you and your life. Many times I hear my friends talk about funny incidents that have happened to them that they would never share in front of people who aren't their good friends. Well, now's your chance.

Here are some quick tips to being funny up there:

>> Focus on what the audience and you have in common.

>> Try it out on friends.

>> Don't be afraid to be vulnerable and open — audiences love that.

>> Don't say, "Have I got a funny joke for you."

>> Don't assume they will laugh. Appreciate it when they do.

>> Once you start the joke, keep going and stay committed to telling it all the way to the end.

- » Use situational humor.

- » Talk about what's bugging you.

- » Keep it clean.

- » Find someone who is funny and ask that person about your story.

- » Don't be the first to laugh, but feel free to laugh at yourself if the audience does.

There's more in Chapter 8.

Telling stories

Everyone loves stories. Using narration helps to get your message across in a fun way that engages the audience. A personal anecdote helps the audience get into your world and relate to you. You can use part of a story as a hook and then wrap it up in the conclusion.

Chapter 6 is devoted to using stories in speeches.

Dealing with the Audience

As a speaker, there is nothing worse than saying something and getting a groan from the audience — especially early in your speech. Avoiding groans starts with knowing your audience. It's your job to find out the kind of audience that will be listening to your speech.

Here are a few things to consider:

WARNING

- » Be sensitive if something tragic has happened in the community.

- » Use appropriate language and tone. If you're talking to a group of seniors about their retirement plan, don't be condescending and don't alienate them.

- » If you're telling a joke, don't *ever* be off-color.

- » Don't pit part of the audience against the other. "Women, don't you think that men . . ." That might work for the professional comedian, but you want the entire audience to be engaged and on your side.

Find out more about audiences in Chapter 8.

DEALING WITH HECKLERS

Don't take it personally. Heckling is just an obstacle you may have to address. Remember that you're the boss up there. Keep your cool and keep breathing.

Address the heckler and ask an open-ended question. "How do you feel about that?" That may lead him to run into a ditch on his own. If he persists, tell him that you will address his concerns after the presentation. (If you do talk to him later, give him a time limit. You have five minutes and then you have to go chat with the organizer.)

If he keeps going, turn to the audience and say, "I think the audience wants to hear more about what I'm saying."

Excelling in Interviews

One fantastic interview away from a major upgrade? Here are some speaking tips for interview situations to get that dream job:

>> Know thyself. The interviewers already have looked at your CV. What can you tell them that they don't know?

>> Dress like you've already got the job.

>> Know the company that you're interviewing for. Find out who the CEO is and who will be interviewing you. Check out the company's website and find its mission statement. Is there a page that shows events that employees do as a company? Maybe they're all on a baseball team or they clean up local parks every year in the spring. These are interesting tidbits that you can sprinkle into the conversation to show that you've done your homework and researched the company.

>> Convince them you will work hard. Employers want to surround themselves with hardworking employees who are interested in the company and want to do well in their position.

>> Know the answers to some important questions. They will almost always ask you why you want the job. What have been your obstacles in other jobs that you've overcome? They may even ask why you left your previous job, or why you want to leave your present one. Be prepared with answers.

WARNING

>> Don't throw in any negatives. Never say something like, "The boss hired his brother so there was no room for me." Be positive about your previous work experience. Focus the conversation back to you.

>> Be ready to ask questions, too.

>> Have an elevator pitch — a description of what you do in the time it takes for a ride on an elevator. Create a clear, succinct description of your career. Make sure it's relevant. See Chapter 18 for more.

>> Keep your body in an up and out position.

>> If there's a question you don't know, admit you don't know the answer and you'll find out. And then follow up — actually find out and get back to the interviewer with the answer.

>> Be gracious and thank the interviewer for taking the time to meet with you.

You find out much more about acing interviews in Chapter 17.

Mastering the Fine Art of Conversation

A speech is a conversation. You're speaking to the audience, and although they may not be giving anything back in the way of words, their attention and their reception is the other side of the coin. Think of talking to a good friend. You use emotion and vocal variety and you have fun. That's what should happen when you give a speech.

It extends to other areas too. Many think that *public speaking* is something that only happens in a presentation. But to me, public speaking is . . . *speaking in public.* That includes party conversations, giving directions to someone on the subway, or even talking to your Internet provider on the phone. Actually, this is where public speaking starts. And it can be just as challenging as the stage.

REMEMBER

Getting out there and mingling can be hard for some, but don't view it as a chore. Have fun and enjoy yourself. Set an objective for what you want to achieve. Maybe it's making a contact for a future sale, but it can be simpler:

I want to talk to three new people. I want to remember what those three do for a living. I want to find out what they do besides work.

Things can get more complicated when there's an event, but remember: Going to a function still counts as speaking in public. It's still a conversation and you want to be your best and show people that you care about them and what they have to say.

Here are a few tips for speaking when meeting people in a functional setting:

>> When you're introduced to people, look them in the eye and smile. Smiling is infectious. Enjoy meeting those people.

>> Shake their hand firmly — don't do the limp or grip or squeeze so hard it makes them wince. Be in the moment. When shaking their hand or talking to them, don't be looking over their shoulder at the other guy you really want to talk to.

>> It is not all about you. Find out stuff about them. Be interested in what they have to say.

Dropping the Ball and Still Managing to Score

Life throws us curveballs sometimes. Have a backup plan for when something goes awry. Maybe the room has changed, or your allotted time is cut, or there's no screen for your slide show.

REMEMBER

The world doesn't need to end. The audience doesn't even need to know. Unless there's some imminent danger, stay cool.

Don't bother apologizing. "Sorry I'm late. Sorry, my PowerPoint doesn't work. Sorry, the organizer told me 30 minutes, and now we only have 15 because our lunch is early, so I'll just rush through this."

People aren't interested in other people's excuses. Plus, saying sorry just puts the audience on edge. Some may feel sorry for you — others might think it's a cop-out. The audience reflects how you feel, and you want them to feel that you are confident and trustworthy.

TIP

Practice some responses if the PowerPoint shuts off. For example, "I'll tell you the story about that slide."

When a problem occurs, have a plan and a comment ready. Breathing helps you to think clearly. The audience wants you to succeed and they want to hear what you have to say. They'll forgive you.

Wearing Clothes That Spell Success

You don't always have to wear the power suit. Going to the opening of the community league barbecue? You're going to look like a dork in a suit. Dress in accordance to how others are dressing, but dress well.

Some tips on dressing for success:

>> Wear something that's comfortable and makes you feel great. Wear clothes that fit you well, not ones that are too big or too tight.

>> Practice in your clothes so you'll feel comfortable in them.

>> You don't want to lift up your arms and rip a sleeve if you haven't worn that shirt in a while. Make sure those new pants don't need a belt.

>> Don't wear anything that will detract from your speech.

>> Hot pants were cool in the 1970s but not so much now. (But if you can still fit in them, kudos to you.) Big bangle-y earrings that have a mind of their own and sway side to side might be great at a party, but not when giving a presentation. Especially if you're using a mic headset.

>> Big patterns on clothes can be distracting. Shiny fabrics can give you a glow that might be too much for the stage.

So, you've now had an overview of the basics of public speaking skills. If you've read this chapter and are now a competent and professional public speaker, you are a genius. If you're more ordinary, like me, it probably wasn't enough to get you signed to that big speaking contract. That's why I've filled the rest of this book with methods to help you go about getting where you need to be. Ready? Turn the page.

Chapter **2**

Getting Your Brain in the Game

Ah, the human mind. One of the most complex systems on the planet. Nearly a hundred billion neurons firing and networking to interpret and navigate and act in the world every second. Here are some things humans have been able to do with their incredible brains: We've landed on the moon, turned black goo from the ground into fuel for transportation machines, created computers that fit in our pockets and that can access nearly every bit of human knowledge. We've done amazing things with our brains over the course of history.

Yet that big wrinkled lump between our ears has trouble doing some very basic things — like public speaking, for instance. Because we were hunters and gatherers and were in constant fear of being ousted by our tribe, that fear still exists in us today. In her book *Overcoming Perfectionism* (Health Communications, 2013), author Ann Smith says we have a need to be attached and feel like we belong in order to survive.

So, even with all that firepower in your head, with all the brilliant things that it's capable of having you write and say, sometimes it's that very brain that's your roadblock to public speaking success.

But it doesn't have to be that way. Your brain putting up roadblocks and also lead-ing you to being a brilliant raconteur aren't so different from one another.

Sometimes all it takes is a little conscious thinking to get your subconscious in check. Whether you suffer from negative thoughts, crippling perfectionism, uncontrolled autonomic response, or are just plain scared, hard as it may be to believe, there's a way past it.

Before we talk about getting past it, let's look more closely at how negative thinking works.

Recognizing the Pitfalls of Negative Thoughts

This may not come as surprise, but it's much easier to hold on to negative thoughts and give them emotional weight than it is to hold on to positive ones. After all, we evolved in a scary, deadly, wild environment. One thing your brain is very good at is alerting you to danger. Pessimism and negative thinking tended to keep you alive a hundred thousand years ago. You had to react instantly to a threat. Positive events don't create the same urgency.

Your DNA, unfortunately, hasn't had time yet to become concerned with your being able to master that presentation to your company without that creeping negativity following you around everywhere. Maybe your distant descendants fared better because of it, but in the meantime you're stuck with your present DNA.

We've all heard of the fear of public speaking. Here are a few of the symptoms, both physical and mental:

>> Stomachache

>> Gritting teeth

>> Fear of opening your mouth

>> Hearing your heart beating

>> Stopping breathing

>> Losing your place in your speech

>> Blanking

>> Negative thinking

Our brains are hardwired to recognize the negatives in every situation. Think about it: You've probably got a lot of positive things going on. First off, you're alive in this world and get to see all the cool stuff it has to offer. If you've got a career you like, that's a positive that you constantly hold with you. Same thing if you have a family and/or a home, if you read good books, or if you're able to go to movies. When you get a dog, you don't just like it the first day it comes home as a puppy. It becomes a constant positive in your life.

Negatives, however, tend to overwhelm your contentment. Maybe there's a blip in your career — maybe you got passed over for that promotion. It's hard to keep something like that in context. We're not really wired to zoom out and weigh the good and the bad equally because historically that would have little value in keeping you alive. Maybe your dog died — after a fantastic life of chasing balls and being jolly. It seems easier sometimes to remember the pain you felt at Rover's death than all the instances of him bounding toward you after a tough day.

TIP

I'm not just saying stop and smell the roses (although feel free, they smell great). I'm saying try to remember to take negative thoughts for what they are — and nothing more. They are fleeting feelings that will take up all the emotional space if you let them.

Saying no to negatives: Avoiding your triggers

How do you take a negative emotion or thought and include it in the feeling of something without allowing it to completely overshadow anything else? Here are a few tips:

>> **Be prepared:** Take it from the Boy Scouts — they know what to bring in case anything goes down. And though you may not be worried about bears coming after the snacks on the table at your presentation, or which way north is as you're facing the audience, it's a good idea to take this scouting advice. Often folks who experience anxiety or negative thoughts surrounding a performance have not prepared to the extent they believe they should.

TIP

Don't let that be you. Be meticulous. If you think the space where you'll be presenting is intimidating, check it out beforehand. Try to get there early enough that you can practice onstage. Know where you have to go, whether you can use notes, where the washroom is. If you're using a PowerPoint or some other visual aid, do a run-through to make sure all the equipment is working. Don't let something you didn't prepare for become a hurdle to your success. I cover practicing in Chapter 9.

>> **Focus on the small victories:** So, it's the night before you hit the stage and present them with a keynote speech you've worked on for weeks. It's a one-time thing, and everything is freaking you out. What if you mess up? What if you start coughing? What if you forget your words? Positive messaging can help you leap these hurdles.

Take out a pen and piece of paper. Write SMALL VICTORIES on top in big, important-looking block letters. Start from the beginning. Why are you doing this speech in the first place? Is it because you're an expert in a certain field? Is there some perspective only you can bring to the subject? Find the context around why you've been chosen to do this speech — chances are, they're all small victories.

>> **Get positive about negative thoughts:** You're worried that the speech will be a failure and you'll be shunned by your social group, and maybe society in general. Maybe there's some small, cold island they send all the speakers to whose PowerPoint cut out or who blanked on a topic — you're sure it's only a matter of time before they send you on a boat without a return ticket.

It's possible to turn such anxiety into motivation. Use it as a reason why you're *not* going to mess up. Have an ego about it. Tell yourself you're not getting on that boat to that island. It exists, people go there, but not you.

The presentation you're about to give is a building block to your success. It isn't a test to determine whether you'll fail — it's something you signed up for as a way to further yourself and your career. When a team plays an important game, there are two types of players: those who go out and try not to lose, and those who go out there and try to win. Successful athletes think about their accomplishments and believe they will succeed. Unsuccessful athletes tend to do the opposite. They ruminate on their failures and worry about their mistakes.

Perfecting perfectionism

Are you the type of person who has to have everything just so? All your ducks have to be in a row, and if they're not, your whole world is destroyed? Maybe asking yourself isn't the best way to figure that out. Find someone who knows you well: your best friend, your partner, or maybe someone you work with closely. Ask them to give it to you straight. Do you seem anxious when things don't go according to plan? Are you extremely hard on yourself and others? Do you compare yourself to others and feel that you fall short of their achievements? Sometimes it takes an outside opinion to determine whether you're a perfectionist or not.

And hey, there's nothing wrong with being meticulous. In fact, it's a trait that — done right — is an important asset to have for many things in life. But we humans often have a way of overdoing things. Sometimes it's hard to let things go, even if we know deep down that there's nothing else to be squeezed out of it. Perfectionists have a way of grinding a problem that has no clear solution into the ground so far that it distorts the problem that existed in the first place. As much as humans and our brains are pretty sharp, we can't think of ourselves as state-of-the-art analytical machines. It's so easy to overanalyze the little things and blow them up.

Nixing those niggling negatives

Everybody complains about something. It's totally natural and it is indeed negative. Sometimes complaining or venting to a confidant can be a perfectly cathartic and rational way to get over something. But it's easy to turn complaints into excuses. Complaining to the extent that it impedes your work is counterproductive. Here are a few tips to help you move on:

>> **Don't waste time complaining about technology failures.**

Anything that happens onstage is directly related to you. Whatever horrible thing goes on up there, you've got to deal with it.

For instance, how many times have you seen a presentation where some piece of technology doesn't work? It's like a cliché at this point: Half a PowerPoint is missing, the mic cuts out, the screen falls off the wall. Many presenters — me included — find technology difficult to work with for this reason. There always seem to be more moving parts than there has to be, and there's always something you can't directly control. Yet often you do have to use a mic, and sometimes PowerPoint is important to your presentation. What can you do when things fail? Well, you can waste in your time wallowing negative thoughts about the technology — or you can press on and make the best of it.

>> **Don't get flustered by things you can't control.** Be smarter than your problems.

>> **Let go of your own mistakes.** And, of course, sometimes the problem really *is* you. So what? We all have an ego. We all have a sense of importance and want to show the world that we are doing a good job. The ego is an important thing for performance — one of the most important things you can wield. But you can't let it get out of hand. We blame others to try to save face or blame ourselves. It's so important to be able to control your ego and save it for when you need to use it the most.

Many people who are new to public speaking find it tough to admit that they're going to make mistakes. But really, it's just math — the law of averages. Everyone on up to the president of the United States makes mistakes while speaking. Pros know it's best to shrug them off and just keep going as if nothing happened. A seasoned musician who plays two shows a day isn't going to get hung up on playing a wrong note every so often — the vast number of right notes far outweighs the bad one, and most of the time the audience doesn't even notice. But for a musician who just started her career, playing bad notes in her first big show can seem devastating.

So it goes with public speaking. The majority of people who end up speaking publicly don't do it very often, and so experiencing a small amount of whatever they gauge as failure can cripple them.

Buck that trend. Instead of being the typical newbie, act like you've done it lots of times before — and act like you'll do it again and again.

Keeping the Brain's Fight, Flight, or Freeze Response in Check

As mentioned earlier, one evolutionary trait that truly doesn't help us when we're getting started in public speaking is the fight, flight, or freeze response. If you remember from science class, this response is the central nervous system responding to protect you from some external terrible thing: a tiger coming through some bushes, a branch cracking above your head, or — nowadays — your name being called to give a speech at your daughter's wedding.

Evolution doesn't know or care, but one of those things is not like the others. If you forget your words to your only daughter's wedding, you're not going to be seriously injured. (Depending on how you raised her, I suppose.) But that fear on a hair trigger is deeply ingrained, and your body responds in the same way. It perceives a threat, and a cocktail of adrenaline and other hormones gets pumped throughout that tell you to

>> Get ready to fight.

>> Get ready to take flight.

>> Freeze.

None of those, especially that last one, is particularly helpful when called on to say a few words. But you may be surprised to learn that you can use that adrenaline to actually help you.

Saying yes to adrenaline

First, a little science lesson. The nervous system consists of nerves and cells that carry messages to and from the brain and spinal cord. As mentioned in Chapter 1, the sympathetic nervous system activates the "fight or flight" response, and the parasympathetic nervous system (often called the "rest and digest" system) is responsible for the "freeze" response. When we detect danger, the amygdala in the brain sends a message to the hypothalamus, an important control center. In turn, the hypothalamus sends a message to the adrenal glands to secrete adrenaline.

Adrenaline, also known as *epinephrine,* is a hormone that the body sends to your muscles when you encounter something that seems like it might mess you up. It's commonly known as the substance your body produces to get you energized — that special superhuman elixir that can supposedly help you lift a fallen tree that has trapped your hiking partner's leg, for example. And that's partly what it is. It increases your heart rate and makes your lungs work harder, which brings more blood to the muscles in case you have to fight off a bear that's sniffed out your basket of berries. We all know the physical sensation adrenaline causes: a tingling feeling in your body and, potentially, a wave of anxiety.

The anxiety is a good thing in the case of threats. It makes you hyper alert and ready to respond. But if you're reading this book, you've gotten to the point in human evolution where you're far more worried about abstract social concepts and their implications than you are about a cougar attack. It will take many thousands of years for our nervous systems to figure out that we're not going to die when the stage lights come on.

What can you do in the meantime? Well, what about taking adrenaline and putting it to good use? I tell my clients to use adrenaline like serious athletes do. When you start to feel that tingly sensation and you don't see a bear in the audience, try using that extra energy. Bring it into your voice and your presentation. That's one way to use a natural system in your body to enhance, rather than hamper, your speech. Of course, if there are actual bears in the audience, reconsider your booking agent.

Stopping cortisol in its tracks

Cortisol is another stress hormone coming out of your adrenal glands. Whereas adrenaline gets you ready to run away or start fighting, cortisol is there in case you have to fight or flee for a long time.

As adrenaline is working on your blood delivery system, cortisol is supplying energy to that blood through glucose. It's there for the long haul, and when you're stressed for an extended period of time, cortisol suppresses your immune system and encourages the production of more cortisol. It's a cycle of stress — not good if you're trying to keep things together.

Here's where you've got to do some mental gymnastics. You have to trick yourself into believing that this audience isn't going to eat you like a bear would, or like a lion would, or like — well, the audience isn't going to eat you. There's a process used in cognitive behavioral therapy that works wonders in cases like this. *Cognitive behavioral therapy* (CBT) is an approach to treatment that focuses on how people think and act. Every time your mind has something pesky to say like "I'm going to fail," you tell yourself, "No, stop it." Then immediately repeat a positive comment like "I am a great speaker." Repeat it *a lot,* until you start believing it. Every time. Eventually, you can break the stress cycle by retraining your mind.

Thinking like a caveperson

Okay, it's time to go back to our roots. There are things that can be gleaned from how our ancestors (or caricatures of them) used to act:

>> **Owning the room:** Society is an important part of everyone's identity, and that involves one kind of hierarchy or another. At work, your place on the hierarchy is in your job title. In your family it might be established by generation or birth order. For our ancestors, the top position was more fluid. The biggest club and the strongest swing might be all it took for a caveperson to become leader of his little clan. I talk about the benefits of body posture in Chapter 15.

TIP

Just as your ancestor "Grog" owned the cave, you must own the room. I'm not talking about clubbing anyone, unless that's what your speech is about. But try visualizing yourself as leader of the pack. Think of it as everyone watching you not to be convinced of something, but for direction. I discuss visualization in more depth in Chapters 11 and 22.

>> **Being big:** When Grog turned a corner and came face to face with a bear, what did he do? Well, he tried to look bigger than the bear. He put up his arms, puffed out his chest, growled, and hoped to hell the bear was dumb enough to believe the transformation.

TIP

You can use a similar method during a presentation. You're not trying to scare your audience into believing whatever it is you have to say (although wouldn't that be wonderful?). But by appearing and feeling as big and as confident as you can, your message *will* carry further. There's more on this in the section about body language in Chapter 15.

Social psychologist Amy Cuddy talks about adopting a *high power pose* that makes you feel more confident. In an experiment, she had participants put their hands on their hips like a superhero or up over their head in a *V* shape. Another group adopted a "low power pose." After just two minutes, the low-power posers felt low self-esteem and self-worth, and the high-power posers felt confident and ready to tackle the world. (See her TED Talk at www. ted.com/talks/amy_cuddy_your_body_language_shapes_who_you_are.)

>> **Letting go of control:** Grog lived in a dangerous world. Saber-toothed tigers, woolly mammoths, the Flintstones' encroaching suburbia. There were no safe days for your prehistoric cousin, so fretting about the small things was not the type of activity that Grog and his pals were into.

In that same way, while you're up on stage — and while you're preparing your talk — remember that things *may* go wrong and there's nothing you can do about them. I discuss this in Chapter 19. A light fixture may fall and destroy the stool where you've put your water. A cell phone may go off, and someone may well answer it and start talking. Grog knew a cougar might sneak into his cave any night.

There are things you can control and things you can't. Of course, we know rationally when we think about it that we can't control everything in the world. You've got to remember it. You can prepare as much as possible, and something still might go wrong. So, worrying about such things, before or during the show, is fruitless. When we let go of negative thoughts and things we can't control, we feel relieved, which leads to feeling happier.

» **Living in the moment:** Grog didn't have a 401(k). He lived day to day, always in the moment. And although our economy (and life expectancy) has improved since his time, it's good to act like Grog when you're up onstage. Plan meticulously *before* you get up there — but once you're onstage, it's time to give in to the moment. I've heard so many people say that when they presented for the first time, it went by extremely fast. Before they knew it, they were done presenting the thing they'd been preparing for such a long time. That moment, believe it or not, is short. Once you're up there, you have to make the most of it because it will be over before you know it.

When you've finished your presentation, reflect on how you did. Did you keep your mind focused on giving your presentation — or did you lose your focus when the dishes crashed in the kitchen or a cell phone rang? When you think of what went "wrong," can you let it go and not judge yourself for making a mistake?

Yes, you made a mistake. Learn from it and move on. I talk more about rolling with mistakes in Chapter 19.

Leveraging the power of neuroplasticity

As much as our brain tries to call the shots on its own, we can fight back. Well, we can work together. One of the biggest problems I see in people is the perceived inability to work with what they've got upstairs. They can control the mind in all the ways that they think they need when it comes to a presentation. They can write one, they can speak it. But the anxiety, nervousness, and fear are traits that many people have just accepted as a cost of business.

That's where the concept of neuroplasticity comes in. There is a perception that an old dog cannot learn tricks, that, when once we hit a certain age, we can't do anything about the bad habits that have plagued us our entire lives. Well, simply put, that's not true. Turns out our brains are more moldable than we thought. *Neuroplasticity* is the ability to change our brains, even as adults. It can occur when we suffer a brain injury or when we learn something new. Neurons *do* form new synapses, scientists are finding.

Adopting a Yes Let's Attitude

Have you ever watched improv? You probably have. Short for *improvisation,* improv is one of the most popular forms of theater in the world. There's a reason for that: Improv may be the only form of theater that doesn't seem rehearsed — because it's not. The actors are making it up on the spot. Players often wear normal clothing, reference timely cultural and world events, and most importantly, act naturally. When improv is good, laughs come from everywhere, and the audience is in on the joke.

Although it is improvised, in improv actors follow some fundamental rules to make the show feel as natural and unrehearsed as possible. Yes, the situations, the jokes, and everyone's reactions are made up in front of the audience. But without the helpful rules of a drama game called Yes Let's, improv would quickly fall apart. Yes Let's can become an important part of any type of performance, whether or not you plan on winging it.

Yes Let's works like this: If a player does or says something, the next actor must respond in a way that furthers the action. If one actor says, "Is that toupee actually stitched to your head?" the second actor has to go with it. "Yes, it's on there nice and tight," he says, pulling at his hair. Part of the comedy that comes from improv is how two or more minds can come together and create something that was totally unexpected for both actors and audience. Yes Let's allows the conversation to continue. In his book *The Intent to Live* (Bantam Dell, 2005), Larry Moss writes that the most important word in acting is *yes.* If the actor says *no,* and is negative about a performance, that actor can't move forward and will be stuck. That's a good thing to remember when you're giving a speech too.

TIP

A Yes Let's attitude can help you to deal with things going wrong too. An improv performer doesn't know where the scene is going and has to accept the twists and turns. When you're giving a presentation, you have a plan, but plans have a way of going awry. They've asked you to cut your one-hour presentation down to 30 minutes, say. Or you're being asked to go first instead of fourth because other presenters are late. A Yes Let's perspective can help you be relaxed no matter what happens during your presentation.

When you get the opportunity to speak — and yes, it's an opportunity — instead of dreading it and thinking, *This is going to be terrible, I don't know what I'm taking about, why did they ask me?* switch it around. You may have to force yourself to make your thoughts more positive: *Wow, this is going to be great! I get to tell my story. Yes Let's!* When you write it, keep that in mind.

Positive self-talk is a technique used with athletes. Positive thoughts create positive results. Negative thoughts create . . . well, guess. Thinking positively may be foreign to you, so start small. If you go through your day expressing positive thoughts about little things, soon this will be your new habit.

A presentation that takes questions can employ the Yes Let's technique in much the same way. Be empathetic — don't judge the person or the question. Allowing people to fully ask the question, even if you disagree with their premise, will give you a chance to fully understand where they're coming from. Your answer will then be better received by the audience.

What if you don't have a Q&A section at the end of your speech? I tell my clients to think of their whole presentation as a conversation. True, the audience isn't talking back. They are, however, giving you nonverbal cues like nodding or shaking their heads.

What you want to come out of any good speech is a bit of a disruption in order — whether that's people left questioning some long-held belief of theirs or another viewpoint directly entering the fray and engaging you.

Don't give the audience an ultimatum, with no room for any other opinion. That's too easily disregarded after the presentation. Instead, see yourself as engaging them in conversation. Trust me, their ears will perk up.

Knowing When to Say No

There may come a time when you have the opportunity to give a speech, but the right answer is *no, thank you.* This section talks about some situations in which signing up to give a presentation may not be the best idea.

> **» It's not me you're looking for.**
>
> I talk plenty in this book about psyching yourself up to give a good speech. I cover *imposter syndrome* in Chapter 5. Some people appear to be confident but are in fact rife with low self-esteem. They don't feel like they belong. They suspect they landed in their position by mistake and soon will be found as a fraud. This can happen even to high achievers. Such mental blocks can eat away at your confidence and cause you to think you aren't the right speaker for the cause. Sometimes, though, maybe you really *aren't* the best person to give a speech. Maybe a manager has tapped you to present on a project that a lower-level team is working on but that you aren't directly involved in. Pride may well make you want to take on that challenge. But are you really the best person to do it? Maybe it's best to defer to someone who's actually working on it. You can say that, of course, you'd love to be there, supporting them and introducing them.

>> When you're set up for failure.

Maybe you've got an ace speech prepared, but the event organizers change the environment of the speech. This scenario is more common than you might think. Say you're asked to speak about your experience in a very particular or specialized industry group — so particular and specialized, in fact, that the organizers can't sell enough tickets. To attract more people, they decide to widen the scope or topic of the event and tell you about it at the last minute. In fact, they widen it so much that your industry group is now a relatively tiny niche that may not be of much interest to the expanded audience.

WARNING

Your answer should be a resounding no. Don't let yourself be put in a position where you're set up for failure. It's not your fault the organizers pivoted. Hey, it happens, but the organizers should have to find a way around their problem.

>> Last-minute preparation.

Preparing a speech or presentation, as Chapter 6 makes clear, takes time — perhaps way more time than you think. Here's a good rule of thumb: If you don't know how long it's going to take you to write and prepare for a speech, it's probably going to take longer than you think. Plan for that. Often people are asked to present on a topic that they know well, but they've never had occasion to write down much about it — or perhaps even thought much about it in detail. All the material has to be created from scratch in that case, which will take extra time.

>> Timing is everything.

Sometimes the timing of your speech is fantastic. For example, your speech on climate change happens the day after big news about the ice caps is released to the public. But news events can also work against you. If you're scheduled to present on a light-hearted topic in a city that experiences a horrible tragedy the night before, ask the organizers or other locals their thoughts about the appropriateness of going on with the speech.

>> You've lost that loving feeling.

Performance is all about passion. If you have passion for a topic, that can outweigh any shortcomings you may otherwise have, such as inexperience. Similarly, if you're asked to speak about something you really don't care about, your lack of passion may come through too. If you're presenting for work on a topic that you feel is inconsequential, that's a problem. Consider deferring to someone who has passion for that particular project or subject matter.

2

Diagnosing and Treating Common Afflictions

IN THIS PART . . .

Discover ways to overcome performance anxiety and the fear of public speaking, reduce tension, and correct your posture to achieve confidence.

Tackle common vocal problems like vocal fry, upspeak, nasal voice, breathiness, devoicing, pushing, and dropping.

Clarify who you are and why you've been chosen to speak, and overcome feelings of being unworthy or fraudulent.

» **Diagnosing and remedying your slouch**

» **Fighting your body . . . with your body**

Chapter **3**

Overcoming Performance Anxiety

f performance anxiety is your problem, I want you to do something for yourself. It's the first thing I ask of anyone who comes into my office. Ready? Here goes: Video yourself presenting a speech for two minutes.

Two minutes may seem too short to figure out problems, and for some things, it is. In two minutes, even I may not be able to determine what to work on, emotion or intonation or other things of that nature. But two minutes is all it takes for someone to go from a comfortable stance to an awkward slouch that inhibits breath, tone, and pretty much all the other speech fundamentals you learn in this book. You may think whatever's ailing you is in your head, that it's anxiety that's doing you in. And you may be right. But without proper physical form, you won't be giving an effective speech no matter what.

After that two-minute test, I put my clients through a little bit of physical activity — just to get limber, and a vocal warmup. Then I have them do the test again. The change is always remarkable. Now, you're not going to always be able to do jumping jacks before a presentation, but understanding your body's role in your performance is critical.

In this chapter, I cover the importance of releasing your tension and how to fix poor form such as slouching.

Staying Loose: Tension Can Ruin a Speech

Consider athletes. Look at the slow-motion videos of elite runners. They look so relaxed, as if they're floating down the track. Uta Pippig, the first woman to win the Boston Marathon three times, says relaxation is the key to winning. Relaxing your mind helps to relax your body. The opposite is also true: Relaxing your body helps to relax the mind. It's a circle of relaxation. Where you start is up to you.

Runners use every bit of energy available to them to propel themselves forward through the air and — they hope — to the podium. Then there are target shooters, whose outfits are a little less revealing (no need for aerodynamics). If you can watch them in high-definition, you should. They maintain such control over their muscles that they can remain perfectly still. Any movement of their body, even a slight sway or an adjustment from the wind, can ruin their shot. They're trained to squeeze the trigger for maximum control rather than pull it with their arm.

Both kinds of athletes are at the top of their game, and both can control the muscles they need to an almost superhuman degree. But although both are perfect for their particular sport, if these athletes switched sports, they couldn't function in the same capacity.

Then there's a sport that combines both kinds of skills. The biathlon has you cross-country ski as hard as you can toward a target, then stop, release all your tension, and shoot. Biathletes have to slow down their heart rate and release muscle tension so it doesn't affect their shot.

TIP

That's how I want you to think of your presentation. No matter how much stress you have before the speech, I want you to be able to release it all once you're up on stage.

Proper posture: Alignment isn't just for cars

Proper *posture* is your first step to releasing unwanted tension. It's essentially the same process your car goes through when you have your wheels aligned. It goes something like this: For whatever reason — maybe you hit a speed bump too hard — your wheels shift slightly out of alignment on the axles. Sometimes it's hard to tell that this has happened until you begin to notice little things. Your steering wheel might not point the car straight anymore, for example, and may pull to one side. Alignment affects your entire vehicle.

Same thing with your body. If you brought your body into the mechanic and told him it's not steering straight, the first thing he would check is your spine. Yes, your spine is the key to alignment in your body.

So what happens when your spine is misaligned? As with a car, your body will try to compensate for it. Muscles that weren't built to carry the load will try to. It will be harder to keep you up straight, and your back may cave in a little bit. Your lungs won't be able to take the full breaths that they would if the spine were aligned correctly. As a result, your vocal energy will be low (read more about the importance of breath in Chapters 4, 14, 20, and 21). Meanwhile, your shoulders and neck may be tense, your knees may hyperextend, and that additional tension will carry through to your voice.

Good posture is what we're looking for, although *posture* sometimes connotes a moral meaning. Like, say, a nun slapping your desktop with a ruler for slouching. And in that same way, whenever you say the word *posture* around people, they seem to straighten up. It certainly works in my workshops. Try it around your friends. They'll all straighten up for the nun.

Most of us are aware of what good posture looks like — but for all the wrong reasons. "Straightening up" can actually do harm to your alignment if you force the movement. When you stand up straight — and I mean the military kind of straight — your knees lock and might even hyperextend, and the rest of your body compensates to keep you from falling.

Try balancing a book on your head: The first thing people do when they try that is stop breathing. Great, look at that, there's a book on your head! But you're not breathing, and you need to do that to speak.

EXERCISE: FINDING YOUR NEUTRAL

Stand with your feet shoulder width apart. Roll forward onto the balls of your feet, eventually putting all your weight forward on your toes. How does it feel? Well, it should feel like you're propelling forward in the world, and pushing everything else behind. Think of the scene with Jack and Rose on the bow of *Titanic* (the ending of the movie doesn't apply here).

Return to your normal stance. Then go the opposite way: Roll back onto your heels as far as you can without falling over. When you're standing on your heels it's like you don't want to be a part of the action. You're holding back. Now go to where you can feel your toes, balls of your feet, and heels equally on the ground. You should have a good feeling of where that neutral stance is, and when you're speaking, that's where you want to be, solidly planted.

In renowned voice teacher Patsy Rodenburg's book *The Right to Speak* (Routledge, 1993), she says, "The natural way of standing is based on achieving balance, ease, and feeling centered."

>> Your head should sit balanced on top of the spine.

>> Your shoulders should be released.

>> Your arms should hang down by your sides.

>> Your upper chest should be open and not tense.

>> Your vertebrae should feel stacked one on top of the other. Your spine is neither slumped forward nor pushed out.

>> Your lower abdominal muscles should be released without being pulled in or out.

>> Your knees should be unlocked.

>> Your feet should be firmly planted.

EXERCISE: FEELING KINESTHETIC LIGHTNESS

Looking to get in touch with your natural alignment? Stand with your feet shoulder width apart. Make sure your feet are flat on the floor and that they're each taking an equal amount of weight. Now imagine roots growing down from the bottom of your feet, going down farther and farther.

In a trance yet? We're about to go deeper. Visualize all the bones in your body. Can you feel them all individually? Your anklebone is growing up into your shinbone. Your shinbone is growing up into your thigh bone. Your thigh bone is growing up into your pelvis. Your vertebrae are growing out of your pelvis, stacked neatly on top of each other. Your shoulders are spread wide across your chest. Your arms are gently down by your side. Your head is floating on the top of it all, like a bobblehead.

Now, imagine a light coursing through your body, flowing through your legs, stomach, arms, neck, all the way through the crown of your head up to the sky. Does that feel good or what? You should *feel* the light. In fact, this effect has a name: *kinesthetic lightness*. You are feeling support from the ground, which leads you to your natural alignment. You're not stiff or rigid and your muscles are not contracted but expanded. This exercise is a technique actors use, and I find that it works to get people physically ready for performance.

Identifying the tension

You're starting to get yourself aligned. Once good posture is established, it's much easier to figure out where any remaining tension is coming from that may inhibit your speech performance. If you're like most of my clients, you're a reasonably healthy person. No serious back problems, able to walk around, pretty active. You may even be thinking, what tension?

The type of tension caused by public speaking doesn't usually exist in your everyday life. But the mere thought of presenting makes it come out. You start to tense up muscles in areas of your body where you wouldn't if you were doing literally anything else. With one of my clients, the mere mention of a speech or presentation has her gripping her abdominal muscles — something that would never happen to her in, say, the grocery store.

That is the tension we're trying to break here, that tension we hold without even knowing we hold it. In many ways, it's the hardest kind of tension to work on. First, you have to acknowledge that it exists.

EXERCISE: MUSCLING THOSE MUSCLES

Do you know what each muscle in your body does? This exercise can help you get to know your muscles better. You can do this either standing up or lying down. Whatever your position, you should be comfortable and as relaxed as you can be.

Start with your toes. Tense them and feel that sensation. Then release them and feel that sensation. Travel up your body, tensing and then releasing every muscle group you come across. Tense your feet muscles, your calves, your quads, your hamstrings, and every little muscle group in your back. If it's difficult to do this on a particular muscle, try pressing it lightly with your fingertip while you tense. Make a note of how each one feels when you tense it, and if each muscle returns back to normal when you release it. If any release feels tense or doesn't release like you think it should, that could be a sign of some unknown tension there. Try it again and see if you can feel a release: I want you to become a scholar on the muscle groups in your body so you'll have a good idea if anything's amiss.

Next, read your speech and imagine thousands of people in the audience — a number far outside your comfort zone. Now stop. Do you feel any tension? Are any muscle groups not releasing? If so, that could be a key to where you need to work (keep reading for what you can do about it).

There's a difference between *relaxing* and *releasing.* Generally, when I speak about relaxation, I'm referring to the mental side of it, and then of course, the physical side follows. Think about coming home from work after a super busy day and sinking into the couch with a glass of wine. That's pure relaxation. But maybe you carried a heavy box at work and one of your back muscles is tight. It's possible to be in a state where your back muscles are tense and also be relaxed. If you're giving a presentation and you've locked your knees, people can hear it in your voice. Your voice sounds tight and restricted, and that can inhibit your performance, even if you're not mentally tense.

TIP

I generally teach my clients to *release,* not relax. You're in a relaxed state just before going to bed. Or maybe with that glass of wine or cup of tea. When your muscles are released, you're not holding any undo tension, and they're ready to fire up at a moment's notice. Sure, it's good to feel relaxed after a long day at work. But that's not what you're going up on stage to do. You want your muscles released, but you also want to be on alert — a cat ready to pounce.

Releasing the tension

You've expertly pinpointed where you hold tension (or you've got a pretty good idea about it). Now, it's all you can feel when you tense that muscle, no matter whether it's during a performance or leading up to it. You squeeze it, and maybe it doesn't release like it should. And it's begun to drive you crazy. You hunt for a cure far and wide and stumble onto this section of the chapter. Nice going: This section offers some tips and tricks to lose that tension.

Physical activity

"Exercise more." I know. It's almost become a cliché, a sort of panacea that drives people crazy and makes them long for the couch even more. Unfortunately, I'm going to join the ranks of those people right now: *It really does help* to be doing some physical activity. If you haven't realized it by now in this chapter, speech is physical. You're not going to excel if you don't have any other physicality in your life.

For one thing, regular exercise gives you a better understanding of your muscle groups. That exercise you did earlier, where you tensed and released all your muscles? That will get easier after you get to know what muscles do and how to use them. Another thing physical activity does for you is release *endorphins,* chemicals that make you feel exhilarated and happy and block feelings of pain.

REMEMBER

You don't have to run five miles a day to get to where you need to be. Going for a walk, doing some yoga poses, or even taking the stairs instead of the elevator can help.

EXERCISE: VISUALIZING TO RELEASE STRESS

You can do this exercise sitting or lying down. Close your eyes. Now think of a white, sandy beach. The sun is warm, but not hot. The waves are close enough to hear, but not close enough to swallow you up. You smell the sea. You're lying on that sand feeling great.

Breathe in and out with the waves. All that tension you have, let it go out with the tide. Let every breath sink you deeper into the sand, until your perfect imprint is all that remains. Remember, incorporate every sense of this place that you can: Imagine the sight, smells, sounds, the feeling of the sand, the taste of salt on your lips. Try to feel like you're actually there.

Stay on the beach for 10–20 minutes and explore all your senses in your new world until you feel completely relaxed. Your body is like a limp rag. Go back to the beach any time you feel stressed.

TIP

Is your yoga mat nowhere in sight? Maybe you're sitting at a conference table, waiting to present that PowerPoint you spent all night working on. It would probably be socially awkward (at the very least) to lay yourself across the floor, close your eyes, and begin tensing every muscle. Well, if you've become an expert on your body, you may have a good idea where your tension is coming from or will come from once you start your presentation. If you're subtle, you can tense it and release it right there at the table. No one will know, and you won't have to splay across any dirty floors!

Chin Up and Don't Slouch

He's no slouch is a compliment. You shouldn't be slouching, but often the slouch isn't a physical problem, it's a mental one. The anxiety of the fight, flight, or freeze response is at it again. Many slouchers are trying to protect themselves, so they start to curl into a ball.

When your spine collapses, your lungs can't fill properly with air. That's going to travel to your neck, and then your jaw. You'll end up looking like Shaggy on *Scooby-Doo.* The dreaded slouch is one of the worst postures in speaking, but luckily, it's one of the easiest to remedy.

Breathing as a sloucher

Remember when you were a baby? No? Okay, think back and remember the last time you saw a baby. Can you visualize how they breathe? Babies do this ingenious thing when they breathe: They follow their instinct. When babies breathe, they have very little tension in their abdominal and back muscles, so they can breathe in and out easily and take deep, uninterrupted breaths. Sometime during the stage between baby and now, we adults have learned a lot of great things and nasty things. One of those things is the horrible habit of shallow breathing, as if from the upper chest.

There are a few reasons for this adult style of breathing, but the big one is stress, which, not surprisingly, babies don't have a lot of. Stress causes the muscles to contract tightly around your abdomen, making you take quick, shallow breaths. Now, guess what happens when you slouch? The problem gets much worse. We'll do something about that in the next exercise.

We slouch is because it's often the most comfortable position we can find. It's often the path of least resistance. It's a way for all our muscles to become dead weight on top of each other. Aligning yourself for good posture goes against all of that.

It will take time and it will be uncomfortable for a while until you wean yourself off the slouch. But once it becomes natural, it begins to feel great.

Why feeling bad ends up sounding bad

We don't yet have the ability to separate our bodies from our voices, even though it may seem that way for some narrators. So we're stuck with having our voices be conduits for any maladies our bodies seem to have on that given day — or conduits for something more chronic, like stress. If your body is tight because you're anxious due to an upcoming speech, your voice will reflect that. You're stressed and think you can fake it? That's a tough one, man. The only way to get rid of that sound is to dig it up from its roots.

EXERCISE: BOWING TO THE SLOUCH

This exercise is meant to prove to you that slouching is a breath killer. Slouching has its time and its place (for example, on the couch during a ball game), but that time and place is *not* during a speech or while preparing for it.

But right now you *are* going to slouch. Ready? One, two, three, slouch. Curve your back. Let your neck scrunch up, like it does when you're binge-watching your favorite show. Now, try to take a deep breath. What? You can't?

Now flip back a few pages and redo the alignment exercise. How do you feel now? Can you feel a huge difference in how you breathe? How your body has positioned itself?

EXERCISE: FINDING YOUR BREATH

Here's another exercise to prove something to you. Let's see "where" you breathe from.

Stand with your feet shoulder width apart and plant those feet like you have roots growing under them, through the foundation of the building your standing in, all the way down into the dirt, and there's a big tree growing out of the crown of your head into the sky. Breathe a few times. Now, put one hand on your upper chest and another on your lower abdomen and breathe again.

Where do you feel the most movement? If it's in that upper chest, try again, this time trying to fill up your lungs with all that air. The belly moves because the diaphragm is expanding fully and the abdominal muscles are released enough to respond fully to this expansion. Take a few more long breaths, in and out, and then pause. Feel where your body is when you take those breaths. That's how you should be positioned when you're performing. I go into more detail on breath in Chapter 14.

You may also want to check out the exercise in Chapter 20 involving Tai Chi.

WARNING

Your voice will betray you. That quiver you feel in your gut on the day of the performance will be heard. That's why I'm focusing so much on getting you to release your tension with these exercises.

Here are some common vocal symptoms of an anxious presenter and suggestions for what you can do about them:

>> **Quiet speaking into a microphone:** This idea that you must use a microphone to be heard is endemic and in many cases it's just wrong. Let's go ahead and say it: You probably don't need a microphone. *But,* you protest, *what if I'm about to speak at a conference for five thousand people?* Well, then you're going to need a microphone. But generally, for a small crowd size, using a microphone is a crutch and often doesn't end well. When you speak quietly, it's often because your muscles are tense and you can't project your voice.

Why shouldn't you use this technology that's made specifically for the projection of the human voice? One reason is that you probably won't use a microphone when you practice your speech. So, you'll practice the speech and get it perfect with a great projected voice, and then get there and see a microphone in your face and have to suddenly figure out a whole new way to do it. Have you ever heard your voice coming out of speakers? If you haven't, it's best not to try it out during a speech. It's horrifying. Your voice doesn't sound like you. Totally weird. So what you'll do is compensate and speak quieter than you should, and because of that you could potentially lose some power.

- **Speed speaking:** It's amazing how fast people can speak when they're just trying to get through something. Logically, what's the best way to get through a very anxiety-ridden speech? To do it as fast as you can, of course. But that's not going to help you in the long run. It's one of the easiest things the audience will pick out about your speech. And it's one of the biggest problems I see in new speakers. Luckily, there's a cure for it: Realize it's going to happen, and slow down.

- **Shaky voice:** Have you ever heard speakers who sound like they're about to cry the whole time? Sometimes that's for effect. Sometimes they *are* going to cry, and it's so completely powerful that the audience cries too. But sometimes you can tell from the beginning that it's not the type of subject matter to get teary-eyed about. A business plan might be beautifully executed, but the board of directors doesn't expect you to cry about it. Having a shaky voice can get awkward.

  The reason for shaky voice is simple: no breath support. If you've ever played an instrument like a trumpet or saxophone, what happens when you don't blow enough air into the horn? A poor sound. The same idea applies to our vocal folds if there's not enough air going through. The vocal folds don't *approximate* (come together) fully and won't vibrate with ease and efficiency.

  The answer: Breathe deep, as if from down from your lower abdomen, not from up in your chest. Take long breaths in, and then out again. Keep your shoulders down and your chest up and out on the inhale. Inhale for a count of four, then exhale on a whispered "ah." Allow the sound to flow freely out of your body. Repeat a few times and then replace the whisper with a spoken "ah." Eventually graduate to a sentence in your presentation.

- **Voice cracking:** Assuming you're not 12 years old, your cracking voice is due to something other than hormones. So, how come you become a preteen throwback every time you go up to speak? The same reason some people get shaky voice. It doesn't happen with everyone. It depends on how deep or high your voice is and the control you have in your voice already. But either way, the cure is proper breathing. Slow down those breaths and bring them in as if from deep in your abdomen. Try to release your abdominal muscles after every sentence. And take a breath after every sentence. This will allow you to fully catch up and also give the audience time to process what they just heard.

- **Dry throat/loss of voice:** This is a physiological response to stress that causes muscles in your body to tighten, and that goes for your throat, vocal folds, and chest as well. This is common enough, as are the remedies, such as hot water with lemon and honey. But what if that doesn't do the trick? If not, it may be that the fight, flight, or freeze response has been activated, and moisture is being diverted elsewhere. So, if you're full to the brim with water and your mouth is still dry as a bone, keep reading for ideas on combatting this sometimes troublesome gift of evolution.

- » **Clearing the throat/coughing:** Not a cougher until you're on stage? That seems mighty suspicious, doesn't it? When you're stressed, you often breathe quickly and shallowly from your upper chest, which can cause your throat to dry. It can also be just a nervous habit.

- » **Yawning when you're not tired:** Do you constantly yawn before you give that presentation? Physiological responses to threat include increased heart rate and tightening of the muscles. When this occurs, our bodies heat up. Yawning is an unconscious way of cooling your brain down.

- » **Trouble putting thoughts into words:** Oh, things may be all fine and dandy when you're just remembering what you wrote. But what if there's an unexpected question period? And you've lost the ability to speak your mother tongue? Breathe deep! And keep reading because the next section discusses how to fight the fight, flight, or freeze response.

Using Your Body to Battle the Fight, Flight, or Freeze Response

Chapter 2 talks about what the fight, flight, or freeze response can do to your mind. What are some things your body can do to fight back? This section includes exercises that will help you regain control when you step in front of those bright lights.

In my workshops, one of the exercises I use to explore the difference in the positions I call *in and down* (slouched) and *up and out* (tall with head held high) involves role play. Each group pairs off and decides to play out a scenario with a problem. For example, it could be a boss reprimanding an employee who always comes late to work.

The pair then decides which one will be in an in and down position and who will be in an up and out position. They tend to conclude that it's more likely the boss would maintain the up and out pose and the lowly employee the down and in. They role-play for a few minutes and then I ask them to keep the characters and problem but switch their body positions.

What happens is interesting. In an up and out position the boss is confident, can articulate clearly why arriving late is a problem, and comes up with solutions — such as set an alarm clock. When she's in a down and in position, though, she can't make eye contact, has trouble stringing two sentences together, and just wants to get the heck out of there.

EXERCISE: ASSUMING THE POSITION

Stand upright in a neutral position. Feel roots growing down to the earth from the bottom of your feet while the rest of your body is growing up to the sky. Now slouch down and droop, like Shaggy from *Scooby Doo*. Try to walk around the room in this position. What happens to your pace? Where's your focus? What are your thoughts? Put one hand on your lower abs and one on your upper chest. Breathe in and out. What hand moves first when you are breathing in?

Give your body a good shake and return to your normal stance. Now stand as tall as you can, with your chest out, and walk around the room again. Notice your pace. Are you moving faster? Is your focus more focused outward, at the world? Where does your breath feel like it's coming in when you inhale? Are you dropping it deeper into your lower abs? What are you thinking about? What are some words that can describe this feeling?

When you hold your head up and stand tall it sends a message to the brain that you are strong and confident, so you actually begin to feel more confident. Before, when you were Shaggy and your body was contracted and slouchy, you were instinctually taking up less room, and your voice sounded smaller and less confident.

When the employee is in the down and in position she feels bad and has little self-esteem, and might even feel that she's going to get fired. When she's in the up and out position, she wonders why there is a problem. She thinks clearly and comes up with answers.

EXERCISE: STANDING UP WITH LESS EFFORT

Sit in a chair with your feet flat on the floor. Put your hand on the back of your neck. Now try to stand up. Are your neck muscles tightening? Do you feel your neck pull forward? Your neck is just an innocent bystander and it shouldn't be involved when you stand up. The Alexander Technique, created by Frederick Matthais Alexander, is a process of initiating movement with ease. We can move in a more comfortable way with no strain.

So, try it again. Sit in a chair, with your hand on your neck. Start to stand up. When you feel a pull from your neck, just roll your neck slightly forward until you don't feel the pull. Then stand. Doesn't that feel easier? It takes less effort, and your neck will thank you.

TIP

As you probably know, you don't need to be standing in front of 1,000 people to feel anxious. Sitting around a conference table explaining the goings on in your department can do it. So sit up straight! A 2009 study in the *European Journal of Social Psychology* held a test for body posture and self-evaluation. Participants were asked to write down their strengths and weaknesses. When they were slumped in a down and in position, they were not as articulate and had difficulty listing their strengths. Those who sat up straight with their feet flat on the floor in an up and out posture wrote more positive qualities about themselves.

REMEMBER

Changing your posture can also change your mood about things, which may be particularly important when you need to include your input in something. When you're in a slumped position sitting around the boardroom table, you're more likely to be persuaded by others even if you know that your idea is better.

Chapter **4**

Curing Common Vocal Problems

D o you remember being a baby? Probably not. But let me tell you how it was, having had two babies of my own. The biggest difference between me and my babies that I noticed (aside from the littleness and not being able to do anything) is that they experience little stress. They might cry over not getting fed immediately, but a few words from me might have them smiling. This is not to say that babies don't experience stress, but definitely not as much as they will when they get older.

As they grow up, with each upsize of shoes, an added layer of stress and worry gets lumped onto them. At first, it's just spelling tests. Then homework and chores. Then standardized tests, more chores, and so on. But with every level of stress they accumulate, they also learn behaviors to mitigate that stress and figure out what needs to be figured out. They may hold their breath, clench their teeth, or tense their facial muscles. Some of those behaviors will be shed as they get older and learn new, better ones. But some will stay put, and some of those will become habitual.

Not all habits are bad. Making your bed every day? That's a good one. Waking up early for a run? No one's going to make you stop that one, especially not in this book. But you may also have bad habits that you didn't even know were there. And when it comes to voice habits, all the bad ones tend to come out when you start public speaking. What is your natural voice anyway? Renowned vocal pedagogue

Kristin Linklater, who wrote *Freeing the Natural Voice* (Drama Publishers, 2006), suggests that getting rid of physical tensions will help us find our natural voice. Whether it's vocal fry, lack of breath support, or any other number of things, bad voice habits can impede your onstage performance. The point of this chapter is to recognize which bad habits may be hurting your speech, and then work on them.

Vanquishing Vocal Fry

Vocal fry, or creaky voice, seems to be everywhere nowadays, from podcast announcers to reality show hosts. What is it? To create sound, air moves past our larynx to the vocal folds, which vibrate smoothly. Vocal fry occurs when you speak in your lowest possible register, as low as you can go. You don't have enough energy or breath to produce the sound. Instead of the vocal folds moving easily together, they are slamming shut. Very little air can pass through. This creates a creak or popping sound, often compared to bacon frying in a pan. Sometimes you can hear it at the end of a phrase or sentence, and sometimes all the way through a sentence. And you hear it from women and men.

Vocal fry is commonly employed by young people, but some older folks have it too. Currently, the criticism of it has sometimes been tangled up with criticism of young people — in particular, girls. However, a study of 18–22-year-olds at Centenary College in Lousiana found that men, too, have vocal fry but tend to use it throughout their speech, whereas women mainly use it at the end of a phrase.

Unfortunately, some people of my generation have found a hill to die on, and that hill is vocal fry. They say it sounds annoying. Some say that the claim that vocal fry is annoying is a sexist argument. Others say, no, it actually is annoying.

I'm not advocating for either side. I'm a vocal coach. My problem with vocal fry is simply that its symptoms are such that they fly in the face of my teachings about breath and projection. So, for that reason alone, I'm going to try to help you stop your vocal fry.

Recognizing vocal fry and its causes

Vocal fry is caused by one of two things that both have the same results:

>> **Holding back and not allowing your breath to flow through your vocal tract fully.** Or you run out of breath and your vocal energy drops into your lowest register. Vocal fry often emerges at the end of phrases because that's when you run out of breath or lose your vocal energy. Think about a guitar. When you tune a guitar, you tighten or loosen the strings until they're

vibrating at the right pitches. When they're out of tune, they sound wrong and clash with each other. They might even smack off each other and the guitar body itself. The same thing happens when you don't have enough breath. Your vocal folds don't tighten properly, so they don't vibrate correctly and can cause popping sounds.

>> **Speaking in your lowest possible pitch:** When you speak in lower pitch, you tend to give it less air than is normally needed, and this can result in vocal fry. Why would anyone speak in a lower pitch? Well, it often has to do with instinct. People often speak lower when they're trying to speak authoritatively. It gives a certain amount of empowerment, for sure. But when what comes out instead is vocal fry, authoritativeness goes out the window — plus it's really hard to hear.

Seeing why vocal fry is perceived negatively

Your seat is fastened and the flight attendants have just done the safety spiel that you didn't listen to. Then, as the plane begins to taxi, on comes a crackly voice that seems caught in a cultural feedback loop: At this point it's hard to determine whether some pilots sound that way because they just do, or because they've heard other pilots talk that way. "Ladies and gentlemen, this is your captain speaking." But he seems barely whispering, and his voice rattles and crackles and trails off at the end. I'm not saying *all* pilots speak with vocal fry; some are pretty darned clear and expressive. The point is that with the fancy sound systems we have these days, we hear their voice very clearly. Plus when we can only hear a voice, we aren't distracted by what the person is wearing or by the spinach in their teeth.

Researchers at Duke University conducted a study to determine how young women who had vocal fry fared in the job market. Men and women were asked to record a message with vocal fry and then one without. Eighty percent of people choosing a candidate for the job picked the message spoken by the non-vocal fry voice, and, unfortunately, women had an even tougher time getting jobs than men when both had vocal fry. These interviewers found candidates more trustworthy when they didn't have vocal fry, even if both candidates were otherwise the same.

Note: This may be partly the result of a generational divide — those who have reached the point in their careers where they are interviewing people are probably a little older.

Regardless, vocal fry shouldn't be part of your public speaking.

To find out if you have vocal fry, try this: Whisper, "One, two, three, four, five," without much pause, as if it were a sentence. Then say those numbers again out loud. Do you hear any croaks or crackles? Does your voice tend to drop off at the end of your sentence?

EXERCISES: DIAGNOSING AND ADDRESSING VOCAL FRY

- **Finding your optimal pitch:** Before I get into diagnosing and addressing vocal fry, you need to find your *optimal pitch*. This is the sound we make when the larynx is released, tongue is relaxed, and body is aligned. It's where you breathe easily and feel comfortable in the placement of your voice. Say an "aaah." Try to vary your pitch and note how it feels. Does your throat tighten or does it feel free and easy? Say, "aaah" in a higher pitch. Do you feel as free and easy as the first time? Go lower and see what happens.

- **Get out!** Whenever Elaine on *Seinfeld* heard something crazy, she would yell, "Get out!" and push one of the male characters aggressively. Say, "Get out!" Gradually slide your pitch up, repeating, "Get out!" each time, resonating it in your chest, your oral cavity (mouth), and your head. Go as high as you can and stop when you feel like you're pushing your voice out in a squeak. Now go back down, repeating, "Get out!" Take note where you feel most comfortable and your voice sounds free and expressive. That's your optimal pitch.

Do it again now, but this time with proper breath support. Take deep breaths as if from your lower abdomen. Your ribs, lungs, and belly should all expand when you inhale. When you start speaking, say your whole sentence to the end with enough breath that you could do it again if you wanted. Imagine you're keeping a balloon suspended in the air when you say a sentence. Keep it suspended with your breath until the end of a sentence.

TIP

It's a good idea to raise your pitch a little higher than your general habit dictates. A slightly higher pitch makes your tone stronger and clearer. There are different ways of describing vocal registers and speech pathologists tend to categorize them as follows, from lowest to highest: vocal fry, modal, falsetto, and whistle. The *modal* range is the middle of your voice range, where it operates more efficiently.

Undoing Upspeak

Upspeak is a high rise in intonation at the end of a sentence that makes it end up sounding like a question. Upspeak perhaps reached its height in the "Valley girl" talk of the 1980s, partly due to Frank Zappa's hit song, "Valley Girl."

Upspeak tends to creep into people's speech now and then due to habit and mimicking others, or when they're not feeling confident. Some of my clients who speak English as a second language (ESL) use upspeak. It's as if they're asking you if what they are saying is correct? Sometimes people say every sentence as if it were a question? Like you're reading this now? Even if it's not a question, but actually a statement? Like for instance? The car is blue? The truck is, like, red?

It's exhausting even writing that way. And unfortunately, once again, women tend to use upspeak more. A study that analyzed the answers given in the game show *Jeopardy!* revealed that women who answered the question correctly used upspeak in their answer 48 percent of the time, whereas men used it in 27 percent of their correct answers. (I know, seems like a weird study; you're *supposed* to answer *Jeopardy!* questions in the form of a question.)

Knowing why we upspeak

For men or women, upspeak is just one of those habits we pick up from people speaking around us, from popular entertainment and media, or when we're not sure if the words we're saying are correct, as in my ESL clients. But upspeak tends to make you sound not confident and monotonous.

If you encounter someone who is asking a question with everything he's saying, you might start to think that person isn't too confident. Whether it's true or not, people who speak with upspeak sound like they're looking for approval from those they're conversing with. And it's really tough to sustain a conversation with someone like that.

I find that upspeak comes out a lot during public speaking, especially when people are unsure they'll get the type of reception they're hoping for. Just the fact that they aren't confident with themselves speaking can bring it out.

Upspeak is also monotonous to listen to. Hearing people speak can be boring if they're using the same intonation the whole time. People crave variety when listening. Even if the topic is compelling, the monotony of upspeak may overwhelm everything else.

The following exercise "Getting rid of that question mark in your voice" can help you lose your intonation, but in a real speech you probably won't be talking about the color of your shirt. You'll need to take your speech and get rid of any question asking there, too. Write every line of your speech on a separate line of a piece of paper, just as you do with the random truths you write for the exercise. You should see a similar structure: barely any questions, I'm guessing.

Find a chair and stand in front of it, but don't sit down yet. Say a line of your speech out loud. Think of each line as an individual statement rather than a part of a larger work. Sit down firmly on the chair at the end of the line. This can help drop your pitch, which is what should happen at the end of a sentence. Sound better?

TIP

Need some more inspiration? Try reading a children's book if you have one handy. Take out your favorite Dr. Seuss, for example, and read it out loud. Children's books are typically full of plain, simple statements. *Aphorisms* are easy on the ears of kids and may just retrain you, too. Our lives are complex things, and our language often reflects that complexity, but when you have a short amount of time to convince someone of something, it's a good idea to turn that nuanced reasoning into pure, cold, statements.

Decomissioning Devoicing

I had braces as an adult — like, deep into adulthood: I had them at age 40. It was my decision to get braces. So when I had to confess to my orthodontist that the reason I broke one of my brackets was because I ate a frozen cookie, the smallest sound came out of my mouth. I didn't *really* want him to hear what I had to say. And this, my friends, is the topic of this section: devoicing.

Recognizing devoicing

Devoicing is when your voice sounds like a whisper and is almost inaudible. But it doesn't just happen out of shame or embarrassment. You often devoice when you soothe someone. Doctors and caregivers use devoicing to sound reassuring and trustworthy. And it's good for these things. But in public speaking, devoicing is problematic. You're *not* soothing your audience (probably not, anyways). And when you devoice, your energy goes completely flat.

If you're a natural devoicer

Devoicing, as I've mentioned, is a legitimate way to speak to someone in certain situations. Maybe you do it a lot. But it's almost impossible to be heard when you devoice to a large crowd — in that situation, your voice *must* have the timbre to sustain a strong message.

Maybe you find it hard to draw attention to yourself. You can't make yourself heard in social scenes. Maybe you're constantly asked to repeat yourself. That gets tiresome. Devoicers can become so hard to communicate with the listener just stops trying. That can damage confidence. So how do you speak sentimentally when you have to use a full voice?

One way I've taught my clients to overcome this is to do away with the idea that emotions have their own volume. Of course, there may be times in a speech where you get *louder*. But the point is to never dip too low, regardless of whether is time to be sentimental or not.

EXERCISES: COMMANDING THE CROWD

You've gotten rid of devoicing, you've found your breath, and you know where to look. It's time to *command* the crowd. How do you do that? With passion, of course. Use your emotional connection to your speech. When you're invested in speaking because it's important to you, you get inspired, and you then transfer that energy to your voice.

It's time to chant. Oh, what's that? I've gone off the deep end? Bear with me, folks.

Take a piece of text. *Any* piece of text. It could be the warning on a coffee cup stating that it's *hot*, or the label on your favorite beer. If you're feeling frisky, it could be a sentence you've written in your speech. Now take video or record yourself speaking the text the way you think you'd say it during your presentation. Pick a pitch that is comfortable for you, right in the middle of your range. Take a breath as if from deep in your abdomen and then let go. *Chant* the sentence. For example: *"Thank you for coming."* Then immediately *speak* the same sentence, quickly enough that you don't have time to analyze your voice. On the video or recording, take a look at both versions. What's different about the second? It should sounds more natural than the first.

Not all devoicing comes from emotion. Where you look with your eyes and body position can cause it, too. Something I see quite a bit is speakers applying one of the most harmful body positions you'll ever see onstage: the *down and in* position mentioned in Chapter 2. This looks exactly the way you picture it: looking down, arms scrunched together, trying their darnedest to sink into those floorboards. And where are they looking? Directly in front of their feet. Not good. Speak to an audience the way you speak to someone — you look at them, or close to them.

Your body position follows your eyes.

Body position is a tricky thing to have to figure out onstage. Sometimes when you're onstage, you can't see anyone anyway, so what are you supposed to look at? If you're around a boardroom table, are you looking at everyone directly in the face? For many, it's easier to sink into themselves and stare at the floor than to stare the boss in the eyes as if over tiramisu on a fantastic date.

Here's a simple solution: Look the audience in the eye. Yup, I mean it. You know the saying "the eyes are the windows to the soul"? Well, they are in Chris Anderson's book *Ted Talks* (HarperCollins, 2016). He writes that the best speakers look at the audience: "Great speakers find a way of making an early connection with their audience. It can be as simple as walking confidently onstage, looking around, making eye contact with two or three people, and smiling." When you look at someone in the audience, you form a connection with that person, if only for a few seconds. It builds trust in you and makes the audience member feel important. It makes you feel more confident and powerful. If you *don't* look people in the eye, that gives them the opportunity to look away from you and focus on something else. So, find someone in the audience and look at that person for no more than 5–6 seconds, then move on. You could even add a smile; why not? You will transfer the same feeling to the other person. It's a win-win. I talk more about this in Chapter 15.

Battling Breathiness

Breathing is the first thing we do in life and the last thing we do in life. It's with us wherever we go. Ever try to regulate your breath? You can, but not for long. When your problem is *breathiness*, you're going to have to get in there and do a little tweaking.

How breathing works

When you take a breath in, or *inhale*, the lungs fill up with air, the ribs expand up and out, and the diaphragm, which is dome-shaped, flattens as the abdominal muscles move down and release. When we exhale, the diaphragm flexes upward, the ribs contract, and the abdominal muscles move in and up as air is expelled from the lungs. The diaphragm has resumed its dome shape.

EXERCISES: BEATING BACK BREATHINESS

Exercise 1: Imagine blowing up a balloon. Note how the bottom of the balloon expands first. Imagine that's how your lungs look too. Breathe in through your nose and try to drop your breath deep into your abdomen. As you fill up your lungs, notice your ribs swing open as you fill up with air. When you exhale, your abdominal muscles should move in and up toward your spine, kind of like rolling up a tube of toothpaste.

I always ask clients to breathe in through their nose because it acts as a *cleansing* breath. When we breathe through our mouths, we often don't take as big a breath in to make it feel like we're filling up the lower abdomen, even though it is our lungs that are actually filling up with air. Breathing through the mouth often causes us to expand only the upper chest, and when you breathe from the upper chest, you can only take short breaths, which aren't enough to sustain your breath through a long sentence. But breathing through the nose isn't always possible during a presentation. You often can't take that time to make sure you have that "belly breath." So, it's important to at least learn what it's like to take that breath in from your nose, and then re-create it while breathing in with your mouth during a speech.

Exercise 2: To feel your abdominal muscles working, try breathing in and exhaling with a "Shhh," like a librarian. Tell that mischievous library patron a few times: "Shhh, shhh, shhh." Can you feel your abdominal muscles pull in and up? That means that they're engaged and working to support your breath.

Exercise 3: This one will help you get that breath support you need, although it takes a bit of math. Well, counting. Anyways: Count to one, and then breathe. Next, count to two, and then breathe. Continue this until you reach 10. How does your body feel? If you feel any tension building up, start over. Do it until you can go all the way through, with no stopping, without any tension building up in your body. Make sure you're counting with energy. Imagine you're playing hide and seek and counting before you go off to catch someone.

Your *core* muscles are used to support the release of air from your lungs. The air then passes through your vocal folds. So where do problems arise? Your body doesn't allow the diaphragm to flatten to its full potential due to tension. You grip those abdominal muscles and exhale all that air that should be coming out of your lungs and into your vocal folds. Instead, you get a wispy sound, called breathiness, kind of like your vacuum makes when the bag's full.

What breathiness does to credibility

The *breathy* person sounds like a lazy person, someone who is holding back in life, who doesn't seem to care. "But it's not true!" you say. "I'm breathy, and the farthest thing from lazy!" Well, now's your time to prove it. Maybe it's not laziness. Maybe it's a lack of trust in others or in yourself. Maybe you just need a little impetus to sound like you know you can. But make no mistake: Speaking without breath support sounds dull. There's no room for inflection or resonance, and without that you're not a very engaging speaker. Breathiness can be caused by lack of breath support and a lack of contact of air at the vocal folds. So to make sure you support your breath at all times, to break that dang habit, see the nearby exercises.

Negating Nasal Voice

There are two main types of nasal problems in speaking. The first is *hyponasality,* which sounds like you have a cold or nasal obstruction caused by allergies. The other is *hypernasality,* which sounds almost like you're talking through your nose. Think Janice from *Friends.* "Oh. My. God. Chandlah."

TECHNICAL STUFF

You've actually got two *palates.* One is the *hard* palate, which extends from the back of your teeth back along the middle of the roof of your mouth. That's the one your tongue is always touching. The *soft* palate, meanwhile, is behind your hard palate, and pretty hard to get at with your tongue. Its job is to close off the nasal passages during swallowing. When it lowers, it lets you make the nasal sounds of *ng, n,* and *m.* These sounds are meant to vibrate through your nose. For a non-nasal sound, the soft palate at the back of the throat stays up there, allowing for the breath to enter more fully in the mouth.

How can you tell if you've got this nasal issue? Start by saying something, literally any sentence. Now put your thumb and another finger gently on each side of your nose. Then pinch your nose and repeat the same sentence. Do you sound different? If you sound drastically different, it's because that sound that is supposed to be coming through your mouth was coming through your nose. Guess what: You've got a sound that's nasal.

EXERCISES: NIXING NASALITY

How do you avoid sounding too nasal? You need to send air and vibration through your mouth as you speak, not through your nose. I know, it's weird thing to try to do. Plug your nose and practice speaking through your mouth without your nose.

Exercise 1: Open your mouth as wide as you can. Pretend you're chewing a mouthful of crackers. (Be careful that when you open your mouth you're not creating tension anywhere else on your body.) Once you have a wide mouth, switch between the nasal sound and non-nasal sound (now that you know the difference). Exaggerate your nasal sound even more when you say, "I am happy to speak with you today." Really feel the vibrations buzzing in your nose. Then drop your jaw and open your mouth, visualizing the sound at your breastbone, and repeat the sentence again. Move between the nasal and the dropped sound and notice the difference.

Exercise 2: To see the opening and closing of the soft palate, take a look in the mirror. Open your mouth wide and yawn. Exercise your soft palate to see how it works by breathing out on a *K* sound.

Exercise 3: Breathe in and on the exhale say, "Aaah." All the air should come from your mouth. Then breathe in again and on the exhale say, "Aaah" from your nose — some of the sound will come out of your nose, then into a long nasal *ng* sound where all the sound comes from your nose. Close your eyes and do this complete round a few times. Can you hear the difference?

Exercise 4: Exaggerate your nasal sound even more. Think of Janice on *Friends* or Fran Drescher in *The Nanny* while you're saying, "I am happy to speak with you today." Really feel the vibrations buzzing in your nose. Then drop your jaw, open your mouth, visualize the sound at your breastbone, and repeat the sentence again. Move between the nasal and the dropped sound and notice the difference.

Preventing the Push: Speaking Evenly

When I started out acting, I got a weird bit of direction. A director once told me that I was *pushing* myself on the other actor, specifically with my chin and neck. I looked around: There was a solid three feet around me and the other player. A total personal bubble. No pushing in sight. "No need to force yourself on him!" the director shouted, as I stood in the corner of the stage by myself, and the other actor was at the front. "It's a quiet scene!"

What was the director talking about? And what was I doing wrong? I should have clued in when he was talking about the intimacy of the scene. Many people who are inexperienced performers tend to push their voices too hard, at all times. They go full tilt, regardless of the tone of the speech. I learned that day that when there is a quiet scene, it's okay to act appropriately quiet. What we want to hear in a speaker is one who speaks with ease, not one who is turning red, is tense all over, and looks like he's gonna blow.

Don't *push* or ram your speech down people's throats. Sometimes speakers do this so they can be heard — they feel they must do it. It happens in the boardroom as well as onstage. In renowned vocal pedagogue Barbara Houseman's book *Finding Your Voice* (Nick Hern Books, 2007), she states, "the brain associates effort with a need to close or constrict the throat." The resulting sound reflects the tension in the body: The tension can wind up in the throat, so speakers lose the ability to adjust much of the range of pitch or tone. They're stuck on one level, and all the audience gets is the monotonous, loud drone of someone who's worried she won't get the message across without it. And it's a horrible cycle: The speaker compensates by getting louder and louder and often becomes physically and vocally drained.

Disconnecting your thoughts and feelings

What does pushing do to your message? Sure, you may feel the emotion, but you're only using one way to express it. The quiet, the soft — it all goes away. It's like the so-called "loudness wars" in music. In the past few decades, there's been a push to engineer popular music to be as loud as it possibly can go on a recording, presumably to grab attention on the radio. All the frequencies are boosted and compressed, which undercuts the difference between the soft parts and the loud parts. What this has done is flatten the dynamics, and make recorded music sound much more monotonous, all the way through a song. You don't have the change in tone from the acoustic part in Led Zeppelin's "Stairway to Heaven" to the heavier parts. When those differences are gone, the differences in emotion go away along with it.

Speech works the same way. When I listen to someone who is pushing, whether it be at a dinner party or at a presentation, it all sounds the same. There are none of those ridges and valleys, those emotional leaps you get when volume or tone changes. The audience is there for the content of the speech, but they want the content to provide that emotion, too, and the emotion often comes from the performance itself. At the very least, the dynamics of the performance enhance the emotion in the content.

Wingin' it

I know nothing about football. If someone were to ask me to describe the mechanics of the game, chances are I would take a deep breath, gather some courage, throw my chest out, and start talking in a really loud voice to muddle my way through it. For some reason, our brains tell us that these things compensate for knowledge.

You may want to review the alignment exercise in Chapter 3. Your feet should be flat on the floor, with roots growing down into the earth. Your shoulders should be relaxed and your arms easily placed down by your sides. Release your neck and note any jaw tension. If so, release that, too (see Chapter 12 for jaw exercises). Try yawning. No, seriously — a yawn helps release the tension in the jaw and is a great way to signal the body to relax. Yawning also involuntarily helps you breathe more deeply.

It's all about breathing. Take the time to breathe deep. Find the support from your abdominal muscles, not your throat. (See more exercises in Chapter 14.)

We push when we're not prepared or when we lack confidence in what we're saying. For example, if you're giving a speech about the benefits of vitamin D, you'd better believe it yourself. (Some *devoice* when they're unprepared, not wanting anyone to hear what they haven't worked on.) Ever been to a school council meeting when the president unexpectedly asks the chair of the playground committee to give an update? First the committee chair says, "My apologies, I wasn't prepared for this." (Never say sorry or give an excuse, by the way — I talk about that in Chapter 19.) But then guess what happens? The chair starts talking loudly. Another example is when comedians are bombing. They'll push and push until they get anything out of the audience.

Stopping Stuttering

We all know what stuttering sounds like. It's a common problem dramatized in movies. In school, stuttering gets made fun of a lot. And that's really a shame, because it makes stutterers even more nervous and self-conscious. But it can get better. James Earl Jones had a stutter and refused to speak when he was young. Imagine the galaxy without Darth Vader.

Stuttering is a disorder where the rhythm of speech is interrupted by repetitions or prolonged sounds. It can start in children as they are exploring how to speak. Often, once a child gets older and more of a seasoned vet when it comes to speech, stuttering can go away. But not always. It can linger into adulthood. You might stutter because you're anxious. Or you may be anxious because you stutter. It's a vicious cycle. Often, a stutterer just wants to get everything out as quickly as possible (hey, that's typical of many non-stutterers, too).

Breathing to alleviate stuttering

"Don't tell me," you're saying. "It all comes down to breathing, doesn't it?" Of course it does. Breath is the thing that makes your speech go round, baby. It's the material you need to make sound.

TIP

As I say elsewhere, *slow down your breath.* Breathe deep as if into your abdomen. When you breathe from your upper chest, it stresses you out. You can't get much air into your body that way — you can start to look like a person on the verge of drowning. You take short gasps of air, which can even make you hyperventilate. Breathing calmly helps you gain control, thereby increasing your confidence.

TIP

Many politicians, actors, and singers stutter, but we never know it until we hear them being interviewed. Singing can help. When a stutterer sings, the rhythm can prevent them from stuttering. In their book *Understanding Stammering or Stuttering* (Jessica Kingsley Publishers, 2012), authors Elaine Kelman and Alison Whyte surmise that the combination of melody and speech, which come from different parts of the brain, may result in greater fluency. Singing words that he had trouble speaking helped King George VI. It was much safer than the advice he was previously given, which was to speak with marbles in his mouth. Poor guy could've choked. So try singing lines from your speech. Try to feel that rhythm when you're speaking.

Rolling with word flubs

It wasn't too long ago that most people believed stutterers had a sort of cognitive delay. To this day, some stutterers and others believe that. A listener may wait patiently for a stutterer to get out those words, but seeing how hard a time the stutterer is having can cause anxiety. Humans are empathy machines a lot of the time, after all.

I have worked with a few people who stutter, and I tell them, like I tell all my clients, that if they feel they haven't presented their speech as well as they practiced, or if they do stutter in the speech — just *let it go.* You really can't do much more than that. Nobody's perfect. As a speaker, you have a story to tell, and we want to hear it. If you appear flustered and frustrated because you stutter when giving a speech, the audience will pick up on that frustration. They'll be worried about you — and that's when they'll lose their grip on your message.

TIP

There could be many reasons for your stutter. Seeking professional help from a speech language pathologist may be beneficial.

EXERCISES: SOOTHING THE STUTTERING STORM

Try to drop your breath deep into your abdomen. Breathe in for a count of four, and then out for a count of four. If you still feel the breath dropping deep into your abdomen after four, go ahead and increase the count — but only count to a number where you can breathe in and out without feeling any tensions in your body.

Now that you're breathing slowly, it's time to speak slowly. Speak some one-syllable words: "Cat, made, time, seam." Then graduate to multi-syllable words: "Doorknob, baseball, crossover, moonlight." Now move along to sentences of some complexity: "The public speaker, who was giving a speech about the health benefits of bananas, was thoroughly engaging."

Take a favorite book and spend some time reading out loud. Find a place in your house where you can be calm. Brew some tea or coffee, then read. And as you read out loud, make the time to breathe and really form your words.

Denying the Drop

Ever listened intently to someone's sentence, but then he drops the last — often most important — bit? Take a guess where that comes from. Yup, it's *breath.* Dropping the ends of sentences and phrases makes speech difficult to understand and can lead to frustration in the listener. For the speaker, the breath support just isn't there by the end of the sentence or phrase. Dropping the end makes it seem like the speakers have little commitment to what they're trying to get across.

REMEMBER

You lose your authority on the subject when you can't even say it completely. "Thank you for coming to . . ." To what?

Dropping sentences means your words lose impact. It's as simple as that. The audience can't hear you. Plus, after a drop, when you do take a breath and begin the next phrase, the volume change can be jarring.

It's much better to maintain a minimum volume consistency all the way through your speech. Those last words of phrases might be your most important. If you don't seem committed to the words, you will appear to lack authority. Why would we buy into that timeshare if you can't even rouse yourself to maintain enough volume to tell us about it?

EXERCISE: DITCHING THE DROP

When you're speaking, visualize a feather suspended in the air. You're keeping it aloft with your breath.

Here's an exercise that will give you an idea of how much air you need for a phrase and also expand your breath capacity. Say every line of the following, and when you run out of breath, go ahead and take a breath:

"Hi." (breathe)

"Hi there." (breathe)

"Hi there, my name is Sharon." (breathe)

"Hi there, my name is Sharon, and you are sitting on my bench." (breathe)

"Hi there, my name is Sharon, and you are sitting on my bench where I eat my lunch." (breathe)

"Hi there, my name is Sharon and you are sitting on my bench where I eat my lunch every day."

Which line did you get to? If you said the whole last line before taking a breath, by all means, add more words. ". . . and I would rather you find somewhere else to sit, please." This is good practice for expanding the number of words you can get out evenly using one breath.

This exercise was inspired by vocal coach Ginny Kopf in the book The Complete Voice and Speech Workout (Applause Theatre & Cinema Books, 2002).

You want to have roughly the same vocal energy at the end of a sentence that you did when you began it. All together now: *Breathe, breathe, breathe.* Sometimes you may need to take a deeper breath because your sentence is long. Sometimes you don't need to take as big a breath because your sentence is short.

Chapter **5**

Conquering Impostor Syndrome: You Are Who You Think You Are

usually meet clients in their workplace. I find it's easiest to work with people where they are most comfortable — there are fewer hurdles to overcome that way.

I received an email from a woman who was looking for public speaking help. She said she was lagging behind in her field because of it. She had difficulty expressing her ideas and had no confidence when it came to presenting her ideas to a group of people. Naturally, I came to her workplace because it was exactly the kind of case I prefer to handle where a person is most comfortable. She worked in a big, imposing glass skyscraper, and waited in her beautiful lobby. I was offered a latte from an expensive coffee machine and was then led to her gigantic corner office, with the best views the downtown has to offer. She was sitting in her big office chair and seemed to be exuding confidence. Yet that's exactly what she needed work on.

This story isn't meant to intimidate those who don't have a swanky office or an Italian espresso machine with a trained barista doubling as an assistant. It's meant to show that confidence is relative. This woman was killing it in her career.

But even she, in her giant tower with its sweeping views, could experience symptoms of what's commonly known as impostor syndrome.

The term *impostor syndrome* was coined by psychologists Pauline Clance and Suzanne Imes in 1978. They used it to describe people who were high achievers and well regarded in their field but who nevertheless felt that they didn't deserve the accolades bestowed upon them. At first it was thought that only women were afflicted by this condition, but they soon found that men too suffered. In their research, Clance and Imes noted that some women with PhDs didn't feel competent enough to hold their job as a professor in a university.

Feeling Like a Phony

If this is your feeling — if you've diagnosed yourself as an "impostor" — it's time to figure out how you got there, what you can do to address the problem, and how to go about it.

Diagnosing yourself

Why do you think you feel like an impostor? In what ways do you feel this? What happens to you when you feel like an impostor? Is it all mental — or are there physical symptoms? Think about when your feeling of being an impostor presents itself. Does it only happen when public speaking? Does just thinking about speaking publicly bring it on, or does it require really standing in front of an audience? Answering questions like these will be crucial to regaining your confidence.

It took the client I mentioned in the introduction a few sessions before she could answer these questions. She eventually was able to tell me exactly where she needed help. She said she felt she "didn't belong," and that she had been "hired by fluke," and one day she was going to "make a big mistake" and her "cover would be blown." That told me that her impostor syndrome wasn't just about public speaking.

Once you've really thought about how this problem manifests itself, you have to find a way to fix it, and a good way to start is to write down your goals. With a piece of paper and a pen, start listing some things you want to accomplish. They can be small steps. Do you have a presentation you have to make at your company's Christmas party? Asked to speak at your daughter's wedding? Maybe your goals aren't that formal. Maybe you feel like an impostor when simply trying to speak with a larger group of friends. No matter the circumstance, it's good to know where your problem lies and where you want to improve.

Critiquing the criticism

Some of the most talented people are that way because they continue to improve, even if it seems like they don't need to. My husband is a career radio broadcaster in my city. He has a great speaking voice. He really is a natural (I'd like to take the credit, but alas, I cannot). Yet whenever he has an opportunity to take a course on improving his vocal technique, his presentation skills, or his on-air conversational style, he jumps at the chance. Why bother? He's already at the top of his game, it seems. His answer is simple: He just wants to be better.

It's good to feel like you always need to improve. But taken too far, that feeling can lead to impostor syndrome. A healthy acknowledgment that there's always room to improve has become a belief that you're hopelessly out of your depth when it comes to almost everything.

Seeing criticism for what it is

It could be that you take criticism too much to heart. Criticism isn't always constructive, after all. Sometimes it's deliberately *destructive*. And for people with a level of impostor syndrome, or who simply lack confidence in a lot of they do, this kind of criticism can really work against them and undermine what confidence they do have. Criticism may validate fears that you already have — maybe somewhere, deep inside, you were waiting for someone else to just say it.

TIP

People with confidence can evaluate and use criticism effectively. Often, even criticism that seems unhelpful can be used productively. People may say something that could help you, even if they say it a stupid way. Sometimes, even with malicious criticism, a confident person has the faculties to take it and figure out if it applies to them — or discard it altogether.

Being overwhelmed by information overload

Public speaking workshops can generate a great deal of criticism, ideas, suggestions, and cautions to keep track of. Maybe you spend one hour every few weeks with a teacher, but in that time the instructor may offer so much criticism and helpful tips it makes your head spin. I admit that I've done this, trying to give my clients their money's worth, but they end up feeling they have so much wrong with them they don't know where to start.

TIP

Some people who receive a lot of criticism have the ability to compartmentalize it all. This is a good mindset to have. They don't let their egos get in the way of processing and acting on information.

Recognizing progress

You should give yourself credit where credit is due. It's difficult to see individuals come so far only to not themselves recognize that they have done so and remain discouraged. But this is a major facet of impostor syndrome — the inability to sort out your success and believe that you're a failure despite it.

I've noticed in my work that progress can be difficult to judge by yourself, and you may not always have a professional around to point out things you have truly gotten better at.

TIP

Take a video of yourself the very first time you say a speech out loud. You don't have to dissect it then if you don't want to, but later, if you're ever feeling down about your progress, video yourself again. Then watch both videos. In the second video, can you point out where you have improved? I bet you have — admit it! This technique will give you a good benchmark and can also show where you need to focus to become successful.

Understanding Why It Happens

To overcome impostor syndrome, it's important to understand why it happens. It's also important to understand that it doesn't happen in a vacuum. None of us is *born* an "impostor." Rather, impostor syndrome is a reaction to some stimuli. You may have a sibling who has been designated the "intelligent" member of the family, while you're told you have "other" gifts. Maybe you're the caring one or the social butterfly of the family. Even if you work hard and sometimes get even better marks in school than your "bright" sibling, your achievements somehow remain unnoticed. That can create doubt in yourself.

Or maybe you were put on a pedestal the day you were born and never removed. You are perfect in every way, your looks, intelligence, and so forth. No one has ever played the tambourine better than you. But once you venture out into the big, bad world out there, you find out that there are actually other people who are smarter, more talented, and better-looking than you. Again, this can plant the seeds of self-doubt.

One of the telltale signs of impostor syndrome is the inability to receive a compliment, because you never received them as a kid (or received too many!). How many times have you brushed off a nicety and said something like, "Thank my tailor," or, "I was just following our company mission statement"? Guess what, folks — a lot of the time, the complimenter may not even mean the compliment in the first place. But the "impostor" behaves in a counterintuitive way here. Instead of analyzing whether someone giving a compliment really meant it or was just being polite, people tend to believe the complimenter, but can't for the life of them attribute that chosen suit or powerful presentation to themselves.

Feeling a failure onstage and off

This section focuses on understanding the feeling of impostor syndrome onstage, but it's important to note that often the feeling doesn't discriminate between public speaking and the regular world. Many people feel like "impostors" both onstage and off — the feeling is only exacerbated by shining lights and a microphone.

Here are some typical reasons why people have this feeling:

» **They feel unworthy:** Remember in *Wayne's World* when Wayne and Garth meet Alice Cooper and get down on their knees, chanting, "We're not worthy, we're not worthy"? That's not much of an exaggeration of how a lot of people feel inside when they have impostor syndrome. Some people put a position in life or a certain success on a such a high pedestal that when they finally achieve it, they feel they there must have been some kind of mistake for them to actually get to that point. There they are, the same old person who just recently had not achieved that particular goal. Must be a fluke, right? Same goes with Wayne and Garth. They feel they're unworthy of speaking to a rock star — but who are the stars of the movie?

» **They feel they don't deserve it:** They've been put down and told indirectly or directly that they'll never succeed. Or they've been pumped up so much that when they find out that they won't get that A in algebra, they doubt themselves and the people who lied. All of these things can build up to a person's insecurities.

» **They feel they have no place to go from here:** This may be a terrifying feeling for some and a comfort to others. Beware that this feeling is pervasive throughout every level of success. There are billionaires who feel this way, professional athletes, Oscar-winning actors. Someone at any level of any profession may have this feeling. I don't mean to terrify or comfort you with this fact; it's just a reminder that this afflicts anyone at every level — and that you can't success your way out of it.

Lucking into success

There's this little lie that I've heard over and over from people I deal with who have impostor syndrome: The success they've had is all because of luck. There they are, in their executive lounge wearing a handmade suit, telling me it's all the result of some lucky divine poker hand. Now that they have to actually present something, anything that has supported them to this point will come crashing down. Their luck has run out.

OVERWORKING YOUR GOALS

When actors put on a play, they're trying to emulate the feeling of opening night every time they step out onstage. For most of the audience, this is the first and only time they are going to see the play, so it *is* actually opening night for much of the audience. The actors have a difficult task: They have to take what worked in past performances and what didn't and incorporate that knowledge into their next performances — while somehow maintaining that opening night energy. Chances are your first performance will be your only performance. Think how much easier you have it than a stage actor!

It's possible to overdo practice and rehearsal, even for a presentation. Some people with impostor syndrome take practice to the extreme — because they're convinced that they are a fraud and must work hard to not be found out — to the point where the speech's delivery starts to stagnate. The speech is honed and practiced to death. It starts to sound boring to the presenter. Because impostor syndrome affects those people who are not easily satisfied with their level of work at anything, grinding a speech into the dirt can create panic that they will be exposed as a fraud. Why are they up there speaking? they wonder. What do they know anyway?

If this is you, it's time to rework what you've got. It's time to be that acting company going into the second night of production. You don't have a director, so it'll be up to you. Video your speech and watch it later with pen and paper. Start with the positives. What are you doing well? Go through the speech a few times and jot down everything you think you excel at. Maybe it's an entire section. Maybe your intro is spot on.

Okay, now for the hard part. Listen to what you can do better. Is there a particular section that stumbles? Do you say "um" in between thoughts or phrases? Jot all of that down, but don't be too hard on yourself. Video yourself again, but practice *only* those sections that gave you grief. Starting from a new spot will remind you about the story structure of the speech and will likely also give that isolated section energy.

I know exactly how that feels. My first bit of success was college. I got into one of the most reputable theater schools that you can apply for. And it was not an easy process: I had to present two monologues, sing, dance, do improv, and go through an interview over the course of two sessions. Unbelievably, I got the acceptance letter that I had made it. I was in. Out of hundreds of applicants, just 16 of us had been chosen. But while my family was congratulating me, dread started creeping in. It must be a mistake! How long would I really last at that school, among the other, actually deserving candidates?

REMEMBER

The truth is, every success, no matter how hard had it is to achieve, contains a bit of luck. That's true for other people as well. It doesn't just apply to you.

Being Yourself

Hopefully you've come to understand a bit about impostor syndrome, and that you're not *actually* an impostor. You may have pinpointed why you feel this way. How do you lose that feeling?

One of the go-to platitudes parents like to trot out when their child enters that socially awkward phase before high school is: *Just be yourself.* Parents love their kids so much that they can see past the pimples and the lanky, cumbersome limbs — but the kids think being themselves is the problem. They think everything about *them* is wrong, not the world.

EXERCISES: ACCEPTING YOUR ACHIEVEMENTS AND OWNING YOUR VICTORIES

You think everything good that has happened to you is not of your doing? Wrong. It's time to combat that type of thinking, and that's what the following exercises are designed to help you do.

Jot it all down: Get comfortable. Sit in your thinking chair. Take out a pen and a sheet of paper and write down why *you* are the right person to be speaking on your subject. Maybe you write down "I'm a banking expert" or "I'm the father of three girls." Or maybe it's something more nebulous, like "I experienced the economic downturn." Whatever it is, don't editorialize. Just get down why you think *you're* writing and presenting this speech. Now think about why *others* think you're the appropriate

(continued)

(continued)

candidate. Feel free to check back through emails folks have sent you. Imagine how they'll introduce you. In big block letters, write that down at the top of the page (whether you agree with it or not).

Remember your history: On a second piece of paper, write down everything in your history that has gotten you to this moment. I'll make it easy for you. If you graduated high school, write that down. Same for college, if you went. What was your first job after college? Write this stuff like you're writing a resume, but in a more linear fashion. Don't leave out the bits that aren't relevant to the position you're looking for — you'll figure that out later. And don't editorialize here either. Just write any job title, any volunteer position, any experience that has either shaped your personality or could be considered a step in the direction of the person you are now.

Get introspective: You've got a bit of a roadmap to your life in front of you. Now it's time to bring out some details. Fill in exactly what you got out of each of those little periods in your life that you just wrote down. Maybe you coached youth soccer one summer. What did that do for you? What did you learn? Did you have to overcome anything to become successful at it? Did you become more comfortable in your teaching abilities? Did you adapt to the behavior of kids? Maybe it wasn't a totally positive experience. That's okay. Write that down as well. Maybe your team did poorly. What did you get from that? Did that give you a better sense of both your strengths and your weaknesses? Did you know your limitations better from that experience?

Apply, apply, apply: Now, go back to that page with the block letters at the top and stare at it really hard until you understand what those words really mean. Then go back to your list of achievements and cross out all the headings you wrote down first — all the positions that got you to where you needed to be. What you'll be left with are just the details of what those experiences taught you. Now take a highlighter and highlight every detail you think applies to what you're being compelled to speak about. Maybe you're speaking about tire-selling tactics and you've highlighted a detail of your life describing why you were named captain of your soccer team. In other words, it doesn't have to directly relate, it just has to be something that helped make you who you are.

Bring it all together and take a long, deep breath: On another piece of paper, copy the block letter heading again at the top, and then under it, copy all those highlighted details down in whatever order you want. It doesn't have to be chronological — life may happen that way, but our buildup of experience doesn't necessarily. Sometimes it takes perspective to realize how your life experience is applicable to what you're being asked to do.

Let's co-opt that platitude and use it in a way your parents probably didn't intend. Go through the exercises here that focus on what exactly it means to *be yourself*. And no, it doesn't necessarily mean *flaunt your oddities*. Mom's heart was in the right place, but to be yourself in this situation is to look inside and see what is truly working — then apply it to the stage.

A lot of traits can be gleaned by practicing some self-deprecating humor. Laughing at aspects of yourself that you may not necessarily like can be a great way to disarm their power. How do you practice humor? Well, the same way you rehearse any other aspect of your speech.

One thing you can do is use humor when things go awry. Have you ever seen a performance where there was a terrible screwup? Maybe you were at a play and an actor forgot his words. Or you were watching a keynote speech and the poor speaker's PowerPoint went down. Such moments seem so crushing that surely they make or break these performances. But what actually happened? Did the mistake *really* ruin everything, or did the performer recover nicely and maybe use humor to get past it?

TIP

Here's a valuable tip: People don't really want you to fail, and it's not even for your sake that they don't want you to. It's uncomfortable for an audience when somebody bombs. Ella Wheeler Wilcox wrote, "Laugh, and the world laughs with you." Even if you don't feel like you deserve to be up there, you actually do. And even if things go badly, nobody wants a mistake like that to ruin the day. Being able to laugh about it in the moment will save your performance.

3

Preparing Your Speech and Training Yourself

Craft your speech for maximum effectiveness, figure out your own voice, mark up your notes to help yourself in your delivery, and work some exercises.

Enhance your speech with visual aids like slide shows (PowerPoint), photos, graphics, bullet points, and audio and video while understanding that these aids, if you choose to use them, are not your speech.

Liven up your presentation with humor, jokes, and anecdotes, loosen up the audience, and find out what to do when you're not that funny.

Discover the importance of practicing your speech out loud, use audio and video to help you practice, and comprehend why it's okay (and advisable) to slow down.

Become a vocal athlete by eating right and exercising to enhance your public speaking performance.

Chapter **6**

Crafting a Captivating Speech

C an you remember the last time you were at a conference and a very interesting keynote speaker with presumably a lot to say droned on mindlessly for what seemed (or really was) hours, spewing information in no particular order? Probably not. Those people are weeded out early in the process, and regardless of their merit and worldliness, they don't often get to go onstage and vomit words. At least not twice.

REMEMBER

This highlights a very important point you must grasp to get anywhere in public speaking: *Presentation is king* — as it is in publishing.

Of course, that's not an absolute rule. You must have something to say in order to say it. I don't know anything about plumbing, and even if I craft the best speech I can about the mechanism below my toilet, it will still come out not great. But the opposite phenomenon also happens: You can have all the clout and respect in the world when it comes to a subject, but without the proper words, structure, argument, and, ultimately, presentation behind it, you will sound like a rookie.

Don't believe me? Pull out your phone (or a recorder) and start talking about the subject you know most about. Then pour yourself a healthy glass of wine and listen to yourself. There's probably some repetition in there, and lots of "ums" and "uhs" as well. Where's the narrative? It was all up there in your mind just a second ago. Did it disappear?

In this chapter, I offer guidance on composing the speech of your dreams about any subject you know well.

Planning and Preparing

You may not be the type of person to plan things meticulously. You are, of course, the expert on the subject you are about to talk about. And certainly, in the public speaking world, there *are* those who can wing a perfect speech and deliver it with a punch. But unless you're one of those people (and if you were, I doubt you would have bought this book), in order to present your expertise in a way that engages your audience, you first have to understand the mechanics of what makes a speech effective.

REMEMBER

Giving a speech is a performance. And if your message is going to be received in the way that you want it to be, you're going to have to give a good performance. If you think of any other performance you've seen onstage, you know that it almost certainly followed a specific script.

My husband and I recently went to Chicago and saw maybe the most famous improv troupe in the world: Second City. *Improv* (short for *improvisation*) is an art form that's built on spontaneity, and the best improv appears to be completely made up on the spot. You may think the performers are winging it, and in some ways they are. But even in improv, a very specific set of rules governs the performance. In a typical improv performance, the actors ask the audience for suggestions for a situation. They use the sacred rule "Yes Let's" as a method to continue action. "Yes Let's" means when one actor says something new, proposing a new direction for the action or creating the situation proposed by the audience, the other actors immediately agree to it — they never push back. This way, everything moves forward smoothly. Before they are ever on stage, the performers work tirelessly in the studio to prepare for anything so that when they perform, it looks as if their performance is completely spontaneous.

So, regardless of whether you want your speech to feel like a meticulously scripted piece of drama or a spontaneous piece of improv, you first need to learn the basics about what makes up a speech.

What's Your Point?

This first thing you have to decide when you're planning your speech is your *point*. This is like the punch line of the joke. It's the reason everyone will gather with eager anticipation to hear you reveal the magic bullet of just whatever it is you do or know. "But," you may say, "There is no magic bullet! I've worked years at learning this skill I'm about to talk about, and in no way can I condense it into a five-minute speech!"

This is the case with many who feel overwhelmed by a speech or presentation they have to give. It's *not* their lack of understanding of the material. Often it's the opposite: It's that their understanding is so *vast*. It's a challenge to reduce a body of knowledge down to a small talk that both demonstrates that knowledge and gives the audience what they need to know, *specifically*.

To determine the overall point you want to make in your speech, answer the following questions:

>> **What do you want to say?** The answer to this question probably popped into your head immediately after you were asked to give a speech. "Well," you thought, "I'll tell them about X."

>> **What does the audience need to hear?** This question gets slightly more complicated, encouraging you to explore the other side. How will *your audience* be better off by hearing about what you, the expert, knows? You may hold the knowledge, but the speech is more about the audience than you.

>> **What language should you use?** A psychiatrist speaking to healthcare providers would use different terminology when speaking to patients about the same topic. Pitch your speech to the audience.

>> **Why are *you* speaking to them?** What makes *you* the right person to be sharing this idea? What is your particular perspective? What do you have to add to the conversation that only you can add?

>> ***What* do you have to say that's so important people will want to hear it?** Does what you want to talk about matter to your audience? If the answer isn't a strong, immediate *yes,* then can you find a way to make it matter? You don't want your audience to leave at the end of your speech (or, worse, in the middle) wondering, "Okay, so what?" Either find a way to make what you have to say relevant to your audience or find a new topic.

>> **Can you say it in one sentence?** The answer to this question is always *yes.* Even the most complicated topic can be summarized in a single sentence. You need to write that sentence down, and that's the hard part.

Hooking Your Audience

Good speakers grab the listeners' attention from the beginning and draw them into the topic. You do this with a *hook*. The hook often comes in the first sentence, but not always.

The hook is the first idea you give to the audience. It establishes the tone for what's to come and sets up your point.

Here are some proven techniques for creating and delivering your hook:

>> **Ask a question.** Asking a question is an easy way to engage an audience. They don't have to answer it, but they will think about the question as you talk. This works to arouse their curiosity about your subject. Be prepared to predict their answer. Don't arouse their curiosity about something you *aren't* going to talk about. Keep it short and sweet: for instance, "What if you went to get your morning coffee and there was no water?" or "How did you travel to this conference today?"

>> **Begin with a powerful quote.** A quotation from someone the audience respects is a way to both introduce and elevate what you're about to talk about. Use the quote to position you as a fellow admirer of the wisdom imparted by this person. Your audience will find it easier to relate to you as a fellow student than as a "teacher."

Don't use a quote in a way that makes you seem to be trying to elevate yourself to the level of the person you're quoting. Audiences are sensitive to that.

For example, in a motivational speech, you might begin with something like, "Amelia Earhart said, 'The most effective way to do it, is to do it.'"

>> **Show a visual.** Presenting a visual is a great way to start a speech, especially if you're nervous. It draws the audience's attention away from you, and it briefly makes you a member of the audience too as you turn to look at what they're looking at. Your visual might be a photograph, short video, or graph. If you're talking about something concrete, showing a good picture of it makes a lot of sense.

If you're stuck, it sometimes works to center your speech around a visual. When I first meet with clients, I ask them to prepare a two-minute speech on anything. One of the most memorable first meetings was with a woman who simply held up a picture of her dog before she started speaking about it. Granted, I'm a dog person, but that picture grabbed me right away. I wanted to know more just looking at it.

>> **Present a surprising fact or statistic.** A statistic can be a great attention-grabber, especially if it refutes a widely held belief or otherwise surprises the audience. For example, did you know that you're more likely to be killed by a falling coconut than by a shark? That might be perfect for a presentation to convince an audience not to be so afraid of sharks (or, I suppose, to be more cautious around coconut trees). A statistic can have an emotional impact on your audience and raise your credibility. Perhaps best of all, your audience might just remember it.

>> **Compliment the audience.** It may sound corny, but one effective way to get an audience on your side is to compliment them or otherwise convey your respect. You want them to respect *you,* and ultimately respect your opinion enough for them to consider it, so starting by throwing a little respect their way can do wonders.

I once heard a speaker begin this way: "It is an honor to be speaking with you today. You are the top sellers in real estate in the city, and I am thrilled to present to this high-achieving group." He had the audience in the palm of his hand.

WARNING

Something to consider with this approach: *Be genuine.* The audience can smell "fake" a mile away. Don't just tell them you're happy to be in front of them — show them. Act like you're seeing an old friend for the first time in a while.

>> **Be humble.** If you've been chosen to speak among esteemed colleagues, or even people with a higher standing than you, don't pretend to be something you aren't. "It's a great honor to be speaking in front of you here today" establishes that you know your place in their world and helps you sidestep any chip-on-the-shoulder issues, especially if you're about to refute an old status quo idea or propose a new one.

>> **Sprinkle some local flavor.** If you're speaking outside your home turf, mention something that demonstrates you have some familiarity with the area. You might say something about a local sports team, a coffee shop or restaurant you stopped at, a local news story you heard that morning, a popular event that's being held, or some other topic of local interest.

On a cold winter night in Edmonton, I saw the comedian Amy Schumer perform. She commented about the weather, and without a beat mentioned that it was way colder in Calgary. She had our attention immediately because she had learned something about the rivalry between Edmonton and Calgary. The audience may know you're not a local, but they'll be on your side.

>> **Tell a story.** Everyone likes a good story, so consider telling a simple (short) story related to the topic you're about to speak about or a story that leads smoothly into that topic. A personal story is best, because it invites the audience to join you in your world.

Some of my most vivid childhood memories are my mother's stories about what it was like as a little girl growing up during the Great Depression. I could imagine her as a little girl in that era, with everything in black-and-white, of course. I could almost see the characters interacting in my mind as she spun her tales about her brothers filling her gloves and shoes with dead mice, and throwing the only ball they had over the schoolhouse. I could almost feel what my mother had felt at the time. Without saying it explicitly, such stories can show what kind of conditions she grew up in.

FIRST IMPRESSIONS ARE EVERYTHING? NOT QUITE

You never get a second chance at a first impression, isn't that what they say? Well, I don't subscribe to that belief. Let's say you spilled red wine on your first date's mother's dress. You're toast, right? Maybe, maybe not. Depends on how quickly and gracefully you recover. If you mumble an apology and act awkward the rest of the time, all she has to go on is that you're some kind of wine-spilling buffoon. But suppose, immediately after the spill, you did something memorable and endearing — such as dumping the rest of the glass on yourself and saying something like, "Well, at least we match now." Assuming it struck her as charming, you'd have a fan for life.

>> **Use sound effects.** Think about how freaky it is to walk into a haunted house around Halloween. Every creak and groan of a floorboard, every witch's cackle can make your spine shiver. You can use sound to build an emotional cue for your audience. You could use music — or not. The clinking of glasses, a door opening, the banging of hammers. What are some sounds related to your subject matter that could grab an audience?

WARNING

Be careful when using sound effects. Test your audio beforehand to make sure it works as planned and so you don't blast everyone's ears. If you've picked music from *2001: A Space Odyssey* to start your speech about trekking through the Arctic, make sure the sound is at a comfortable level. You'll find material on using copyrighted material in Chapter 7.

>> **Use humor.** Yes, tell a joke! (Make sure it's a good one.) A good joke softens a crowd and makes them more willing to like you and, just maybe, what you have to say. I talk more about using jokes in Chapter 8.

WARNING

Be careful here too. The key to using humor is knowing your audience. Nothing's worse than crickets after a punch line, especially when you're using the joke to start your speech. Don't alienate anyone. Be professional. Stay away from jokes that pit one group against another — or you against the audience.

Supporting Your Point: The PIE Method

Once you've decided on your main point and hooked your audience, now it's time to get down to the nitty-gritty. You've got to pack your speech with arguments that back up your main point. Treat an audience that has come to see you as being open to your ideas, but skeptical until convinced otherwise.

Remember writing essays in school? You may have thought that procedure was tedious and pointless at the time, but it did instill in you're the basics of building an argument. A speech in which you are trying to persuade someone of your point should operate on some — but not all — of the same principles as an essay.

This section applies mostly to persuasive speeches — those times when you're trying to get the audience to sympathize with one side of an issue. But the advice here can be used in any other kinds of speeches as well.

Enter the PIE method. No, I'm not talking dessert. But your argument should be just as enticing. I'm kidding, of course — nothing can compete with pie. *PIE* is an acronym for focusing on three important components in your speech:

>> Point

>> Illustration

>> Explanation

Now, a persuasive argument will have a main point, of course. But embedded in that is a line of logic that makes a number of smaller points. You have to back all of those up. The PIE method is a good method to use for your overall speech, but I'm going to show you how to apply it to the minutiae of your argument.

Point

I discuss finding the main point of your speech earlier in this chapter. Now let's take a look at how to fit your point into your speech effectively.

In an essay, your point, or *thesis,* comes in the first paragraph. It's one of the very first things you should see on the page. But a speech, it turns out, is not an essay.

REMEMBER

A speech is a performance. As such, it requires a certain measure of entertainment — unlike an essay.

In a speech, your point doesn't necessarily come first. If you've taken the advice of starting with an anecdote, say, it may be a while before you get around to your point. That's fine. But don't put it off for too long.

TIP

Make your point sooner rather than later. Why? Because it's hard to support an argument before you've made it. (It *can* be done, but it's tricky.)

Let's try a noncontroversial example. The point we'll try to make and support isn't a tough one:

I believe pie is tasty.

To make it a little tougher, suppose the audience is from a horrible island where (shudder) pie doesn't exist. In fact, these poor folks have never even heard of pie before.

Illustration

This part — the *I* in the PIE method — is where we start to get into the argument. You've made your point: *I'm here to tell you, pie is tasty, ladies and gentlemen.* Now it's time to give examples of, or otherwise illustrate, why they should agree that your point is correct.

The illustration step is fairly rudimentary, but it's crucial to the whole of the argument. You'll see that once we get to the explanation portion of the argument.

So, to help illustrate the point, let's add the following:

> *Some pies are made out of berries, and other pies are made out of apples.*

Now, this isn't going to convince anyone of anything yet. Sure, of course pies are made with berries, and some pies are made of apples. That's indisputable. Many of the illustrations you'll make using facts aren't necessarily groundbreaking, even if your argument is (hopefully) a little more nuanced and complex than that one. In fact, choosing illustrations that the audience either knows or can relate to is key here. If you've established a point that can cause others to be skeptical, and your illustration of that point feeds into that same skepticism, your point is lost. Even people who hate pie must concede that it is in fact made with berries or apples some of the time. And the folks on this island are learning something new with this fact, but it's not something they can dispute because it's just a fact.

But you're not done here. One illustration is not going to do it for most audiences. You have to give them enough so that they're going to believe you in the end. That's not all that's in a pie, right? Maybe your next illustration is this:

> *Pie is usually made with pastry.*

Then something else:

> *Pie sometimes has sugar sprinkled on top.*

And another for good measure:

> *Pie is baked to make it crispy on the outside and soft and warm in the middle.*

Explanation

This is where you start bringing in your opinion. You're starting to analyze the facts you illustrated in the last section that few in the audience would dispute. You're beginning to engage in your argument, on the way to finalizing your point.

Here's an example:

> *Berries and apples taste good.*

It's not a fact anymore — it's an opinion that these two fruits taste good. But it's still a pretty easy argument to make. You have to start small, before you get to the big one.

Let's keep going with this:

> *Pastry is delicious on its own.*

And:

> *Everyone loves a bit of sugar.*

Finally:

> *Crispiness and warmth are the most important attributes a dessert can have.*

It's important to choose a more universally accepted position than your main point, which is an original thought that maybe the audience hadn't heard before they saw you onstage. For the folks on this island who have tasted both berries and apples, like sugar, and know about warm, crispy dessert, your assertion that they taste good should make your argument more accessible.

So what?

We've completed PIE, right? Well, sort of. But there's one final step to really hammer home your point, and that's the "So what?" part of the argument. *So what* if what you say is true? How is it significant to the overall message you're trying to get across? Let's continue the pie example:

> *Because berries and apples are tasty, and berries and apples are in pie, then pie must be tasty as well.*

We're bringing it all together here. In this admittedly very simple example, we've successfully explained to them why pie is tasty. We took an indisputable fact and applied it to the argument so the audience can both relate to it and, hopefully, believe it.

Conclusion: Ending with a bang

You've checked your watch or the organizer is giving you a cue, and it's now time to wrap up your speech. You're pretty sure you've convinced the audience that you're right about your point. You've got them in your pocket. It's time to make this a *memorable* speech for the audience — not just a persuasive, entertaining, or informative one. How do you do that? It's all in the conclusion.

The *conclusion* is one of the most important parts of your speech. It's the last thing you'll say, and chances are, it's the part of the speech the audience will remember most. So it's important to make the conclusion count. Think of it as another hook. With your first statement, you're trying to grab the audience so they hold on tight during the rest of your speech. The stakes in the conclusion are even higher: You're trying to grab the audience *beyond* the speech — maybe for the rest of their lives, if you've done it correctly. And it all starts by bringing them back to the whole reason they're watching you speak: your point.

TAKE IT FROM POLITICIANS: STAY ON MESSAGE

Politicians are often good at public speaking, and political speeches are worth studying as examples of persuasive argument. A political speech may go on for 20 minutes, an hour, or longer. It may outline all the politician's values, what they think they can do for voters, how they'll do it, and why. It may talk about their humble upbringing and their dogged rise to leadership, and how they did it as a testament to the spirit of the people. Or maybe the speech explains the hardships of people and offers proposals to help them. Whatever it is they're saying, successful political speeches end with a punchy, digestible version of the message, or *takeaway*. In fact, this ability of politicians to never stray too far from their core argument is even called *staying on message* or *staying on point*.

Say someone is running for city council, purely on the "bike lane" ticket. Many residents of the city are fed up with the lack of proper cycling infrastructure. This candidate has stated his *point* that he will represent the long neglected cyclist in the city and has *illustrated* and *explained* how he's the right man for the job. He needs to solidify that in the minds of voters and attach his point to his name when they fill out their ballot. He could say something like this:

*If elected **I will** change the bike lane laws, **I will** construct more bike lanes, and **I will** make our city a safe place for cyclists."*

Here, he's using the powerful repetition of "I will" to solidify and make memorable the idea that he is the bike lane candidate.

As in an essay, when you restate your thesis at the end, it's vitally important to remind people why they've been listening to you for the past few minutes. And as with your hook, it's important to convey your point in a catchy, digestible way that your audience will take away from your speech and use it as kind if a keepsake for the speech as a whole.

TIP

If you start your speech with a story, you may want to wrap it up with one too — or give the ending of the story you began earlier at the end of your speech. In the same way that you used the story to help the audience relate to an abstract notion, you can use the story to tie back to your point.

Writing in Your Own Voice

When I began my master's thesis, I gave it to my son to look over some early drafts. I'm not an academic, and my public speaking degree was a practical one — nevertheless, I had to develop and write a large document to graduate. My son, who was studying English literature at the time, took one look at it and said, "These aren't your words." And he was right. I was writing to sound like the academics that I had read for my degree and the academics I was presenting to. By doing that, I had lost the very thing I was trying to go out and teach: my voice.

We've gotten out of the habit of writing. Sure, we text that we need milk and bread, we email to remind someone of a meeting, and we congratulate our kid on social media for winning a softball game, and . . . that's about it. It wasn't so long ago that people wrote all kinds of elaborate letters all the time. They wrote to loved ones who were traveling or serving in the armed forces. They wrote to friends, foes, newspapers, radio stations, companies, movie and TV stars, sports heroes, and politicians. If you go back and read correspondence from, say, the middle of the last century and earlier, you can really hear the unique voices of the writers.

The same should go for a speech. You want to make your point in your own voice. But because writing is a bit of a lost art these days, speeches can easily end up sounding like they're coming from someone other than the writer.

I once had a client who worked on oil rigs as a safety inspector. Part of his job duties included giving demonstrations every day to the workers on his oil rig. I ask all my clients to bring in a prepared speech for our first session. When this guy spoke, his eyes were glued to the page. He used big words like *paramount,* and he seemed almost disinterested in the topic. I asked him to put down the paper and tell me in his own words what the point of his message was — what he was trying to get across to the workers he had to speak to every morning. What I found then was a passionate person, with great knowledge and experience, who would never in a million years use a word like *paramount* sitting next to colleagues at lunch. What's more, his points were concise and well thought out. He knew what he had to say all along, but just got bogged down trying to fiddle with the structure of the speech. He was boring those poor workers. (Especially if it's your job to keep people from dying on the job, try to be at least interesting.)

Keeping it simple

Part of the process of writing in your own words is to consider how the audience is going to react to the information you have to give. I've noticed many speeches go off the rails early, using esoteric lingo or jargon or making logical leaps that the audience can't follow because they just don't have the fundamental understanding of the subject that the speaker does. Worse, because speakers are reading off their speech, they can't backtrack even if it becomes evident the audience is lost. They just power through.

In a conversation, when it becomes clear that the person you're talking to is beginning to lose the plot, you can stop, go back, and explain the missing pieces. This is pretty easy to tell in a conversation because the person you're talking to will say something like, "Wait, what do you mean?" Your speech is a conversation between you and the audience, and they will respond with nonverbals, but one element is missing — the audience will be very reluctant to stop you and ask you to go back and clarify something. So when writing your speech, it's important to compensate for that lack of verbal feedback.

There are plenty of reasons somebody might not understand what you're talking about. If you're an expert in a subject, there are fundamental building blocks of knowledge about it that were formed in your mind years ago. This is called the *curse of knowledge.* It refers to a cognitive bias whereby an expert in something simply assumes other people have sufficient background to understand what she's talking about. Chances are, you unconsciously take a lot of what you know for granted when you speak to someone about the bigger picture. There's a line that Denzel Washington says in the movie *Philadelphia* that I always think of when I want to explain this phenomenon: "All right, explain this to me like I'm a 2-year-old, okay? Because there's an element to this thing I just cannot get through my thick head." In the movie, he plays a lawyer, and he realizes that in order to represent his client and understand his client's case, he needs to know the whole story as well as the client does.

REMEMBER

Keeping it simple, or "dumbing it down," means not taking your audience's background knowledge of your subject for granted. Think of them as a blank slate that you're going to fill in with the information that only you provide. It's a fine line, though. Don't assume they know too *little* either. The audience is smart, not dumb. They just haven't spent as much time on your particular subject as you have.

Writing and reading out loud

Before you hit pen to paper, spend some time thinking and talking out loud about what you're going to speak on. Speaking and writing are not the same things. As mentioned earlier, people nowadays may be intimidated by extended, complex writing or out of practice with it.

TIP

Never forget that the medium you will present your ideas in is *speech*, not writing, so it makes sense not to begin explicitly with that other, different medium.

For myself, the following activities help free up ideas for when I actually have to get to my computer and write the thing up:

>> **Take a walk and make your points to yourself.** When I have to develop a speech, the first thing I do, of course, is take my dog Artie for a walk. This helps in two ways. One, he needs a walk, so I feel like I'm accomplishing something that needs to be done. And two, it allows me to free up my headspace to toss around ideas. When I first started writing speeches for myself, I would begin by sitting down at the computer and trying to bang out ideas. More often than not, I found myself staring at a black computer screen with that horrible little blinking cursor taunting me. It was horribly frustrating. I became aware of the seconds ticking down, and that frustration often led to a panic of lost productivity.

That's when I started going for walks with Artie — to get my mind off the task. Soon I found that I would start thinking about what I wanted to talk about in between picking up poop. Remember, though, it's important to have a general sense of what you want to speak about before you go out on a walk. Once you get home, write it all down.

>> **Talk to yourself in the shower.** Ever have an argument with yourself in the shower? I bet you always win. Once you've figured out a few ideas in your head, it's time to start verbalizing. And where is it better and more socially acceptable to talk to yourself than in the shower? Crank that faucet, lather up, and, instead of singing your way through Shania Twain's catalog, vocalize the ideas that are bouncing around in your head. How do they sound to you? If they're lame, no worries — try again, rework them. Sound better? Is there something that sticks? Dry off and write it down.

>> **String ideas together out loud.** Once you've got a few loose ideas that you've spoken to yourself about, try figuring out where they should go in relation to each other. Talk to yourself when you brush your teeth. Have a conversation with yourself in the car on the way to work. How does this one sound paired with another one? Should you move them around? Maybe an idea doesn't actually fit with the message you're trying to get across. Toss it. It's much easier to tell what works and what doesn't if you can hear it for yourself — out loud. Write down what seems to work and jettison what doesn't.

>> **Come up with an ending.** Once you've got the general idea of how things are going to go, try thinking about how you're going to end it. It doesn't need to be polished, but is there something in your normal vernacular that will help you end on the right message? With many of my clients, the conclusion is of the biggest hurdles. I suspect that conclusions are difficult because in life, we don't often stop doing something that abruptly. As a result, many people find themselves writing a conclusion using language they would never say in real life, and find it grating when they speak it out loud later.

Show, Don't Tell

We've all heard the advice *Show, don't tell.* It's often given to writers. What it means when it comes to speeches is twofold. First, being extremely technical and strenuously logical about every little bit of information can come across as very boring. And why don't you want to be boring?

A speech is a performance.

Second, to show and not tell, you must give people room to make leaps in their own heads. You don't have to spell out everything in prose if you can get the audience picturing what you're talking about in a story. People actually like making connections and having surprising thoughts of their own. They, too, bring some energy to your speech. If you can lead them *just* up to the point where they can make the connection you're after on their own, you're going to become an audience favorite. Your speech is supposed to be appreciated, not spoon fed.

Painting a picture in the audience's mind

In 2017, for the first time in years, there was a total solar eclipse that spanned across the continental United States. The moon, a big round space rock, passed slowly in front of the sun, temporarily casting a huge shadow on the earth.

But if you were to go in front of a group of people and describe the importance of taking part in the event, would you explain it like that? Of course not. You'd paint a picture of the entire scenario: millions of people flooding into the countryside to get a clear view, many of whom have waited years to see something like that. The stories are endless. Some people dressed in costumes or wore funny hats. There's the couple who coincided their wedding vows with the moment of total eclipse. There's the old man who first saw one over a half century ago and the young child who will one day tell her children about it — and urge that they see one too.

HEMINGWAY'S ICEBERG THEORY

The "iceberg theory" was popularized by the American writer Ernest Hemingway. It described his own writing: He would give his readers the tip of the iceberg of the story, just the surface events, and expect them to understand on their own how the events connected underneath it all. Hemingway's prose was quite stark, and I don't recommend that you completely emulate his technique. But you can learn from it.

Allow the audience to come to their own understanding of the events. Allow them to work a little. When you guide people like this and they come to their own conclusions, not only is there a better chance they'll get on board with your ideas, they'll also feel a sense of pride that they figured it out.

TIP

Earlier in this chapter, I mention hooking your audience with a story or anecdote. That's a great way to employ this principle of showing instead of telling. Yes, you *tell* a story, but what you're really doing, if you spin a tale properly, is offering the audience a screenplay and letting them cast and direct the film in their minds. This is also a great way to give the benefit of the doubt to the audience and trust them to take your story and apply it to the subject of your speech.

The next section talks about the importance of story in greater detail.

Crafting Your Narrative: Story Time

Our culture is literally built on story. In fact, all cultures are. The big three — religion, mythology, and history — are nothing but stories. And sometimes, as storytellers, we get lucky. A perfect story, one with a beginning, middle, and end with just enough conflict falls right onto your lap. All you have to do is tie it up in a neat little bow and present it in whatever medium it needs to be in. But more often, we have to take the raw materials of a story and construct them into something that *looks* as if it fell into your lap.

My mother grew up on a farm on the prairies during the Great Depression. She has a story about an injured fawn she found, which her family took in and raised. Fanny survived and grew up and lived for years in the farmhouse. Many of my mother's stories involved the deer's antics. My mother, like many others of her era, experienced great hardship and struggle during that time. But her stories didn't describe the stark minutiae of that era. Instead, Fanny served as a conduit for both the strife — and sometimes the hope — that filled her family's life. A pet deer eating a week's worth of barley may not be a perfect story, but in the context of the times, it's a good way to suggest the hard times without spelling things out too much.

You're the boss: Acting like a protagonist

Let's face it: On a certain level, your speech is going to be about you. Whether it's about your company and its products, or the effects of climate change on drinking water, or a park that should or shouldn't be built in a certain neighborhood, what brings together that story and your audience is *you*.

The *protagonist* of a story is the hero. That's not necessarily your role in the actual story you're telling. You could be speaking in more of a narrator capacity, with knowledge of the subject but without a hand in the movement of the plot. Or you could be right in there, telling your own story. Or maybe you're telling a story about someone else from your personal point of view — like the character Nick Carraway in *The Great Gatsby*. In any sense, treating yourself like a character in the story is an important step to engaging with the audience. To them, you are their connection to the story, so you want to keep yourself involved in the story as much as you can.

Here are a few tips to keep the *you* in the narrative:

>> **Use "I."** This may be the simplest way to keep the story about you: Talk about yourself. This is easy if you're telling a story about something you did, or some experience you went through. It gets a little trickier when you're explaining something that someone else did. Regardless of where the story came from, though, you are the one up on the stage. Using phrases like "I saw" or "I heard" places you in the narrative.

>> **Clarify your participation.** There's the one extreme where you are the instigator of the conflict in a story, are the one affected by it, or are the one who bears the consequences. And then there is the story where you're really just an observer, or you're being told the story well after it happened. It's important to establish for your audience where you fit on that spectrum. If you claim to have more influence over the story than you really did, an audience will sense it and be suspicious. Don't be flattered by the stage. Tell the truth. But make sure you don't *downplay* your participation. It might look like you don't deserve the credit, and an audience will question that.

>> **Be subjective.** The information in your speech may be extremely dry by its nature. That's not your fault. But if your speech is boring, it is definitely your fault. Perhaps you're being asked to turn a business report into a speech. No one, absolutely no one, is looking for you to just read that damn report. The

problem with the report is not that your colleagues are illiterate. How do you take such a dry topic and turn it into something with even a little bit of juice? Again, connect yourself to the story. Be subjective.

That report may be as factual as the sky is blue, or it could paint a far too rosy picture of your business's future. It doesn't matter where your information falls on that scale — acting as though that information is yours and is coming from you and your perspective allows you to be the conduit for the information, and therefore a conduit for the audience. And — hopefully — not too boring.

Telling the story of your business

So you've got a company. Invariably, that company has a story. Every company does. In fact, thanks to the web, the story of a company has become part of the company's identity in ways it never could have before the "About Us" tab appeared on websites.

This is both good news and bad news. I'll give you the bad news first: You won't be breaking any ground by telling your business's origin story. It's been done to death. But that's also good news, because it's become easier to tell what works and what really doesn't.

Here are a few questions the story of your business must answer:

>> **Why does your company exist?** This seems like an easy question. And it is, once you understand it. No, it doesn't exist to help you pay the bills (at least, not in this context). What you're looking for here is *what your company can give to the audience.* If your audience is your potential market, why does it exist for *them?* If it's for a group of investors, how can its existence enrich all of you?

For instance, maybe your company buys wholesale socks in one country and sells them to another. If you're pitching Socks Without Borders to a group of sockless potential customers, the business exists to sock the barefoot. If it's a group of investors you're talking to, it exists because of a market that doesn't have access to socks. Your company exists for both reasons, but each reason is tailored to the audience.

>> **What is your product and how did it come to be?** If you're an inventor, this is a pretty easy story to tell. But for other companies that sell products that are well known or are abstract (say, sock futures), this question calls for a little more thinking. If it's a common item and you just seem to be selling it, why did you think to sell it in the first place? Where did you get the idea that this service would not only be needed, but make you successful?

Back to the sock example. Maybe the CEO saw the need for socks, plain and simple. She saw a bunch of barefooted people walking around begging for socks, and she gave them to them. It doesn't matter that socks were already a thing — she provided socks in a way no one had done before.

>> **Who are your customers?** This may be an internal question, and maybe you're giving an internal speech, but regardless, this is important to know. Consider what kind of speech this is. Are you trying to tell them the story of your business, or are you trying to sell them on it?

Socks again. Say the CEO is giving the speech. She's said her piece about the origin of her company, relating why she is where she is. But to what end? If she's speaking to her alma mater, the idea is most certainly to inspire the students to make businesses themselves in a similar way.

The message must change depending on whom you're talking to.

>> **What motivates you?** No matter whom you tell this speech to, you're going to have to go into it knowing why you do what you do. If you had the option to do something else but you didn't, why is that? What helps you get up in the morning and start selling those socks on your own?

REMEMBER

Getting real: Enhancing your story

Sometimes you need to "get real" with part of your speech. That's not to say that other parts aren't real or true, but getting down into the dirty aspects of why something is the way it is can make the difference between showing and telling (see the earlier section "Show, Don't Tell").

Getting personal

I'm sure you're familiar with the term *TMI*, meaning *too much information*. It's a phrase we tend to hear a lot as children. Few of us are born with the social inhibition needed to get anywhere in society. As kids, we tend to just say whatever pops into our heads until told otherwise, and then we adjust next time (that's the theory, anyway). At some point we're all told that a certain detail or story we've just mentioned is too much information, and we should have kept that to ourselves. Being wary of TMI is something many of us have internalized. But what if the TMI thing really matters?

Try this. When you're thinking of a speech about yourself, say, and you get to a part that you feel uncomfortable telling, flag it. Go ahead and write it out and highlight it. Try recording yourself giving the speech including that piece of information. Now think: Does it need to be there? Perform both versions for someone you trust. Can he understand the story without that detail? Or is it a true building block for your narrative? His answer may be your answer.

Of course, there's personal, and then there's *personal.* It's not worth a painful dive into your soul if it only makes the audience uncomfortable. I once attended a comedy festival where local celebrities came on the stage and did standup. A well-known personality came up to the mic and talked about why he divorced his wife. And it was messy. Certainly, messy is par for the course in standup comedy. But the messy part also has to be funny, which, in this case, neither the details nor the delivery were. Into the teeth of very little laughter, still he pushed through. The audience just stared at each other and tried to get through it. We truly were a compassionate audience, looking back on it. But it's never good when something like that happens.

Getting dramatic

How do you take a personal tidbit and turn it into something you can use? Drama helps. And not the kind around the lunch table in high school. Not necessarily, anyways. No, getting *dramatic* with your story can enhance the vulnerability of a personal narrative or bring its suspense to the forefront. Drama can best be used to enhance what's already there — a great narrative that just needs a little help. Remember, every speech is a performance, whether you're talking about tires or tutus.

Here are a couple things to keep in mind when looking for that perfect piece of drama:

>> **Draw out the suspense.** Make the audience feel like they *need* that punch line. Many times in speeches that I review, people possess fantastic information that they give away too quickly — or they disclose it in such a way that it comes and goes without giving the audience time to register it.

If your speech is based on one shocking or wonderful event, let it breathe. Give the idea time to mature in the audience's heads, so that when they hear it, they're totally ready.

>> **Study others.** It's important to know how successful speakers really do it. Grab a pen and pad next time and take notes. Watch it once, and just mark all the information you get from it, in double-spaced point form — every bit of the story they're trying to tell. On your second viewing (assuming you're watching a video), write how the speakers treat each piece of information below it. Do they get really quiet? Does their voice change? Use such techniques in your own speech and see if it makes a difference.

USING PUNCTUATION (YES, IT MATTERS)

Writers use punctuation, like I'm doing in this book, to organize and clarify the message — and as clues to rhythm, pronunciation, pausing, emphasis, and so on. When you read these sentences in your head, note that you are actually hearing them. Reading is a lot like listening. Pay particular attention to what your brain does when it encounters marks of punctuation. How would you read this sentence if. I. Did. This? What happens to the voice in your head when you expect a question mark but none appears. Wrong punctuation can frustrate — the reader and send; the meaning the writer is trying to, get across astray. See?

But preparing a speech isn't the same as writing for the page — it's writing to be *heard*. In fact, many people who write speeches write them in shorthand. They may write them in point form or use punchy keywords to keep them on the right track. Now, I'm *not* advocating for you to read off the page at your next speaking engagement, but it is important to at least map out everything in your speech, especially if you're just starting out. And the way you write it down can affect the way you give the speech.

Punctuation on the page is like markings on a musician's sheet music. For a piano player with sheet music in front of her during a performance, every crescendo, every staccato phrase and dramatic rest can be mapped out on the page ahead of time.

There are two main areas to consider regarding punctuation and speech: emphasis and breathing. New speech writers are generally confident with the knowledge that punctuation is used for emphasis — it's the use of punctuation as markers for breathing that stumps most people. This section offers an overview of how certain punctuation works in speech.

- **Periods (.):** I don't have to tell you what periods are for in writing, although I'm going to anyways: Periods indicate the end of a sentence. What does that mean for a speech? Pretty much the same thing, with a slightly different lingo. You should treat periods in a written speech much the same as you would in any other writing, but you need to be aware of what you're going to use them for. Periods, for your speech, will indicate the end of a phrase or statement and a chance to breathe. In writing, it's possible to have a sentence run much longer than you can read aloud — you only have two lungs and limited lung capacity, after all, and some authors' sentences run on for a page or more. Often sentences vary in length. If there's a sentence that you need to say in one breath, make sure you take enough breath to sustain your speech until the end of that sentence. You find exercises on breath support in Chapter 14.

- **Commas (,):** Commas are used to separate phrases, sometimes to emphasize a certain part of the phrase and sometimes to list things. For speech, we should think of the comma as "period light." You're not going to stop the progression of your phrase, but you're not going to power through it either. You should use a comma as a signal to slow down. You can also use commas as a chance to breathe, but don't breathe on *every* comma like you do a period. Often when you resume speaking after a comma, you change the pitch of your voice. So, the comma can be used for dramatic purposes and for other reasons of emphasis (see Chapter 14 for more on breathing).

- **Colons (:):** Generally in speech, we use a colon before we get into some sort of list. A colon is a very helpful tool when it comes to pacing. For many speeches that include colons, the phrase leading up to it prepares the audience for the list to come. It's necessary, but it's what's *in* the list that counts. That's why I instruct many of my clients to take longer pauses at a colon as a mental reminder to the audience of something important coming up. Colons can also be employed when used as visual aids (see Chapter 7 for more on visual aids).

- **Question marks (?):** You may want to present a rhetorical question to the audience — meaning one you're not really expecting an answer to. It may seem trivial, but it's important to remind yourself of that in your speech. Vocally, a question mark indicates a rise in your pitch at the end of the sentence.

  Question marks are also a perfect time to slow down your read. Allow yourself a few beats between question and answer, enough time for the audience to realize that you don't know the answer, if that's the case.

- **Quotation marks ("..."):** Say this sentence aloud to yourself: *He sure seemed like the "best" candidate.* How did you say the word *best*? Chances are, your intonation changed to reflect the quotations around that word. Or maybe you said *quote unquote best* or even did "air quotes" with your fingers. Think about how you would say that sentence to yourself if there were no quotation marks around that word. We often use quotation marks in this way to imply something, and to really emphasize its presence.

- **Exclamation marks (!):** This one's a no-brainer. If you're looking to exclaim, this is your mark. The issue with this one, especially when people first begin to write speeches, is that they're so nervous about expressing any emotion they forget when it's right to exclaim. We do this all the time in real life. "My dog's breath is so smelly!" and "My kid ate all the leftovers!" In real life we're committed to our emotion and show exactly how we feel in how we talk. Your pitch goes higher in your voice, volume increases, and I bet you gesture with those hands. So don't feel silly about it: Put that exclamation mark on the page and go for it!

- **Italics and bold font:** We use these to emphasize *key* words, and they **pop** off the page when you're reading. When you write your speech and use italics or bold, you should emphasize them **more** than the other words *when you're speaking*. For example: That speech was incredible! When you put it in italics, it's even more *incredible!* If you use italics and bold, it becomes amazingly ***incredible!***

Chapter **7**

Using Visual Aids

ood old-fashioned Microsoft PowerPoint (https://products.office.com/en-us/powerpoint) has been joined by other kinds of presentation software options. You can try Prezi (www.prezi.com), Google Slides (https://gsuite.google.com/products/slides/), LibreOffice Impress (www.libreoffice.org), and Apache OpenOffice Impress (www.openoffice.org/product/impress.html) for starters. Most people probably still think of slide presentations as all being "PowerPoint." It's sort of the Kleenex or Xerox of its field.

But the variety of options doesn't change the age-old question of presentations: Do you need a visual aid? Generally, the thinking goes like this: Some people feel that just standing in front of an audience and delivering their message is not enough. They need something more to entice and captivate the audience.

Sometimes that's true. It's hard to describe a picture. Plus it's worth a thousand words, right? Why not just show it? But other times, feeling compelled to use a slide show has to do with what a lot of this book has to do with: anxiety.

Some presenters are afraid that if they don't inundate the audience with information, they run the risk of not looking like they don't know what they're talking about. It's similar to the freshman essay in college. Load the paper with information to impress the teacher. But does that work? No — not likely, anyway. And some presenters may be drawn to using a slide show as a way of distracting the audience from staring at them the whole time.

I have a client who works in human resources who told me that without having a *deck* — hip presenter lingo for *slides* — at a meeting, my client believes the audience will think, "What are you here for?" This kind of thinking is common. The slide show *validates* the message and, ultimately, validates *you.*

Anyone who's ever put a slide show together knows that validation comes at a price. I have many clients who, before they worked with me, spent more time on their slides than on practicing their actual presentation out loud. That's not a good way to go about giving a speech.

So back to the questions: Do you *really* need that visual aid? Do you *really* need PowerPoint? Is it *really* adding to your story — or might it be confusing? Does it *really* help to get your message across — or does it get in the way? In the end, only you can answer these questions.

WARNING

Whatever your answer, don't try to make your slide show the star. *You* are the star. Don't let your slide show take away from what you are saying. And don't get too carried away by those fancy pictures and graphs — they won't take the place of your speech.

The late Steve Jobs was apparently not a fan of PowerPoint. In Walter Isaacson's biography *Steve Jobs* (Simon & Schuster, 2011), he quotes the co-founder of Apple: "People who know what they're talking about don't need PowerPoint."

There's something to that sentiment. Still, sometimes a slide show may be able to help you get across your message to an audience. Here are a few general tips:

>> You'll get about ten seconds out of a slide. That's all you can expect people to pay attention to it.

>> For bullets, only use five or six lines of text, revealing one line at a time, as you speak about it, and no more than five or six words per line.

>> Consider carefully whether your information would be presented better with a picture or with text — or neither.

>> Less is more when it comes to slides. Don't overwhelm the audience. They can only remember so much. They want to find out about you and your message.

>> Don't repeat what's on the slide word for word. The audience can read. Your message is the meat and potatoes. The slide is the side dish.

WRITE FIRST, ADD SLIDES LATER

When I was in theater, the *last* thing that was added to our performance was our costume. If we had received our costumes first thing in rehearsal, they would have taken precedence over what we were saying and who we were as a character. The costume helps create the character, of course. But it can't be allowed to impose upon the character. It should only be used to augment the actor's performance — to add just a bit of reality to it.

Yes, at times women would wear skirts to rehearsal to get used to the feel of wearing a skirt. If a specific piece of clothing was instrumental in how the actor moved or was vital to create his character, they would wear that piece as soon as possible so that it became a part of them and felt like something they would wear everyday. And if it was a Shakespearean play, men would wear tights or leggings in rehearsal just so they could get familiar with them, so they became second nature. I wouldn't know, but wearing the codpieces must have taken a while to get used to.

It's the same way with slides. If anything, they are only there to augment your performance, not become your performance. Take away the slides, and you should have the same basic presentation. It's best to add slides *after* you've already written your speech. That way, they aren't building blocks in your presentation, and you won't depend on them.

But just like in theater, there are exceptions. If you know that you have a slide with a picture that you need to write about first, that's fine. And if you're telling the story of your fabulous vacation in Egypt through pictures — sure, in that case write to the pictures. But if the slides contain nothing but words, don't worry about writing the slides after you've written your speech. And don't create too many slides — don't try to have a slide for every sentence. Your slides aren't your speech.

A Picture's Worth a Thousand Words

I'm going to be frank with you. I don't use slides in my painless public speaking and presentation skills workshops. Companies always ask me to send them "my deck" when it's ready. Sometimes I feel a little pressure to use slides. For my talks, for example, I could have a picture of someone with hands on his upper chest and lower abdomen with arrows to show how and where to breathe in and out for best results, and I could show a picture of a person in an up and out position and another in a down and in position. But for me, my work is experiential. Many a client has come with a coffee and muffin just ready to sit down and listen, but quite often we get up and do stuff. I often ask the participants to walk around assuming this or that pose instead of showing slides.

If I'm asked to give a keynote speech instead of teaching public speaking, however, I *do* often use slides — PowerPoint, to be specific. I have a speech on "grit," or gutting it out through tough times in life, and for that one, I start with a smiley picture of me at about 5 years old, then a picture of me at about 13 performing in a musical, followed by a picture of me in college working toward my BFA. Guess how the pictures change through the years? Yup, the smile goes away.

Note that all three of my references are pictures. Some people shy away from using just pictures. They feel they need some info up there to explain everything to the audience.

REMEMBER

Give the audience some credit. Don't spoon-feed them. Let them figure some things out on their own. People feel proud when they connect the dots for themselves. Many of my clients who used to be staunch "info slide" presenters have turned to simply using pictures instead. They love the results, and their audiences do too.

Knowing when a picture works and when it doesn't

Let's say I'm giving a speech on how our dog, Artie, has brightened our lives. (When I exclaimed to my husband that he has given us so much joy, he said, "Didn't we have joy before? Ahh, not this much!") I have two slides. One is of Artie frolicking in a ravine with his buddy, a black lab named Indy. The second slide is the same picture except superimposed on top are these words: *Artie and Indy enjoy playing together.*

Now, think about it. Didn't you get that information from the first slide? You should have. Chapter 6 talks about showing, not telling. You can see that there are two dogs and they're having fun. As an audience member, I can then can take the image and relate it to my own life. *My dog needs a buddy, She likes to run and play too,* or *How I really want a dog!* Trust that the picture alone will affect the audience in some way. Remember, always be critical of not just the type of information, but the amount you put on a slide, too.

TIP

Don't worry too much about connecting the dogs — or whatever image you show — with your message directly with every slide. It doesn't all have to be so on the nose. Allow the audience to engage with the slide without being hammered with your message.

Not all pictures are great. Here are some things to avoid:

>> **Too small:** If the whole audience can't see the picture, then it's too small. If you're in a boardroom, you know what kind of space that is, and you can be

confident everyone in the room will see your picture. The same isn't always true for a larger space. Always test out the equipment and your slide presentation to make sure everybody will be able to see them. Telling the audience "Some of you won't be able to see this, but . . ." is bad. You're alienating those who can't see it.

Chapter 16 talks more about scoping out the venue where you'll be presenting.

>> **Too much detail:** Some photos are like those *Where's Waldo* books — spot Waldo and you win. But if the audience has to spend time looking for the equivalent of a man with black-rimmed glasses and a red toque, they're going to miss what you're saying. Better to crop such pictures (cropping is covered in the next section).

>> **Poor quality:** You've spent the time to write a great presentation, so take the time to find a clear picture. If you have to explain or apologize for a fuzzy photo, you've lost the audience.

Cropping pictures to fit ideas

Cropping pictures has become much easier in the digital age. I mean, you used to need actual scissors. Now you stretch a box around a picture in an image editor and click a Crop button.

With cropping, you're trying to get rid of some of the less important bits so the eyes focus on what you're trying to showcase. In a slide show, cropping means trying to highlight something in each slide while cropping away noise that may distract.

TIP

A simple rule of thumb is to crop an image so it very clearly shows just one thing. Strive for one main thing per image.

Considering color

Go ahead and add some color to your slides. Maybe your message is colorful. It's your slide show, after all.

TIP

It's a good idea to pick a consistent color scheme that uses just a few colors, and uses them consistently, rather than having the text a different color in each slide, say. This general design principle applies to everything from website design to marketing, advertising, and publishing. Choose one color or a few colors that go well together and stick to that. It makes your presentation look professional and is easy on the audience's eyes.

Be mindful about the different types of feelings in the audience that may be provoked by different colors. The psychology of color is not an exact art, and there's lots of room for different philosophies about which colors are good for which themes.

For instance, here's how the ancient art of *feng shui*, which at least has a long history behind it, views certain colors:

>> **Yellow:** Generates happiness and intellect and stimulates the mind

>> **Orange:** Expressive, lively, dynamic

>> **Blue:** Serene, peaceful

>> **Purple:** Royalty, riches, quietude, knowledge

>> **Pink:** Love, joy

>> **Brown:** Grounding, being rooted

>> **Green:** Harmony, growth, bounty

>> **Red:** Hot, courageous, dominant

You may not agree about how these colors make you feel — or even whether colors make you personally feel anything at all. But it's always good to consider these things. For example, I have a client who hates red because to her it conjures up the feeling of danger and fire.

WARNING

Certain colors, when combined, can definitely clash. Hopefully, you know it when you see it. Use common sense.

There's also the issue of color blindness. People with color blindness (or color *deficiency*, as my son's optometrist diagnosed him with) have a problem discerning among some combinations of colors. Sometimes they can't distinguish certain colors at all.

The issue of colorblindness is perhaps most important to keep in mind when you're using text on a slide. If you use text, make sure the color of the text stands out in contrast to the background image on your slide. Colors can even cause problems with some people who have fine vision. If you have a light background, don't use light color text. And if you use a dark text on a dark background, the audience won't be able to read anything.

MAKE YOUR TEXT EASY TO READ

Back in the day, people used to handwrite everything. Letters, essays, the Declaration of Independence. Personally, I'm glad I was born into an era with typing machines. My handwriting is appalling, perhaps because I'm left-handed (which my husband believes is merely an excuse). Deciphering my handwriting can be difficult. And I'm not alone — *many* people have horrible handwriting that is near impossible to read.

Luckily, it's easy to add text fresh from a keyboard to your slides in just about any type-face, font, and color you can imagine. But some fonts are harder to read than others. Pick clear, familiar, easy-to-read fonts. Don't use unusual or weird-looking fonts on your slides. Make it easy for the audience or they will be distracted or zone out. The words are there to be easily read and understood. Your message is what's important, and you don't want to mess with that.

Place your text smack in the middle of your slides, or as near to that as you can without interfering with an image. Putting text way up or down in a corner of the slide isn't easy to read. And it should go without saying — size your text big enough so that everyone can read it.

(There are also people who are completely colorblind. Sometimes it's not all bad for these people. I was upset when our son was diagnosed, but the optometrist informed me that he could actually see minute details which people who see the full color spectrum can't. This has actually proven useful through the years when it comes to finding lost items — such as my husband's glasses, hanging on a bike handlebar in the garage, or coins in the sand.)

Mastering Essential Slide Show Skills

This section is kind of a hodge-podge of advice I've gathered from years of helping people put together presentations.

>> **Let the slide speak for itself.** You may have been to a presentation where the speaker puts the slide up of bullet points and proceeds to read them out loud. Often, you've already scanned the bullets by the time he's done reading the first one. Never forget that the audience is smart. We can read. Reading aloud bullets that all people in the room can see for themselves gives the audience the opportunity to zone out. Some might even mutter, "Why don't you just send us the slide deck and let us go home?"

>> **Remember the ten-second rule.** Earlier I mentioned that an audience will engage in a slide for no more than ten seconds. That means they'd better be able to read everything on the slide in that amount of time. That means you need to limit the amount of text you place on each slide. A good rule of thumb is no more than five or six short lines per slide, with each one being revealed as you talk about it. If you can't make your point with that amount of info, consider breaking the slide into two.

TIP

One handy trick is to use the function, available in most slide show software, that makes bullet points appear (and perhaps disappear) as you talk about them. This trick takes advantage of the ten-second rule and gives a little more life to your slide. Speak about each point as it comes up. You can use this function like a cue card.

>> **Resist the urge to read the slide.** It bears repeating. The slide, like an old-fashioned cue card for a speech, is a jumping-off point. It's not your script. Let the audience read the slide. You can embellish the point that's on the slide.

>> **Don't turn your back on the audience.** It's not that they might stage a sneak attack on you, or at least most audiences won't. It's more a matter of professionalism and presentation. What's more exciting to look at, your back or your face? A good rule, if you need to look at the slide, is to stand at a 45-degree angle from the slide and cock your head to look at it.

>> **Use one slide per idea.** Each of your slides should represent one idea. The slide should represent one beat in the overall rhythm and structure of your speech. There is no better place to look at how this can be done successfully than with the presentation style called PechaKucha (see the nearby sidebar).

>> **Make sure you can see your notes.** The room is usually dark when you show slides. Unfortunately, that gives the audience an excuse to shut their eyes for a minute because no one will see. Try to make sure the room is just dark enough to see the screen but light enough to see your notes — and for you and the audience to see each other.

>> **Stand away from the screen.** You need to choreograph where you're going to stand as you present your slides and be sure you're out of the way. You don't want the graph of the Realtors Association statistics projected on your head, do you? A good rule is to stand at a 45-degree angle from the screen. That way you can refer to your slides while still sort of facing the audience.

>> **Back everything up.** This should go without saying. Technologies like the cloud make it easier than ever to back up your data. You may think it'll never happen to you, but every day lots of people learn the hard way that they should have backed up their work. Even if you've sent your slides to the organizer, and even if they've already played them on their end, make sure you always have access to your own copies.

>> **Be prepared for your slides to not work.** Never fully rely on your slides. Here's a cautionary tale: I attended a conference with the theme of promoting entrepreneurship and innovation. I was excited to hear one of the speakers particularly. She had started a company that makes a spread out of a very unique vegetable. She mounted the stage and, like many before her, appeared nervous. (That's okay. It's shows you care. I provide tips on dealing with nervousness in Chapters 2 and 3.) She began to talk, and a slide came up. Then — horrors! — the same slide stayed up there. It was frozen. And she froze too. A nightmare scenario. But it didn't have to be. This was a familiar story for her. Speak to the audience as if they're at your dinner table.

They don't really need the slides — not if you've prepared your speech properly. They need you. Never count on technology to get you through. And never rely on your slides to tell your story.

>> **Think outside the box.** You could show a slide with the following information: "According to the National Eye Institute, colorblindness affects approximately 1 in 12 boys and 1 in 200 girls in the world. The gene is passed on by the mother." That may be true, but it's boring on a slide.

What if, instead, you showed a picture of boys and girls playing in a play-ground with a caption: "8% of boys and .5% of girls are colorblind." In your speech, then, you expand upon those stats.

Stats can be fine to include on slides, but make them succinct. Try to think of new or unusual ways to present them. Don't try to put the abstract of a scientific study on there. Just sum up the results in an interesting way.

Here's a pretty typical scenario: The audience looks at the speaker, who's about to give a speech. Up pops the first slide with a whole bunch of bullet points. She starts talking about the downfall of oil and gas in 2016 — but her slides are all about the price of gas in 1980.

Sure, that's probably relevant information somehow. It might tie in later. But right now it's confusing to the viewer. What does the audience do? Read the information on the slide or listen to the speaker? They're confused! Many of them simply shut down. They can't be bothered to think through that stuff. They zone out and don't register anything.

Try listening to your favorite podcast or radio show and reading an article at the same time. Can you do it? I can't either. I zone out and daydream. When we're reading, we're probably not in sync with speakers even if they're talking about the same thing we're reading. If we read the slides too fast, we may wait around and think of something else while the speaker is speaking. If we're reading the slides and the speaker has finished and is going on to the next slide, we feel frustrated.

PECHAKUCHA: SPEED PRESENTING

PechaKucha ("chit-chat") is a presentation style created in 2003 by Astrid Klein and Mark Dytham of Klein Dytham Architecture in Tokyo. The form aims to speed things along by constraining a presentation to 20 slides with 20 seconds per slide, for a total of 6 minutes and 40 seconds. The slides contain mainly images, with little or no text.

PechaKucha presentations require you to be really precise and to the point. Slides need to do two things to be effective in this form: impact the audience and transition smoothly to the next slide. PechaKucha forces you to do something I stress a lot: You need to become completely confident with your content. You have to stay on your message because you have so little time. PechaKucha forces you to practice your presentation over and over to nail down the timing. By the time you present, you know the entire thing inside and out.

Presenters using this style often tend to talk really fast to pack everything they want to say into each 20-second time allotment. Again, the constraint encourages being concise and pithy — which is a good thing. If you need to cut something, well then, cut it. This form is all about content management.

TIP

One technique I like is to repeat the bullet point and then expand on that. Once that happens, if the listeners are lost, they can just look back at the slide to figure out where they are.

Above all, it's you and your message that need to resonate with the audience — not your slides. I have a friend who is an English professor at a university. She used to provide her students with the PowerPoint slides she used in class but found that the students relied on them too much. Ultimately, attendance dropped. The students would find the slides online and not go to class. So she stopped giving out the slides online.

The Do's and Don'ts of Audio

Using audio can enhance your presentation as much as slides — but here, too, make sure it doesn't become the star of the production. Running onto the stage to the theme song from *Rocky* could be great. Trying to *speak* over that music? Not so great.

We'll start with the don'ts.

Don't let music play for a long time

We've all heard "Gonna Fly Now" (the *Rocky* theme song) before, and we certainly don't need to hear the entire song again. We get it — in fact, we got it with the first few notes. Plus, you're on a time restraint. Don't waste time. Playing a piece of music for five or six seconds is ample time for the audience to feel the emotion or reaction you're (presumably) going for. Fade the music out when you're about to speak. If you can't do that yourself beforehand in software, if possible have the technician or organizer fade out the song when he sees you onstage ready to start.

WARNING

Remember that any music you play, unless you wrote and recorded it yourself, is almost certainly protected under a copyright law, and that needs to be addressed. If you find that you *must* use a copyrighted piece of music in your presentation, give yourself plenty of time (as in weeks, at least) to track down the rights holder (probably the publisher, but not always) and secure written permission. Music copyright laws are well beyond the scope of this book. Here are some links to get you started on understanding copyright law: Check out `www.rbs2.com/copyrm.pdf` for info on U.S. copyright law and `www.socan.ca/licensees/faq-licensing` in Canada.

WARNING

What you want to avoid at all costs is standing awkwardly onstage waiting for the sound to stop.

Don't play music too loud or soft

Don't damage the audience's ears, please. If it's too loud, they'll be irritated and resistant to your message. Once the music is over, all they'll think about is how loud that bloody song was. On the other hand, if you intend it to be heard, let it be heard. Always test volume levels beforehand if at all possible.

Don't play music during your whole presentation

I used to go to a yoga class where the instructor played music. That's normal enough. But it wasn't the calming, set-the-mood music usually used in yoga class. This guy played rock and other bouncy music. It made me want to dance, which isn't very conducive to yoga. It's not easy staying in Downward Dog while listening to Van Morrison's "Brown-Eyed Girl."

The same principle goes for playing music while you're giving your presentation. Music can cause listeners to go into their own worlds — you want them coming to your world.

And now for a couple of do's.

Do have a sound check in the space prior to your speech

This is by far the most important thing you should do regarding the audio component of your speech. If you're lucky there will be a technician on hand, but often it's just the organizer and you. You will need someone at the soundboard for the venue's sound system to raise and lower the volume. A good idea, although it may not be practical, is to bring someone else to your speech who can cue the technician to raise the volume or lower it. You may have to ask the organizer to be your helper. Remember that the room will sound different when it's full of people; bodies tend to absorb and muffle sound.

Do check your equipment

Choose the right equipment for the job, whether it's a laptop, phone, or tablet. If it needs power, make sure you have access to a working electrical outlet. In any case, be sure to fully charge any and all devices before your speech.

PLAYING EXCERPTS FROM OTHER SPEECHES DURING YOUR SPEECH

Maybe you're in the middle of a presentation about achieving your goals and you want to insert Martin Luther King's "I have a dream" speech, or something like Kurt Russell's speech as Herb Brooks from the movie *Miracle*. This kind of thing can be tricky. But if you insist, here are some guidelines:

- Don't recite the entire speech. A few lines will get the message across.

- If you use recording, don't use a bad one. You want the audience to hear it above all, and if it was recorded some time in the last century, the quality may not be the best. Tread carefully.

- Don't walk around aimlessly while a recording plays, grabbing water or looking at your notes. That gives the audience permission to zone out and check their phones. Rather, be an example: Stand and listen to what is being said so that you're just as affected by it as the audience. Be in awe. Guide the audience in how they should feel.

- Don't play the whole thing. This is *your* speech, remember? Find a short section that pertains to your message and recite that. That way, it can be vague enough that it might just have to do with what you're talking about.

- Find and play only the section in the speech that gives the most impact to your message.

Using Video . . . If You Must

I don't recommend using video during a speech. If you do, though, use it to your full advantage, and don't let its many drawbacks harm your speech.

TIP

Make sure the video is vital to your speech. And make sure it's short.

Here's a scenario where you may want to use video. The CEO of your company is away and can't attend the meeting. Maybe you have a video of her announcing to the audience (who are the employees) that they will indeed receive the Christmas bonus. As a matter of fact, because the shares have doubled, they're getting 30 percent more than last year! It doesn't have to be fancy or elaborate. You could record her with your phone in her office, or anywhere else that makes sense. (Don't shoot her playing golf.)

WARNING

Make sure there's no extraneous noise that could distract from her message — a phone ringing, a copy machine churning out photocopies, somebody laughing down the hall. All of those things would be captured by the mic.

If you can't get video in a situation like this, you could try voiceover. *Voiceover* is when a voice gives a narrative story that plays on the audio. In the case of the CEO, maybe all the audience would see on the screen is her picture displayed while a recording of her plays as the voiceover. And maybe that's the best you could do.

WARNING

Make sure to keep this kind of thing as short as possible — it can be boring to just stare at a picture.

I want to repeat that I'm not a big fan of using video in speeches. "But," you may say, "a video would be more engaging!" Well, just because it's a video doesn't mean it's more engaging. In fact, video can put people to sleep.

A client of mine used to teach high school. One of the subjects he covered was the history of metals. He created a cool video where he shot drawings of people in the Bronze Age and Iron Age. He added narration in his own voice. On the day he would present the film, the plan was he'd just press the play button and then sit back and watch. But he noticed the students weren't engaged. And, yes, this was high school — they often aren't engaged at the best of times. But these kids were especially drowsy. So the next year he scrapped the video. He showed pictures and talked about them live and in person. And guess what? The kids were much more engaged than they were during his fancy movie.

BEWARE OF ANIMATING SLIDES

So, you want to show an animation of a dancing girl at the corner of your slide as the CEO announces the bonus. Beware! Just like strobe lights can quickly become annoying, so can animation.

Here's a good rule to live by: Don't have anything shake or move onscreen for more than five or six seconds. And *don't* use slides that move in and out of focus — they'll make the audience dizzy. Your organizer will not appreciate the cleanup.

Still not convinced? Have you ever been on Facebook or a website and some dumb icon comes up and starts flashing? It's like a mosquito, right? You just want to swat it away. Use animation briefly and sparingly, if at all.

And remember your audience: If you're giving a presentation to high school kids and parents on fundraising for the prom, don't think you're cute by showing a couple dancing in the corner of the slide. You *do* want the kids to come to prom, right?

Using Other Visual Aids

Sometimes you don't want to display something onscreen. You want to show something real and physical. This section offers a little advice on doing that effectively.

Properly using props

A *prop*, as you know, is an object you can use with your hands. It could be almost anything: a phone, a dishtowel, a toothbrush, a painting. If you've run 100 marathons and are giving a speech about the benefits of running, you could bring your first pair of running shoes that you had dipped in bronze.

If you bring a prop, find a way to let everyone in on it. It's not going to be displayed on a big giant screen the way your slides are. Make sure everyone can see it. Shoes are small, so that might not be a great idea after all. Remember to think outside the box — why not costume up and wear your running gear instead?

REMEMBER Put visual aids where everyone can see them.

Are you talking numbers and showing graphical data on some kind of whiteboard or display board? We'd better be able to see it. Make the graph *big*. Don't be that speaker who has to say, "You can't really see this, but what this looks like is . . ."

And keep it simple. If these aren't math majors, make it something that a kid could read. Big letters, bright colors. Make the image clear with no distracting lines or extraneous stuff.

Going old school with flip charts

Before there was PowerPoint, there was . . . the flip chart. I still see charts in a fair amount of boardrooms, and it's not hard to catch a member of Congress pointing to one on C-SPAN. But they aren't used as much as they once were. Now everyone is high tech — but don't forget about that long-lost pal, the flip chart.

I used a flip chart a lot when teaching drama in schools because, well, back in the day that was all there *was*. If you're in a boardroom or have a small audience, then they can all probably see what you write on your flip chart.

When I was an actor, I toured with children's plays for a time. Most of them incorporated audience participation — you know, where the audience gets to shout out answers or ideas? Flip charts are a perfect aid for kids' plays, because it keeps them engaged. And although you may not be speaking to kids, you can use this idea for adults, too.

You can use flip charts to directly engage the audience. For example, you might ask someone in the audience or around the boardroom table to come up and write something. (In schools, I used those scented markers, which were always a big hit. You might not need to entice adults with scented markers, but, hey, you might just want to have them on hand just in case.) Make sure you use dark markers with various colors and that they aren't dried up. Bring several so you have plenty of backups.

When writing on a flip chart, use your very best printing technique. Even if you won a penmanship award in third grade, *don't* write in cursive. It's much more difficult to read cursive — plus writing cursive with a marker on a vertical surface is hard to do. So win a Gold Star with your printing.

Flip charts are great for brainstorming ideas. Be prepared to write quickly. When you ask a question of your audience without a flip chart, you may get a few answers. When you start writing down the answers, you'll get *more* answers, because while you're writing them down, the audience has time to think of more while they're looking at what has already been said.

You might also have graphs and other graphical information that you wrote on the charts previously. During your presentation, you can just flip to them at the appropriate times. You can often endear yourself to an audience by creating your own graph on the spot. Be sure to practice doing it before your presentation. You don't have to be perfect, and unless you are an artist trained in flip chart art, you probably won't be. But you're a human, and humans aren't perfect. The audience knows that.

TIP

Here are two final flip chart tips:

>> **Position the flip chart where everyone can see it.** Make sure the flip chart is the focus. Turn off any other slides you may have used previously.

>> **Don't use a flip chart if you have to describe it.** If what you're writing can't be seen by everyone because the venue is too big, don't use a flip chart. You want everyone to be engaged.

Chapter **8**

Being Funny (or Trying To)

W hat makes someone or something funny? I've had this conversation with clients, friends, and family many times over the years. I'm lucky; I've got an inside track on humor. I'm surrounded by very funny people in my personal and professional life.

My husband and sons have great senses of humor. Others I've worked with over the years are also extremely funny people. Actors, educators — it doesn't matter. People can be funny no matter their profession or skills. But the question of *what* exactly makes something funny only gets harder for me as I think about all the funny people in my life. They're all funny in different ways, for different stages, and for different types of audiences. Many of the actors I know are, not surprisingly, *physical* comedians — they use their bodies to express humor. Charlie Chaplin was one of the originals, and Jim Carrey is one of the best. My husband is talented at purely speech-based comedy, as he works as a radio host. And others I've interacted with over the years use comedy in ways that best suit their careers. All of which convinces me that it's really hard to pin down why something is funny.

What I've said so far might give you the impression that I believe being funny is innate. In some ways, I do. As with any other ability, there are those who have a certain aptitude for being funny. But comedy itself is not an instinct. Those with that certain something still have to put in the work. And it is worth it. Comedy is a way to draw people in. It adds humor and adds a spark your already fabulous content.

Getting Personal: Revealing Who You Really Are

You want to be funny? Prepare to get personal. And I don't necessarily mean giving away the nitty-gritty of your home life (although that can work too). No, by *personal*, what I really mean is *vulnerable*. Any time you're trying to get someone — or in the case of an audience, a group of people — to react with an emotional gesture such as laughing, there is always a chance that it might fall flat.

Scared yet? Here's the good news: If you *do* make people laugh, it can affect how they view the rest of your presentation. People will cut you a lot of slack if you bare a bit of your hilarious soul.

With all of that in mind, here are a few starting tips for using comedy in speeches:

>> **Recognize that comedy is serious business.** This sounds like a classic word-play cliché. But it's got some truth. You want to be funny? You have to work at it like a job. You ever see a standup comedian who absolutely killed it? He just had the whole crowd going, and you told all your friends? Well, that's not the whole story for that guy. He's toiled in sweaty basement clubs and had awkward nights where no one laughed. But he kept working on it, and he got to a point where he can have the whole crowd rolling.

Now, those may not be your aspirations. And you probably don't have the spare time to sweat it out in clubs anyway. The first time you hit the stage or a boardroom for a presentation, you want to already have that funny bone. But there's always time to practice, as long as you're serious about it.

TIP

Next time you're with your friends and an opportunity for a joke comes up, take the chance. Look up some jokes and memorize a few you like. If they don't laugh, reflect later about it. How can you tweak your approach? Were they the wrong type of audience? Heck, ask how your telling of the joke could be improved. If they do laugh, store that away, too. Comedy has to be something you work at if you really want to get better.

>> **Don't sell yourself as funny — let others decide that.** Some of the worst speeches I've ever seen are those where the presenter says he's funny. Don't raise expectations like that — you're bound to disappoint. In my experience, it's much better to walk into a presentation with some comedy secretly in your back pocket.

>> **You have to be 100 percent committed to telling a joke or story.** You want someone to laugh? You have to be *all in*. If you're not in the mood to be funny, you won't be. I liken it to these sorts of situations: Someone tells a story at a

party and everyone laughs. Then someone else goes, "Hey, this was just like that other story!" and point at a third person, who just doesn't want to tell the story, for whatever reason. That will suck the air out of a room quick.

» **You have to believe you're funny.** Having a *sense of humor* is different than *being funny*. They have some overlap, but a sense of humor is more about being able to find things funny. Not everyone finds things funny. If you want to be funny, you have to *believe* that whatever you're going to say is going to make people laugh.

» **Humor will bring smiles and maybe laughs, but jokes might bring groans.** Have an idea of the reaction you're going to get. If you're going to be slinging "dad jokes" all night, be prepared for people to groan. That's okay if that's what you're looking for.

» **A humorous story is often more successful than a joke.** You're probably not up there to tell jokes. Relating a humorous story is often more conducive to a presentation. If you're already telling personal stories about your career or your business, it doesn't hurt to liven them up a bit with humor. Add a punch line or two. On the other hand, telling a joke just to tell a joke, without any of your presentation's context layered in there, stands a good chance of falling flat.

» **Test your stories beforehand.** There's a risk in everything, especially when it comes to being funny. Here's a rule of thumb I offer to most of my clients: If you think a story is going to be funny, try it out on people in casual conversation first. It will give you a pretty good indication as to whether an audience is going to enjoy it or not, and it will give you a bit of practice to boot.

If a story falls flat with a jury of your peers, consider leaving it out. It might do more harm than good. Rewrite it, practice it some more, and then try again.

» **Be yourself.** This is a platitude, of course, but there's no way around it: Your only path to comedy is through your own personality. I know you want to sound intelligent and hilarious. We all do. But you must find out how to get there on your own terms. People can see right through a put-on persona. They want you to be a relatable human being.

Writing Stories and Jokes

It's time to start writing some comedy. Where to begin? I suggest asking yourself some questions to get things rolling.

Questions to help you prep

Here's a handy checklist to get you thinking about getting that audience doubled over in laughter. Take a pen and a pad of paper and jot down your answer to each of the following questions:

>> **What do you and the audience have in common?**

Chapters 11 and 15 talk about ways of relating to your audience. You want to get into their heads. Think about two very different speeches. The first is a presentation to your bosses in which you propose a new, more efficient system that you think will save the company money. The second is at a 20-year high school reunion.

Think about how those audiences differ. Think about the power dynamics. Your bosses are, well, your superiors. A story about throwing up in the bushes before chemistry in 11th grade probably won't resonate with them as it would with your high school reunion class.

>> **What are you trying to accomplish?**

In Chapters 5, 6, and 11, I go over goals of speeches. What do you want the audience to do after they hear you — what is their call to action? You have to think about your goals when you're adding in a bit of comedy, too.

Let's go back to our previous example of the two different speeches. With your bosses, you're giving a *rhetorical* or *persuasive speech.* You're trying to convince them that system B is superior to system A. This really limits the types of comedy you can offer them. In this scenario, you're trying to detach the audience from one idea and give them another one to chew on. There could be complications. It might have to be delicate. What if someone in the room came up with the idea you're trying to change? What if there's an emotional attachment to the idea in the room? Using comedy to disparage that idea would do your presentation harm. So, there's a case where you might want to avoid it.

Your 20th high school reunion, though, is totally about entertainment. You're looking for people to laugh at the stupid things that all used to do as kids. So have at it!

>> **Can you use situational and observational humor?**

You may be in a meeting with the most intimidating people in your company at a career make-or-break moment. You're allowed to make light of that situation. Don't make fun of anyone in particular, but everyone knows what the score is. Joking about it can ease the tension.

Same goes for the high school reunion, although that's going to be a little more lax. You can easily talk about how old you are, for example. You're all thinking about that, anyway.

>> **What do you know and what have you experienced?**

It's much easier making yourself the object of the comedy rather than others (including the audience). First, there's the self-deprecation angle, which I get to later in the chapter. But there's also the fact that you may only really have a good enough idea of your own experience to be able to turn it into comedy.

Boss example again. Don't presume to know their experience when coming up with some comedy. You don't really know how they react to things in their job, because you don't have their job. Chances are, though, you have a great deal of knowledge about your *own* job. And your bosses do too. They manage you — plus they have probably also had a similar position earlier in their career.

>> **Are there frustrating things you could focus on?**

All good stories involve a problem. Stories always involve something at stake. And there's always some failure or struggle in there that reveals the stakes — *ta da,* you're a genius. There's humor in failures and struggles. That frustration you felt while coming up with the solution that you're now presenting to your bosses? Exaggerate them. Blow them up! Make them the stupidest mistakes you've ever made. Make them funny.

>> **Have you written a rough draft yet?**

Content always comes first. You need to know what you're going to say and why you're saying it before you can start making it funny. After you decide what you're going to say, then you can sprinkle in the humor.

>> **Can you keep it clean?**

This shouldn't have to be said, but keep it clean. Certainly no sexist, racist, or xenophobic jokes should be going into your presentation — ever. Raunchy humor is also very probably not a good idea. As for cursing, well, that's up to you — but don't do it at work. It adds nothing and it can only harm your presentation. At the high school reunion, use your best judgement.

Figuring out your own sense of humor

First, what makes *you* laugh? Think about and identify things, situations, and entertainment styles that make you laugh. These might include movies, TV shows, and standup comedians.

Observe people and comedians whom you find funny. Observe how they seem to be saying even more than what they're actually saying. Why are you laughing at that? Try to figure it out. You can learn style, structure, and pacing through watching things you find funny.

EXERCISE: KEEP A COMEDY NOTEBOOK

Try keeping a notebook with you and write down jokes or stories that you may use in the future. File these in your comedy vault. Joan Rivers filed every joke she ever wrote in filing cabinets. She wrote over a million of them. On each file card, her secretary also wrote where and when the joke was told. I don't propose you become obsessive about it like she did, but writing stuff down so you don't forget it is one way to get in the habit of being serious about comedy.

Once you've got a few funny anecdotes in the vault, try them out. But don't let your audience know that you're about to tell a joke — that's a laugh killer. Just be casual. You can try out the gems from your vault with family, friends, or really anybody. See how the joke works on them.

Is there someone that you know that makes others laugh? Give them a buzz and ask them their thoughts on being funny.

Comedy is in part cultural. The things we found funny decades ago are often lost on modern audiences. But there's still a personal element to comedy too. Try to be specific about what you find funny.

Do you ever make people laugh? Was it intentional or not? When you're out with your friends and they laugh at something you did or said, make a mental note of that.

Try to determine where you find the things that make you laugh the most. Is it in books? Television? Social media? Other people?

Breaking It Down: Elements of Humor

Don't feel you have to be perfect. Perfection is boring — and besides, who can relate to it? For people to find something funny, they have to be able to relate to it.

WARNING

Never make the audience the butt of your joke. You want them on your side, remember? Likewise, don't divide the audience. You know the classic comedy trope "Men do this, but women do this"? Yeah, don't do that. Why alienate a portion, if not all, of your audience that way?

Don't start a story by letting the audience know it's a joke. That can spoil it because now the audience is waiting expectantly for your supposedly hilarious story. What if it isn't all that funny? Instead, let the audience come to realize you're telling a joke on their own. And try not to laugh first. If the audience laughs, *then* feel free to laugh along.

While waiting to give your speech, you may hear something from the previous speakers that inspires you to try and say something funny about their presentation. *Don't do it* unless you're great at improvisation and can fit it in seamlessly.

Memorize your jokes. Practice them. Forgetting how a joke goes halfway through telling it is just about the best way to lose an audience.

Don't take it too hard if your humor falls flat. Sometimes it's the luck of the draw. When I was performing in a show, each performance was different, so audience reactions were also different. I could never assume that the audience would react the same each night. Don't expect the same laughter every time.

The rule of three

There's something about the number three. Ever notice things always happen in threes in fairy tales? This is sometimes called the *rule of three.* It's often found in jokes as well.

Three men walk into a bar. The first one does something specific. The second man does something similar, though a little different, and the listeners can see the pattern forming. When the third man does something that deviates unexpectedly from that pattern, that's where the *punch line* comes in.

The rule of three works because you get just enough to establish a pattern — and then you get a surprising deviation from that pattern. All in a nice little three-example package.

The importance of practice

You can't expect to be funny right off the bat, just like you can't expect to dunk a basketball the first time you're handed one. The practice regime to be able to dunk a ball might seem fairly obvious, but how do you practice being funny without looking like a total idiot?

Here are some tips:

>> **Practice telling your joke or story in different ways.** You have a funny anecdote you want to tell at your son's wedding? Try it first on some

unsuspecting guinea pigs. Maybe they're your coworkers, or maybe they're extended family. Try it a few times, in as many ways as you can without straying from the facts. Notice the reaction of your audience to each version. Start with the simplest version and then experiment.

>> **Slow down.** Don't be in a hurry to get to the punch line. People can stand a little anticipation, and anticipation can even make it better once you reveal the joke.

>> **Practice your exact wording as much as you can.** Musicians have a saying: *To play fast, you've got to play slow.* What it means is that to be able to eventually play something fast, you *must* know how to play it correctly to begin with. And that means playing it correctly every time, no matter how slow you have to go — otherwise, you're just practicing mistakes. Find the most effective wording for your joke or story, practice that, and try not to deviate too much from it.

>> **Practice your timing.** Try changing up the pace, playing with where to speed up or slow down and where to pause. Try emphasizing different words in different places.

>> **Say the punch line loud and clear.** You can even increase your volume and really emphasize the last word. Sometimes it's not what you say but how you say it. Keep the punch line clean. When you deliver it, don't say any extra words. It doesn't need any extra, last-minute additions. Deliver what you practiced. Just land the thought.

Brevity is the soul of wit. You'd better believe Shakespeare knew what he was talking about when he said that.

REMEMBER

>> **Memorize it.** Reading it off the page doesn't have nearly the same impact as speaking from memory.

The power of the pause

Comedic timing isn't just when and how you say things; it's also about the *absence* of speech. Pauses play a huge role in whether something can be funny or not.

First off, a pause can add tension, especially in the audience — they're waiting for you to say the punch line, or really *anything* to break the tension created by your pause. Tension is also usually present between characters in your story.

You can also use a pause to wait for an audience reaction. The most classic example of that is waiting for audience laughter to begin or die down, but you can also pause to allow the audience to really ponder something you've said.

The charm of self-deprecating humor and laughing at yourself

Ah, we all know about this, that ego-busting, making-fun-of-yourself type of comedy. But it's not just as simple as calling yourself an idiot. What you're really trying to do with self-deprecation is *disarm the audience.* When you make fun of something about you, the audience can relate, and that empathy creates a bond between the audience and you. They know that you're an expert in whatever it is you're speaking about — they find it charming to know you're also human, like they are.

But what about you should you poke fun at? What's the first thing people notice about you? Try these ideas:

>> **Height:** Are you really short or extremely tall? If so, you know it's noticeable. Does your height contradict your message, maybe? Use that!

>> **Looks or lack of style:** We all try, but we can't all be cool. In order for some of us to be cool, some of us have to look like nerds. If that's you, use it. Maybe you're talking about science, or maybe about fancy basketball stats — whatever it is, rock your nerdiness.

>> **Being bald:** As Jerry Seinfeld says about George, "He knows he's bald." Yup, you're bald. So what? It happens to a lot of guys, and it doesn't affect a thing except your follicles. Use that.

>> **Being boring:** Maybe you're an average person. No one wants to be average, right? But maybe average fits you to a T. Let them know how average you are. Emphasize it! Then stun them with your expertise.

WARNING

Don't go overboard with self-deprecating humor into the realm of self-loathing. You're not Rodney Dangerfield. The audience can become confused and uncomfortable and may not know whether they should laugh or not.

Do you text your kids all the time to find out where they are and what they're doing, what they're eating, what's going on their lives? You can laugh at yourself for being an overbearing mom. Are you a geek who loves comic books and video games? Are you totally out of place demographically in your profession? Good news. You have something to laugh at yourself about.

Laughing at yourself shouldn't be conflated with self-deprecating humor. They *do* overlap, but it's important to distinguish what's funny about you that others will find funny, and something about you that you can harp on yourself about to comedic effect.

One of the best things to do is talk about certain failures in your life that have led you to this moment. I was at a choir concert, and while sitting in the audience I read in the program that the choir director had been replaced due to illness. The MC came on and began introducing the original choir director — the wrong person. He was reading the director's biography, and suddenly the audience started rumbling, and someone from the wings whispered, "He's not here," and ran out to give the MC the correct bio. The MC made a joke and laughed at his own mistake and immediately had the audience on his side.

The value of acting it out

Sometimes it takes more than words to tell a story properly. Sometimes you have to put your whole body into it. Yeah, it's a leap for some people. How can you go into outright acting when you still feel pretty anxious about just speaking? Admittedly, it's a tough thing to master. But I've found with my clients that at least they're more comfortable acting out the stories that they've personally experienced.

Here's an example of a story I've told that lends itself to re-creating my body language onstage. The situation: The time I went to see the hit Broadway musical *The Book of Mormon* in New York. I paid a lot of money for the ticket, and when I got to my row, someone was sitting in my seat.

Needless to say, I was anxious and surprised. What was my body language like? I walked along the row with purpose as I counted the seat numbers. When I found my seat occupied, my body language changed. I became physically smaller. I didn't want to create a scene. My voice became quieter and I tried to sound as pleasant as possible, but I showed her my ticket and said in a small, *devoiced* whisper (discussed in Chapter 4), "Um, I think you're in my seat." This was an encounter between me and an older woman. That creates an opportunity to use different voices for effect. I even had props: my purse held tightly on my shoulder, my program, and my ticket in my hand.

TIP

If you find yourself telling a story about yourself, don't be afraid to use body language, different voices, and even props to re-create the scene a little for your audience.

The art of modesty

You know the first line to that old Mac Davis song? "Oh Lord, it's hard to be humble, when you're perfect in every way"? The artist is of course being facetious — that's where the humor comes from. Because in fact, it's modesty that is the attractive trait. You can use modesty to win the favor with your audience.

Here are some tips for staying humble during your performance:

>> **Downplay your abilities and never boast or brag.**

I keep telling you you're the expert up there, and sooner or later you're going to believe it. But there's a way to *imply* that expertise without proclaiming from the mountaintop that you're a gift to your profession. Many of my clients have a problem with this. It's not that they're overly cocky, because many of them suffer from real anxiety. Instead, they're so worried the audience won't believe them that they go totally overboard and start babbling about their accomplishments. Don't do that. People are smart. They pick up on implicit actions and words. Chapter 6 talks about showing, not telling when it comes to stories. That goes for your accomplishments, too. Do your job up there with good content, and the audience will catch on that you're an expert.

>> **Be confident in what you can do.**

None of this is to say that you shouldn't have confidence up there. In fact, confidence is actually important when it comes to modesty. Those who talk about their abilities ad nauseum are seen as being *less* confident. So go ahead and be confident — but without bragging.

>> **Accept that you may be wrong sometimes.**

Yeah you're the expert. But you're also human. You're going to make mistakes. You've made them before, and you'll make them again. That's gold in the comedy realm. Making mistakes is something the audience can relate to. They're just glad it's you, and not them.

>> **Accept compliments, especially laughter.**

I've noticed that many of my clients have a tough time soaking up applause or laughter. Some feel the need to cut it off by resuming their speech. Some feel they don't deserve it. But remember, a speech is a kind of conversation. You need to allow the audience to speak back to you. Sometimes they do that by clapping and laughing. Let them. Enjoy it.

>> **Put the needs of others before you.**

That joke, that funny story, that anecdote? They're not for you. They're for the audience. You can laugh and you can have fun, but remember who it's all supposed to be for.

>> **It's not about you, it's about your message.**

I've said a few times that a speech is a performance, and it is. Just don't forget the purpose of the performance: *to enhance the message*. Don't get carried away. You're there to do a job, and although that job involves being yourself, and being funny, and being confident, the message is what it's all about. The message always has to come first.

The dreaded cringe and how to avoid it

My husband was named class historian for his graduation in high school. Essentially, he was told to write and give a speech that summed up the social life of the student body. Apparently it was very funny. Yes, he named names. That was sort of the point. He got some great laughter from the crowd, and it's one of the things people still remember him by today.

Years later, he went back to the high school for another graduation, that of his youngest sister. The class historian for her class went up and gave a speech as well. The only problem was . . . it was the same speech my husband had written years earlier, just with the names changed. This time it flopped. It was just a total failure for the poor plagiarist. He barely got any laughs — maybe a couple of pity chuckles from what looked like his family table. My husband sure wasn't laughing.

My point is that the same, identical material can be delivered by two different people, on two different nights, and receive totally different audience reactions. Maybe this time it was the audience. Maybe it was the presentation. Sooner or later, if you do this sort of thing long enough, there *will* be moments when the audience cringes. That's *going* to happen if you keep speaking in public. You'd better know what to do when it does.

When jokes bomb, it's a real bummer. My husband and I once attended the Just for Laughs festival in Montreal. A comedian came onstage and started her set, and unfortunately it just wasn't funny. It was really hard to laugh or even respond, and this was in a really big theater. Out of courtesy, we eked out a few chuckles, but it was hard not to be embarrassed for her. You could feel her frustration. Finally she told us, "I don't know why you guys aren't laughing. Last night's audience loved it!"

Following are a couple tips for keeping yourself above the cringe-inducing threshold when using humor:

>> **Be brief.** Don't let a joke take up so much time that the audience forgets what your speech is about.

>> **Be culturally appropriate.** Once you alienate the audience, it's very hard to get them back.

Here are some things *not* to do:

>> **Don't tell a joke about the organizer.** Or someone in his family who may have died. Or the CEO who just got fired.

>> **Don't recycle.** Don't tell an old joke that people have heard before.

>> **Don't tell inside jokes.** Some in the audience will have no idea what you're talking about, which will make them feel alienated and annoyed.

>> **Don't tell a joke you already know isn't funny.** If you don't think it's funny yourself, there's no way you'll convince the audience.

Loosening up the audience

As you know by now, telling a joke or hilarious story is a great way to loosen up the audience — especially after a tense or serious subject.

Here are some guidelines that should help you break the ice:

>> **Engage the audience.** The audience wants you to *engage* with them. Especially if you have all just come off a very serious presentation.

   You might be next up after a speech that was definitely not funny. Maybe a colleague just gave a super boring presentation. Maybe very grave or sad matters were discussed. Either way, being funny right off the bat — if done right — can set a great new tone for your own presentation. You may need a sharp juxtaposition to get people ready for your speech. Just stay respectful.

>> **Don't disparage the previous presenter.** Yeah, the first presenter was boring. Or sad. Or both. It doesn't matter. *Don't make fun of that speaker.* It makes you look juvenile, and like you're trying to take advantage and get a leg up. Even if the audience secretly agrees with you, it's a bad look.

>> **Don't set the wrong tone.** Is your presentation about something really heavy? Will there be no funny bits? Then definitely don't start with one. You're trying to set the tone here. Don't set the *wrong* one.

TIP

Please don't tell your joke to the mirror. When you look in the mirror, you're thinking about your hair, your skin, your body — you can't possibly really focus on telling your joke. The joke becomes secondary. Videotape is a different story. You're looking at a neutral camera, not your zits and waistline.

Enjoy yourself and don't take it too seriously

On at least some level, you should be enjoying yourself — especially if something is going to be funny, or try to be. You need to be able to laugh in order to be funny.

EXERCISE: RECORD YOURSELF AND LISTEN

I mention this in other chapters — now it's time to do what so few people love to do: Record yourself. Yup, it's awkward. And weird. But it's invaluable too. Using the tools we're afforded today to get better at the craft of public speaking is an advantage you shouldn't pass on.

This one's a bit hard, though. I admit that. Trying to determine whether you're funny or not is a little bit like trying to tickle yourself. But you can at least go through a checklist to see if you're doing it correctly, and then get someone else to determine if it's funny or not.

While listening, note the important parts and then later expand on them. Do the same for the bits that lag or don't add to your story: Leave them out.

Listen to yourself, hard as it may be, and answer some questions:

- Have you set up your joke?
- Are you expressive with your vocal variety?
- Is your speech clear and understandable?
- Have you queued up the punch line?
- Is the punch line clear?

Here are some ways I've found that may help you have fun with this:

>> **Don't be so hard on yourself.** So what? You flopped a joke. Not the end of the world. We've all done it. Shrug it off. The show must go on.

>> **It is okay to feel nervous — it means you care.** Think about interviewing for your dream job. Would you be nervous? Yeah, but it's a good type of nervous. Try for that feeling and feed off it during your performance.

>> **Make it look easy.** Be cool out there. Make it look like it's not your first time.

>> **Feel confident.** You get to share your humor with the audience. How cool is that?

>> **Trust yourself.** If so many other people manage to do it, you can definitely do it. It really will be okay.

>> **Use big gestures.** Don't worry about looking silly. You won't if you're committed to what you're saying in your presentation.

>> **Don't worry about the audience not liking you.** To be honest, they don't care that much. They're more interested in what you have to say than they are in you. So relax.

>> **Don't laugh at your jokes before the audience laughs.** It's the audience's job to find it funny. If they do, *then* you can go ahead and laugh with them if you want. But laughing before they do just comes off as weird.

>> **Don't try hard to be funny.** Don't force it. Tell your story as you would to your friends.

>> **Slow down.** Take your time. Pause just before the punch line for full effect.

>> **Look up at audience.** You're talking to them, not to your notes.

CUTTING TENSION FOR HEAVY TOPICS

Sometimes using humor is a good way of broaching heavy topics, like death or serious illness. I've found that people are naturally uncomfortable around certain ideas, and that includes audiences. You, as the speaker and performer, may also feel naturally uncomfortable around these topics. Humor can be a great way to release some of these feelings.

Here are some things to think about when using humor to reduce tension:

- **It shouldn't feel forced.** If you're trying to *force* an audience to feel feelings, whatever they are, rarely will you succeed. That includes trying to make them laugh when you've already taken them to a place of sadness or contemplation. If you force it, your attempt will seem cheap.

- **Humor gives the audience time to breathe.** You know the release valve on a steam engine? Sometimes the pressure gets so much that you need to hit that lever and let it go. Humor can work in the same way. Sometimes an audience just wants to let emotion out. Laughter is a great way of doing that.

- **Take it from other professionals.** Cops and doctors often use morbid humor to make situations that are painful and upsetting more bearable.

- **Laughter is a form of power.** Laughing at a problem gives you control over it.

- **Use multiple characters.** In a story, it can be a good idea to have at least two characters. Be the narrator. Separating your voice away from the heavy topic can make it easier to be funny.

- **Things can turn funny eventually.** Once when I was in Mexico, I stepped off a curb and fell. Turned out I broke my wrist. It wasn't funny at the time. Later, once I got some distance from the incident, telling the story became funny. I often end it by revealing that I'd only had one shot of tequila.

In your post-mortem, answer the following questions:

>> How did the audience receive my jokes and stories?

>> Could any of my jokes been told better? How?

>> What joke or story received the best reaction? Why was that?

Save your post-mortem and look it over the next time you're asked to speak.

Chapter **9**

Practicing Your Speech

Your speech is on paper — and it's spectacular. Seriously, it's looking like a longer version of the Gettysburg Address. Even the punctuation is spot on and in all the right places. It's in a font that tickles your eyes, you love it so much. And the paper is that beautiful texture, the expensive kind you get at that really nice stationery store downtown.

So what do you do with this glorious document? How do you get from the page to the stage?

Practice.

The old adage says practice makes perfect. Forget that — you're not looking for perfect, you're looking for *human*. You practice so that you can sound like an augmented version of yourself. Still yourself, but a more eloquent, more confident version. Worthy of that speech you've got in your hands. Worthy, if someone were to transcribe it, of the transcription to be on a similar type of paper, with a similar font.

This chapter talks about getting to that level.

Practicing Out Loud

It sounds like an obvious thing, but when I ask most of my clients whether they've practiced their speech aloud, the answer is usually no. Why is that? A speech is absolutely an oral performance. Good speakers look like they didn't even write it, that it's just done on the spot. So why do so many practice public speaking by silently reading to themselves?

The answers I get most of the time include the following:

>> They feel silly speaking out loud to themselves.

>> They have no place to do it.

>> They have no time to do it.

>> It never occurred to them that practicing aloud could be important.

REMEMBER

Get it through your head now: You *have* to practice your speech by reading it out loud. Many times. Not only that, you need to also record yourself giving your speech on video, and watch it. If not on video, on audio, and listen to it. Many times.

Admittedly, it is a strange experience to hear your own voice played back to you. Some people have problems merely talking to themselves. It may feel like you're marooned on an island, and talking to yourself is the last resort for company.

To repeat: You have to practice what you write. It's the only way to improve. Think of how gymnasts practice a big maneuver: over and over, correcting every little movement, conscious of where every body part is and how every muscle is firing. They may *know* the trick inside and out. They may have seen video of the trick, know how it's supposed to be performed, know every little pitfall of a wrong hand placement. But if they don't feel what it's like to actually *do* it, they will fail. On top of that, if they aren't conscious of how they're supposed to do it, they won't be able to adjust on the fly. Speaking is the same way.

But you're not just practicing over and over like a robot. You do *not* want to sound like a robot. You want to sound like a human being — an ambitious, curious, gem of a person. And to make that adjustment, you need to speak to the audience as if they are speaking back to you.

TIP

My overall tip is this: Take parts of your speech and practice it when you're driving in the car, in the shower, doing the dishes. The more you practice it, the more you'll embody it.

The rest of this section offers advice for getting you into the idea of having a conversation with the audience:

Hear yourself

Oh, I know, this is a weird one. Your voice that you hear in your head when you speak and your voice that the camera or recorder picks up are two vastly different things. It seems like they're not even related. That whiny, high-pitched squeal or hoarse, muffled mumbling can't be your voice! No way, no how.

I'm sorry to say that it is. The reason you hear a different voice from the microphone isn't the microphone's fault. When you feel the need to speak, the brain sends a message to the vocal folds to join together and lightly form a closure across the larynx. Breath travels up from the lungs, and the air pressure builds up until there is so much pressure that your vocal folds open. The sound you hear travels through your skull and eardrum. As the vibrations travel through the bone, the sound spreads out, and the frequency, which is the number of vibrations of the vocal folds move in one second, drops. That's why you think you have a lower and richer voice. You hear your voice vibrating through your neck, skull, and face, *as well as* through the air, which gives it a much richer quality. All the microphone hears is your voice vibrating through the air. And I hate to tell you this, but that's what everyone else hears, mic or no mic. That's what you're working with.

Later in this chapter, I talk about recording yourself in more detail.

That beautiful, rich timbre you normally hear is an illusion. You have to know what you sound like to a microphone, what your speech sounds like to a microphone and through speakers, because that's how an audience is going to hear it.

Stand up

It seems trivial, and yes, it's harder than lounging on the couch, but you really need to stand up when you say that speech aloud. Sure, it's okay to write sitting down (even though there are standing desks nowadays). But there are a few key reasons why standing while you practice is a must.

First, it signals a shift from writing mode to speaking mode. They are two different things. You've done the writing. Now it's the presentation that matters.

Second, your breath can totally change if you sit in a slumped, down and in position with your head pulled down and neck tensed. Your lungs are squished, and you can't breathe to your full capacity. If you're sitting in an up and out position, as discussed in Chapter 15, with feet flat on the floor and sitting on your "sitting bones," with your body lengthening up to the sky, that is fine and can be just as good as standing. You're way more open, and there is more available lung capacity to hit all those fancy college words you threw in there to impress your boss.

Third — and this is a recurring theme in this chapter — you will be standing when you speak. You might as well get used to it.

I know there are exceptions. There will be times when you're giving your sales pitch about the new home lottery to a client and you're all sitting around the boardroom table. However, most of the time, you speak standing up.

Prepare those props

Have any sort of props or set pieces? Then you'd better know how you're going to use them.

Before actors use props on stage, they improvise without them. They put tape on the stage floor so they know where a table is, or a couch, so they get used to working around (or with) them. Actors first get used to acting by themselves, and then eventually they work with the props. That's so they don't use the props as crutches for the performance.

TIP

Treat your props the same way. If you're speaking about your marathon, and intend to raise up your worn-out shoes, how would you do it? Practice it in your head a few times, and then practice without the shoes, and then pick them up. Once you do, you'll see how you're holding them, and what you're holding them for. And you won't be hiding behind them, either.

Power up those slides

If you're using a slide show, be prepared. Some dread doing slide shows, and some rely too heavily on them. Chapter 7 talks about visual aids. Like it or not, technology is likely going to be part of your speech, especially if you're going to be doing a lot of public speaking.

People who hate technology often hate the variables and the unpredictability involved. They don't understand why something would go wrong and almost panic when something goes awry. Others understand that it's just a computer. It's only doing what it's told. As often as not, the problem turns out to be human-caused.

Because computers only do what they're told to do, that means it's up to you to tell it the right things. So, even if you know the ins and the outs of the program you're using, you must practice with it beforehand. You may know what to do when the program crashes on your desk — but what will you do when it catches you flatfooted onstage? Will you know how to continue without it?

Be prepared for the very real possibility that, for one reason or another, your slides will just not work. If that happens, be ready to smile, shrug it off, and give your speech. I discuss how to deal with things that go awry in Chapter 19.

Maybe the most important thing you need to know is exactly when to go to the next slide. Is it a particular word or picture that should trigger it? Sometimes, slide shows are used as a sort of reveal — like the picture of the new home for the lottery that you are pitching to the client, for example. Maybe you focus a certain portion of your speech around a picture or a word. With the new home, there is a man cave complete with a bar, an ottoman, and signed sports jerseys hanging on the wall. Practice aloud to yourself and find out where your slides best fit which parts of your speech.

Don't use the slides as a crutch or a fig leaf. Try not to hide from the audience by looking at your slides — or worse yet, reading off them — during your speech. Practice without looking at your slides.

Find an empty room

This could be a room in your home, an empty boardroom at work, a janitor's closet in your child's school. Wherever it is, ideally it has become your own personal bubble where you feel you can scream and no one will hear you. It's a safe place. You need such a spot, where you can totally mess up, where you can video yourself and it's no big deal. This is your practice room — it's the room you prepare yourself in before facing the audience. It's the secondary space. Here is where you practice as if there's an audience.

Do everything you would do onstage. And act like it *is* a stage (Chapter 15 talks more about stages). Come in from stage left if that's how you're going to do it. (Remember, stage left is the area of the stage to the left of center stage when you're facing the audience.) If you're about to present in a boardroom, get some chairs in there. Can you get some crash test dummies in suits? I'm only half-kidding. Act as if this is the real thing, while knowing it's not. It will get you prepared when you have to step out under those lights or in front of those bosses.

Time yourself

This is one of the concepts my clients find hard to figure out. Let's say you're given 20 minutes for your talk. How do you translate that into content? Do you even have 20 minutes in your arsenal? When you're onstage, it's often hard to differentiate 15 minutes from 5. When we write, we split everything up into pages or words — those are easy to count. It's important to know how long you're going to speak, and then you can go from there.

One of the first things you have to do once you're finished writing the speech is time yourself reading it. If the organizers say five minutes and your read takes seven minutes, you're going to have to cut. This can be a good thing in that it may force you to get rid of everything except what is essential. Maybe a certain section is just an ancillary point, and can be cut.

Better to finish with time left over than feel like you have to rush. Get your message out, but slowly and clearly.

Get someone to watch you

It's great to review your own performance, but you should also get some sort of second opinion before hopping up in front of your colleagues and spilling all your great ideas. This is a scary one: recruiting your first bit of audience. And I say *bit* because this person or couple of people will be the smallest audience you're ever going to face.

MIRROR, MIRROR, ON THE WALL

If you've ever been in a dance studio, you'll notice two things. The dancers can contort the human body in ways that seem painfully impossible, and there are floor-to-ceiling mirrors so all the dancers can watch every side of them do that. The mirrors aren't there as just an ego thing. If they didn't have those mirrors, it would be hard to know what they were doing.

The *feeling* of doing something with your body can only go so far. In order to really understand it and be able to correct anything you're doing wrong, you need to be able to see yourself. Earlier in this chapter, I outline how and why you should be recording your voice. It's time to dig a little deeper and put those two things together.

Looking in a mirror isn't really natural for speakers, or for people in general. I had a stint of teaching drama to dancers in a dancing studio. They looked in mirrors and saw things to work on. I saw a rip in my jeans and too much eye shadow. We mostly use mirrors in bathrooms and maybe bedrooms as we dress. And when we look at ourselves in the mirror, we typically begin to criticize everything we see in our appearance.

Luckily, we've got technology on our side, so why not use it to our advantage? Better to record yourself on video and/or audio and critique later — not while trying to give a speech in front of a mirror.

For my clients, it's easy: I'm that person. But you'll have to choose someone who's going to help you, not just act as a stand-in. It's important you give that person some guidelines to work with.

For example: Is my message getting through? How is my posture? Am I moving aimlessly without purpose? Things like that are tough to spot on your own.

Recording and Critiquing Yourself

This section focuses on using recording technology (instead of the old-fashioned mirror) to help you practice.

Take video of yourself presenting

If you're going to take a video of yourself to help improve your speaking, there are a few things you should know. First of all, if you want to use video as a public tool, either on your website or in social media, get a professional to help you. You want a video like that to be produced professionally.

But here are some tips to shoot your own video to help critique yourself:

>> **Use a tripod:** If you're recording a video with your phone, a small tripod would be useful. Set it up so you frame yourself in the middle of the shot.

>> **Shoot close up:** Be within six feet of the camera — that will make sure you're getting good audio.

>> **Use good lighting:** Do it in a quiet, well-lit room. Soft light that comes from a source level with or slightly higher than your face works best. Use the light on the camera while on "auto exposure." Ceiling lights are not flattering and won't give you a good look.

>> **Don't use "selfie" mode:** The front-facing camera on most phones will reverse the image (try it when you have writing on a t-shirt). Use the main camera.

>> **Pretend there's an audience:** Take the video facing the phone but don't stare into it the whole time. Pretend you're addressing your audience and feel free to move (within the shot). You don't have to be stuck to one place.

>> **Don't practice in shorts and t-shirt:** Wear the clothing you intend to wear during your speech. That way you can critique your "look" and get comfortable with what you're wearing.

TIP

A recording of your presentation before an actual audience will be invaluable.

You're not done learning or growing just because you made your speech. It may be easy to move on after presenting and never critique or revisit it, but that's no way to improve. Was that the only speech you're ever going to give? Unlikely. If you were compelled to do one, you'll be compelled, at some future date, to do another. So, why not learn from that first one? It may be super weird to watch the video later, but trust me, that's part of getting comfortable with yourself and your performance.

TIP

Find out if the presentation is going to be officially recorded, and whether you'll get a copy or a link online. It's also a good idea to record it yourself. Either set up a camera on a tripod in the back or ask someone sitting toward the front in the audience to record it with her phone. Make sure that person gets a nice tight shot of you and the audio is decent enough to work with.

At home, take a nap. Then look at the video and take notes. What worked for you? How was your breath? Your volume? Did you do any weird things with your hands you didn't expect? The next time you practice for a speech, look over those notes.

Record your voice

It's important to listen to just your voice, in isolation and without seeing your body language and whatever it is you may be doing with your hands (I get to that eventually, too).

Record your voice using your phone or another recording device, but don't hold it in your hand while you're saying your speech. There are a few reasons for this. You may distort the audio if you wave your hands around. It's also a distraction you don't need while you give your speech.

TIP

Put the phone or recorder somewhere high, on something secure, like the top of a dresser, and stand a few feet away from it. Yes, stand — don't sit — because you'll be standing when you speak for real.

Later, when you listen back, reflect on a few things:

>> Do your words make sense?

>> Are you speaking in a monotonous pitch? Is your voice too high or too low?

>> Is your volume varied, or is it too loud or quiet?

>> Is your tone of voice appropriate for your subject matter?

>> Are your energy and passion coming through?

>> Does your breathing seem easy and free?

>> Do you maintain a conversational tone, and does your voice flow easily from one change of thought to another?

Work on your face and nonverbals

Ever heard communication experts talk about body language? Psychologist Albert Mehrabian's study of nonverbal communication is cited a lot. His findings on how we perceive the meaning of words boils down to 7 percent from the word itself, 38 percent from tone of voice, and 55 percent from body language. Nonverbal communication is a thing, and it's a thing you will need to master to become a public speaking guru. So how do you do that?

TIP

Take a look at your recorded presentation again. Go through the entire thing with the sound off. Look at your hands first. Do they move at all when you speak? Does it look like they're moving naturally and are a part of you?

Try talking to a person in front of you as if you are having an argument. Maybe it's your boss or a coworker. Do you move your hands? In your speech, when your hands are down by your sides, body language specialist Mark Bowden calls this the *grotesque plane* in his book *Winning Body Language* (McGraw-Hill, 2010). It affects many aspects of your body, and not in a good way. Your breath is shallow due to breathing from your upper chest, your neck is jutted forward, and your muscles in your face feel heavy, as does your entire body. And do you know what all that does to your audience? It makes them tired too.

What you want to do is move your hands in a horizontal plane extending outward from your navel, what Bowden calls the *truth plane.* What happens to your breath when you use your hands this way? You are probably dropping your breath deeper into your lower abdomen. How are you feeling? It should make you calmer and in control. The audience will feel it too.

Next, take a look at your posture. Are you in a closed-off position, or do you look open to the world and to ideas? (More on that in Chapter 15.) Notice your face. Are the proper emotions showing through? Is there *any* emotion? Make sure your face matches the content and the emotions you want it to elicit. Don't smile at a drop in stock price, for example.

Mark My Words: Adjusting Your Script for Emphasis

So there that golden document lies. It's beautiful. That speech is the thing that is going to launch you into success, bringing accolades, promotions, and just general good things your way. It's your ticket upward. But wait a second. Before you laminate your masterpiece, make a copy. I'm going to need you to mangle that great piece of literature.

There's a saying in the arts: *A professional writes it down. An amateur says they'll remember.* Have you ever seen the sheet music of a classical violinist? There are pencil marks all over it. How about the manuscript of a famous novelist? Same thing. Notes make this world go round, and nothing is too pretty to annotate.

To turn your speech into a masterpiece on stage or in the boardroom, you're going to want to do what the professionals do: Mark up your work for emphasis. You want to emphasize the part or parts of your speech that you want the audience to really pay attention to, and optimize your language there that you want to carry the farthest.

Here are some things to mark up in your speech for emphasis:

TIP

>> **Mark for intensity.**

Some of your lines probably need a little extra *oomph* to get going. They could use a bit of raw intensity that will separate them from the rest. This means you want to hit a few words with more energy than normal.

You can mark sections for intensity by highlighting certain words or underlining them. Just make sure you mark them in some way that will get your attention and cue you to add some energy in those parts.

>> **Mark for volume.**

It's okay to raise your volume, but only when appropriate. And it's okay to be quieter too, if that subject matter calls for it. You need variation to avoid boring the audience. You don't want to give your whole speech and use the same volume throughout.

TIP

Getting louder and then quieter is a good way to contrast ideas. If you're mad about something, show it! If you're getting into a sad topic, it's okay to lower your voice a bit, as long as the audience can hear you. Mark those sections with your own choice of symbols that mean louder or quieter to you. Maybe it's all caps for louder.

Pair movement with volume. When you're loud, *look* loud. Jump up. Take big steps. Use large, sweeping hand movements. When you're quiet, get smaller. Be more conservative with your steps. Use smaller hand movements.

» **Emphasize the big message.**

When you know you have to hit that important point, make sure you know when it's coming. If there's a certain phrase or line you really want to be heard, underline or highlight it. That way, it'll give you an idea in practice of what you're going toward. How you emphasize that is your choice. But be sure you know it's coming.

» **Mark for pitch.**

Pitch refers to how high or low you're speaking. Pitch is dependent upon the frequency of the vocal folds vibrating together. As the number of vibrations increase in time span, the pitch goes higher, and vice versa. The keys on the left side of a piano produce low-pitched notes, and the keys on the right side produce high-pitched notes. The human voice also varies in pitch. Usually that variation is natural — it's something we all learn as we learn to speak. One thing you shouldn't do is just settle in the same pitch range of two or three notes for the whole speech. That would sound monotonous. You don't want to sound like a robot.

To indicate pitch changes on your speech, use up and down arrows. If you're excited about something and want to get them on board, bring your pitch up and put an up arrow beside that line. If you want to sound authoritative, get deep. Write in a couple of down arrows.

» **Mark for inflection.**

It's important to know where you're going in terms of inflection before you get to the end of a sentence. *Inflection* is the bend of your voice on a certain syllable or syllables for a certain emphasis. Some of it is built into punctuation already. For instance, a question mark tells you to raise your pitch at the end of a sentence. Because question marks come at the end of sentences, though, sometimes it's hard to tell which sentence will be a question or not.

If you are asking a question, put an indication of that right in that top of that line. Make sure you know that you're asking something before you actually have to ask it. If there is another bit of inflection you want to use, you can use a scooping up or down arrow to indicate that. Chapter 14 talks more about inflection.

» **Mark for rate of speech.**

Sometimes you need to speed things up a bit, and sometimes you need to slow them down. A speech usually contains a mix of speeds. What is for certain is that if you are speaking the same speed for your whole speech, your audience will get bored. There's no two ways about it. The next section talks more about the importance of slowing down.

In general, slow down during the most important parts. If there's a subordinate phrase, or one that only supports the main idea, make that bit faster than the main ideas. You want to get to the good bits, don't you? Write a big fat *SLOW* or *FAST* on top of bits where you want to regulate the speed. But remember, you still need to be understood, no matter the speed.

>> **Mark your pauses.**

Sometimes we all need a little silence in our lives and in our speeches. Have you given your audience a lot to digest? Give them a beat to think about it. Put a nice big pause in between ideas. Pausing also lets them know there will be a slight change of topic.

To indicate pauses in your speech, put a slash (/) right before the word where you want to pause. You can also use pauses in sentences, and before big words for similar effect.

Slowing Down: Speed Kills

On the highway, speed kills. Same for your speech. Well, sort of. You won't die if you go too fast, but your message will. Fast speakers tend to rush through so quickly that it sometimes feels as if they weren't up speaking there at all.

Some presenters lament about having to give boring stats, for example. So they barrel through those parts, fast and furious, making the audience dizzy with all the information. Does that sound like you? Slow down — your audience wants to hear what you have to say.

Cutting your speech when your time is cut

Sometimes speakers don't end up having as much time as they thought they would. Maybe things are running late. That's life. It happens.

What you shouldn't do is tell the audience, though. It makes them uncomfortable and it looks unprofessional. The show must go on. If you continue professionally, what the audience doesn't know won't hurt them. But if you have less time, *shorten* your speech — don't read it faster. It will be disaster if you think you can just speed up your speech to fit everything in.

It's a good idea to always have your speech on 3×5 cue cards with the main points in your pocket or purse handy, just in case you need to cut or move around some info.

Resisting the urge to rush

Many presenters are so fearful that they just want to say their speech and get it over with. So they rattle through it. But you might as well hand out a brochure and go home. You have been asked to *speak.* And unless you're speaking to a junior high school audience who, from my experience having a couple of sons, may well hate you the minute you step onstage, the audience wants you to succeed. The audience came to hear what you have to say.

German psychologist Hermann Ebbinghaus studied memory and coined *the forgetting curve,* which refers to how much information we retain over time. According to Ebbinghaus, 20 minutes after hearing a speech for the first time, people retain 58 percent, after one hour it's 44 percent, and after a day only 33 percent is remembered. So you need to go beyond that. You have to give the audience a *feeling. That* they will remember.

Think of reading a story to a child. Take the time to land your thoughts. That gives you time to settle into your speech and breathe, and gives the audience time to register what you are saying. If you speak too fast, the audience won't be able to follow and will lose interest. Record yourself speaking for at least five minutes. Are you tired of keeping up with yourself? So is the audience.

EXERCISES IN SPEED

- **Decreasing your need for speed:** Find an object like a computer (with the screen turned off) and sit in front of it. Look down at your first sentence in your speech. Look up and take a good look at the object. Really take that object in. Then say the sentence to the object just like you would to a real audience. Then wait, as if to check that the sentence has registered with the audience. Then look down and start the process again with the next sentence.

- **Reading lists:** Take a line like "Thank you to the sponsors, teachers, and parents who have made this event possible." If you race through that, those people aren't going to get the credit they deserve. So I'm trying to make you feel guilty for going too fast. For this exercise, find a spot on the floor. You're going to move with the list, a bit like a dance. "Thank you to sponsors (move left), teachers (move right), and parents (move to the center)." This will slow you down because it takes time to move. Think of that when you're speaking. If there are a few important things to say in each sentence, give them all the proper time they need. You don't need to move when you're actually giving the speech, but you can remember how that movement slowed you down.

Making the most of tactical pauses

Pauses in speech can be tricky. To some, they seem like just the absence of something — *dead air*, in radio speak, where nothing is going on even though something really *should* be going on. And in some instances, a dead air effect is what you want. A perfectly placed pause can do so much for a speech that has the perfect content to support it. Pauses can create suspense and build excitement. Pausing displays control. It allows the audience to reflect on what you just said. It gives you time to breathe.

WARNING

But of course, there are also pitfalls to pauses. Too many pauses suggest a hesitancy and insecurity. You might look unprepared, or worse, that you forgot your lines.

So what's the right balance? How do you insert perfect pauses in your speech? The following are a few examples of when pauses can achieve an effect that words might not:

>> **After a comma:** Commas are grammatical cues to pause slightly. It's okay to take a small breath at a comma. Let it linger a bit before getting to the next thing on the list.

>> **After a sentence:** In written speech, a period, exclamation point, or question mark at the end of a sentence signifies the end of the thought. Almost always take a pause after that. It doesn't have to be long. But you do need to breathe, remember. A slightly longer pause can be used to allow the audience to think about that sentence and anticipate the next one. Often speakers neglect the poor period and barrel through.

>> **Before starting a new paragraph:** A well written speech is organized into paragraphs that separate the main ideas. Know where your paragraphs are, why they are there, and how to pause between them for your audience. Your speech should still flow, but paragraphs are there for a reason. Finish your thought and allow space for a segue.

>> **For a visual:** If a visual pops up out of nowhere on the screen behind you, you need to pause to let your audience digest it for a second. Regardless of whether you're talking about it right then, or if you've fired the slide too early, let them see what it is first, and then continue on.

>> **For laughter:** Ever been to a really funny movie in a packed theatre? You may have to see it twice to hear everything. It's often so hard to hear the full jokes over all that laughter. That's unavoidable for movie stars, but you can prevent it. If you expect that people are going to laugh at a joke you make, give them space to laugh. Pick up once again when it does down. And if people laugh

unexpectedly, let them while you pause. Otherwise they won't catch the next thing you say.

» **For a sip of water:** I tell all my clients to have some water handy during their performance. Better to have it and not need it than need it and not have it. If you don't have water, you'll be sorry if you need it. Water also gives you an opportunity to pause when changing topics. Taking a sip of water lets people ruffle in their seats a little bit, and get comfortable again. Once you put down your bottle, they're ready to go.

» **For a rhetorical question:** When you ask your audience a question, you have to give them time to formulate an answer. They will be frustrated if they can't. It may give them the idea that you think only *you* have that answer.

The same is true when you ask the audience to visualize something or think about something. Allow them the time to think about it.

TIP

My clients often ask how long they should pause for. As in writing, the comma in the middle of a sentence is a shorter break than the end of the sentence. Each pause should be appropriate to its intended effect. Have fun and vary them. Pause longer than you think. The audience will wait.

Avoiding filler words: Ums and ahs

There is a politician in my area who is extremely smart and can be quite charismatic. When he reads a speech from the page, his intonation is perfect. He uses pauses to great effect. And, unlike some people, when he speaks to an audience it sounds as if he's speaking in a conversation. Sometimes the odd "um" sneaks in. But after his prepared speech, once he begins to answer questions from the audience, those *um*s and *ah*s explode. They're everywhere, in between sentences, within sentences. Anytime he can't think of an answer, a long *ummm* creeps in. It's difficult to focus on his message when his sentences are so disrupted.

What this does is take him from being an authority figure when he reads that speech to seeming unsure of himself — a babbling mess. Lack of confidence doesn't appeal to voters.

The same is true if you use filler words in a presentation. *Um*s and *ah*s happen when you feel the need to think and speak at the same time. It means you're searching for the right word. You're thinking out loud. But up on that stage, you need to look as if you've already thought about the subject and you're sharing the conclusion you've come to. If you look like you're winging it, you have little credibility.

If you're using filler words, you might not even know it. Many of my clients came to me for a different reason, only to learn later they have this affliction. The first thing you really need to do is to determine whether you use filler words. Here are a few tips to finding out if you do, and then getting rid of filler all together:

>> **Check your video:** You recorded your speech on video, right? How many filler words did you use? What kind were they? Where did they come? Write notes indicating whether they appeared in the middle of sentences or at the ends, for example. Maybe it was just in a particular sentence. Where they occur can provide clues as to why you're putting in filler words. For instance, maybe you don't understand the concept behind a particular section well enough, and you're just saying the words. That's a problem.

>> **Get a spotter:** Recite your speech to a colleague. Don't make that person actually *count* the filler words, but let her know that's what you want her to focus on before you recite it to her. After you do your speech, get her to ask some questions about the subject matter that you will answer. See if you use more filler words. Now it's your turn to ask questions. What did she notice most about the filler words? Where did they come in most? In connection with a certain topic? When you switched from one idea to the next? That information can give you a better idea of what you need to work on.

>> **Position your body:** When people are in a down and in posture, they tend to say more filler words. Try putting your hands in your pockets and watch those *ums* soar! Adopt an up and out body posture and see what happens. You are confidently looking out at the world. This won't cure you, but you will definitely have fewer *ums*.

>> **Practice, practice, practice:** Yup. It always comes down to practice. The more you practice, the more you'll know what you're going to say. It's going to cut down on your anxiety, too. Be totally prepared.

Speaking, not reading

We've all listened to speakers who pull out their notes and proceed to read them word for word. They may not even look up to see if the audience is there. If they do, they often look lost or fearful, and then settle back to their notes.

Don't do that. It makes you seem as if you don't care about the audience. If you don't care about them, why should they care about you and what you have to say?

Communication is between you and the audience, not you and your notes.

When you don't connect with your audience, you'll get no response from them. It also looks like you don't really know what you're talking about if you need to be engrossed in the page.

If you can't tear yourself away from your notes in order to engage with your audience because you're afraid of them, see Chapters 2, 5, and 11 for some tips.

There are many other pitfalls to reading word for word. You can stumble over your words. Often you read too fast. It's extremely hard to read in a conversational style. Reading is reading. Reading is not speaking.

You're communicating your ideas more than your words. The audience doesn't have the luxury of reading your speech. You need to help them out and lift that speech off the page.

You may not always have the luxury of a perfectly prepared speech. You may even get tapped to speak right before it's supposed to happen, and all you have time to do is write up a script. In that case, here are a few do's and don'ts for reading from the stage:

>> **Don't memorize — familiarize.**

Try to familiarize yourself with the speech as much as you can.

It's not always easy to do this, but make it a priority. If you're going to say this speech, you might as well look like you know what you're going to say. Get familiar with it. Try to only look down to find your place in the speech. If you have a general idea of the flow of what you're going for, then use it.

Many of my clients work on their speech so much (and good for them) that they have it memorized. But even if you memorize, you still need spontaneity in your speech. If you practice it *too much* word-for-word, it can sound stilted. What happens if you miss a word in the actual presentation? To avoid this, consider keeping the same points but varying them slightly in practice.

Always have a copy of your presentation up there. It can be the entire speech or the main points written on index cards. If you lose your focus because a cell phone rings or a baby cries, you can always look down on your page and find your place.

>> **Don't look down at embarrassing times.**

This happens more often than you might think. Some speakers start off their presentation like this: "Hi everyone, thanks for coming today, my name is . . ."

and then they look down. We know they know their name. That's not in dispute. But it sort of *looks* like they need a refresher on that. And that just looks terrible. This can happen with any number of things you should just know. Needless to say, look at the audience when you say your name.

Think of your speech as a conversation between you and the audience. Don't look down at your notes in the middle of a sentence.

>> **Pick someone to look at.**

When you look up from your page, don't just scan the crowd. It looks like you're not interested in connecting with them. Instead, look at certain people. You don't have to stare into their eyes — just make eye contact for a few seconds. Give people a sense that you're addressing your message to them. When you just sweep your eyes and scan the crowd, people feel like wallpaper.

>> **Don't read verbatim.**

As I've said, it's the message you're trying to give people, not the words. If you try to read verbatim, you will mess up eventually. That looks bad. Instead, try to go for a flow. You know what you have to say. It's all right if you don't say the exact words on the page.

Unless you're the author at your book reading, your speech is not a novel to be read. It's written to be spoken. So, when you're writing it, say it out loud to hear how it sounds.

Breathing just enough

In breathing exercises so far, I've told you to breathe in through your nose, which is a cleansing breath and filters out pollutants in the air and helps achieve the feeling of dropping your breath into your lower abdomen. However, in everyday speech, we keep our mouths open, and that's what you need to do when you give a speech. Inhaling with your mouth closed tight looks odd to the audience and stops the flow of your speech. Also, breathing through your nose takes more time than breathing through your mouth. We shouldn't be aware of you taking a breath in and out. It should be easy.

Before you begin your speech, take a deep breath. If you have the chance because the MC is introducing you, take a couple of deep breaths. This helps you relax and gives you the breath you need to start speaking.

EXERCISE: FIND OUT HOW MUCH BREATH YOU NEED

Align yourself with your feet planted, shoulder width apart, and your energy beaming up to the sky. Take a deep breath in through your nose. Count out loud to 5, and exhale all your breath. Try not to collapse in your body when you are breathing out. Count higher up to 20 if you can and avoid any tension. How far can you count on one breath?

Every sentence is different and needs a different amount of breath. Apply this exercise in a sentence with a few words, and then with a longer sentence.

For example: "Let's give a special thanks to the sponsors of today's events." That needs more breath than "Special thanks to the sponsors."

EXERCISE: TAKING A WALK

This is an exercise inspired by an exercise called Walking the Sentences from Barbara Houseman that I learned in theater school. Basically, you do what it says. You *walk* your sentences. For each of your sentences, you walk and only stop when you reach the end of your sentence. You will find the best places to breathe within a sentence that won't disrupt the flow of your thought. Your breathing will flow naturally, but you'll also find out how big of a breath you need for each sentence.

Take the first sentence of your speech. As you walk, move with purpose and imagine there's someone a few feet ahead of you that you want to talk to. Say the first sentence, and when it has ended, come to a full stop. Then start the next sentence and change direction. Don't rush your words or your pace. You can change direction every time there is a comma in the sentence as well. You will soon find out how much or little breath you need.

Chapter **10**

Becoming a Vocal Athlete

We generally think of athletes as those who push their bodies to the limits. Higher, faster, stronger. It's the Olympic way. We as a society view these people and how they achieve such feats of excellence with awe. Every time athletes do something tremendous on the international stage, there are articles upon articles about their eating habits and training regimen.

I'm not asking you to start deadlifting or to become a marathon runner. But so many of the people who walk into my office think that everything to do with speaking (and their problems with it) has to do with their mentality. It's true, the mental aspects are important. But to discount the physical aspect of the act is wrong. We speak with our bodies. And though it's not necessary to be a professional athlete to speak properly, it is important to be mindful of how you treat your body.

It's not swimming, it's not running, and it certainly isn't football. But public speaking *is* a sport — or at least, it's a good idea to think of it as one. You're using your body to do something perfectly athletic. You're using your strength, your agility, your endurance. Are you not sweating up there a little bit? Face it. That body of yours is putting in work. Maybe you're not going to be the best speaker right off the bat. But why not be the best conditioned?

Understanding the Importance of Nutrition

Okay, you knew it was coming. This is the part where I tell you to improve your diet. Yeah, I know. It's cliche. But when it comes to speaking, nutrition actually matters. We're about to delve into a little science here.

REMEMBER

My advice in this section comes from personal experience. I don't claim to be a doctor. For proper advice on nutrition, talk to your doctor or nutritionist.

Cutting down on refined sugar

This is not a new one, but guess what? Sugar doesn't do you many favors when it comes to being your best self onstage. At first, you may think, "It makes me energetic, happy, and quick. What's wrong with that?" For one thing, consuming a lot of sugar eventually makes you crash. It can also affect your memory and your attention span, it can affect your mood, and, of course, you can gain weight with sugar.

The big issue I want to point out is that sugar crash. Think of a little kid and candy. The kid is fine until some numbskull hands over a big lollipop, and then the kid is running around like crazy until he eventually crashes, and the rest of the lollipop gets stuck in the carpet.

Your body does need sugar, just not necessarily the refined type you put on your cornflakes. Rather, your body obtains sugar from foods that, when broken down, become glucose. Your brain needs glucose to do some pretty important processes up there — a lot of which you're going to need for public speaking, including memory. The problem arises when there's just too much sugar coming from your foods than necessary for your brain and other parts of your body to use.

What happens to make you have that sugar crash? It all starts in an important organ known as the pancreas. Your pancreas is in charge of secreting insulin, which compels tissue to absorb glucose when your blood sugar level gets too high. When your blood glucose levels get too high, your pancreas can produce more insulin than usual. Your blood sugar drops, and with that you may begin to feel jittery and weak, your mind can become cloudy, and you'll feel sleepy. Definitely *not* what you want to feel like on stage.

One of the biggest culprits for refined sugar is good old-fashioned soda pop. Soft drinks make up a huge percentage of the amount of sugar people consume around the world. One can of regular soda can contain the equivalent of more than *nine teaspoons of sugar!* That's an insane amount of sugar for something you're going to consume with a meal and that you don't even count as a side. Not to mention the extra calories that represents. When you're taking in that much sugar, and you're doing it before a performance, be prepared for a sugar crash.

Diet soda isn't much better, by the way. Although it contains artificial sweeteners instead of sugar, it's going to trick your brain into thinking you got that shot of sugar, but then that sugar is not going to come. So your brain is going to go looking for that sugar, and when it doesn't find it, it's going to think this glucose shortage is really just a calorie deficit, and your body is going to go looking for more sugar. It's a vicious circle.

Cutting back on carbs

You may think you know a lot about carbs. But a lot of contradictory stuff has been said about this particular nutritional component, and sometimes it's hard to know what to think. *Carbohydrates* are a main source of energy in the form of glucose for your body. And just as you need sugars to do your thing, carbs can help you swim — or sink you. It mostly depends what type you're eating:

>> **Simple carbs:** Simple carbs are short chains of sugar molecules called monosaccahrides, which are digested quickly. Examples include glucose, fructose, and galactose. Simple carbs can give you fast energy — maybe a little bit of a sugar high, and then a crash when they're done being digested. Foods containing simple carbs include white bread, white pasta, and straight-up sugar.

>> **Complex carbs:** Complex carbs are also made up of sugars, though these are strung together in longer, more complex chains. Their molecular structure is such that they take longer to digest. They're more of a slow, time-released type of sugar. The idea is that your brain and the rest of your body get the sugars they need, without being totally overloaded. You can find complex carbs in whole wheat pasta, whole wheat bread, brown rice, lentils, apples, nuts, seeds, chickpeas, and a whole lot of other foods.

Refraining from alcohol before speaking

That first sip of alcohol hits your brain and begins slowing down the communication between your brain and body. So your reflexes slow down, and you can't think as clearly. It should be a no-brainer, but I have to say it: Leave the booze for your celebration after the speech. For me, one glass of wine isn't guaranteed to kill my chances of killing it up there. But two might. Of course, at many if not most speaking events, there is no alcohol to be seen. But be careful at events where booze is available and you're going to have to make a speech. Weddings come to mind.

TIP

If you're speaking at a wedding, have a drink with dinner, but then lay off of it until after the speech. Alcohol can mess with your memory, your attention, and your ability to speak clearly — exactly what you don't want during public speaking.

Hydrating with water

Another no-brainer. Drink water! We've all heard that we should drink eight full glasses of water a day. I'm not a very big person. Eight glasses is way too much for me. So there's going to be an amount you need to figure out for yourself. My rule of thumb is that I always have water close by. If you're a bit thirsty and you need to go to another room to get water, you may put it off.

Besides thirst, here are some signs that show you may need to drink more water:

>> Headache

>> Very yellow urine

>> More lethargic/tired than normal

>> Drier mouth than normal

TIP

By the time you're feeling thirsty, dehydration has already begun. Watch for those signs before you get thirsty to stay at proper levels of hydration.

The issue with being dehydrated is that it will hinder your performance, and what's more important than your speech? Water for your speaking voice is like oil in your car. You need it to keep the thing running smoothly like it should. When you don't have enough water in your body, your throat can become dry, and your voice can be raspy.

TECHNICAL
STUFF

You may feel you already know this from experience, but voice scientists (I hope they like that term) have done studies (like this one: www.ncbi.nlm.nih.gov/pmc/articles/PMC2925668/) showing that dehydration can be detrimental to vocal fold physiology. Keep your vocal folds hydrated and you'll avoid dehydration problems.

TIP

For dry throat, take a series of tiny sips of water and hold them in your mouth for a second before swallowing.

Chilling out with the coffee

Coffee and its effects feel like a miracle for millions of people around the world. It certainly is for me. But like all things purported to be miracles (especially substances), there's more to the story. What we're really talking about when we talk about coffee is the caffeine.

Caffeine is a stimulant. It makes the heart beat faster and it causes you to use energy at a fast rate. But it's not a cure-all for energy. Caffeine carries risks, too. It can make you anxious, give you headaches, and cause the runs due to its laxative effect.

Here are a few symptoms of caffeine use that might have you thinking twice about drinking it before a performance:

>> **It might make you have to pee.** Yup, that's right. It sure makes me pee. Caffeine is a *diuretic.* There's no problem with that at work, where you can simply go to the bathroom. But you've got enough to think about your speech. Hold off on the coffee until after.

>> **It might make you nervous.** That's right. Other than giving you that extra boost, too much caffeine might actually make you a little anxious. I've seen this in a few of my clients. So many of the people who see me for performance anxiety have a big coffee in their hand when they walk into my office. And I understand that. We're working people. Sometimes we need pep. But being nervous contributes to performance anxiety.

>> **It might give you heartburn or acid reflux.** Oh, your poor throat. Maybe it's already dry from anxiety, maybe you haven't had enough water today, and then you go have a coffee. All of a sudden, instead of relief you get . . . *acid reflux.* That's the horrible burning sensation in your esophagus, as if there was, well, acid, in there. If this is a problem for you, don't drink coffee before a performance. If you don't trust yourself to avoid coffee, bring some antacids.

Dialing down the dairy

Milk is a great source of protein. I'm not going to tell you whether to drink milk or not, but I am going to ask that you refrain from doing so before a speech. When you drink milk, you may feel like you're producing mucous in your mouth and throat, but it's not mucus that gives you that hard-to-swallow feeling and makes you want to clear your throat. That's due to the texture and thickness of the milk.

The problem with milk and speaking is that when it goes down your throat, a bit of it stays there. Think about pouring a glass of milk into the sink. That white film that stays in the glass? That's also on your throat. And then you may feel compelled to clear your throat. Not great for public speaking.

Properly using protein

There's a reason bodybuilders love protein: Protein repairs damaged tissue. Lifting weights damages muscle tissue. A big protein shake provides the material the body can use to repair that tissue. When the tissues heal, they come back bigger and stronger. So, you may say, "But I'm not a bodybuilder." What does protein have to do with public speaking? A lot, actually.

>> **Protein provides backup energy.** The body wants to burn carbs first for quick access to energy, but when carbs are exhausted, your body starts looking for protein, which it can also use for energy.

>> **Protein helps you feel full longer.** Ever eat a meal and then an hour later you're hungry again? For me, that happens when I eat certain kinds of soup, like tomato, cabbage, and other kinds that don't include a protein. Eating enough protein makes you full for a long time, which means it can prevent you from grabbing a bag of chips later. And that's important before a performance: You don't want your stomach grumble to be caught in the microphone.

>> **Protein helps muscular performance.** Public speaking is a physical activity, as pointed out at the beginning of this chapter. Everything about speaking involves muscles. For those muscles to work the way they should, they need fuel, and protein is muscles' favorite fuel. Protein doesn't just repair muscles; it's also important in maintaining them and giving them the fuel they need.

Making Sure You're Fed

Everyone knows you have to eat. Three square meals a day, right? You've got a natural nag called hunger telling you that you have to keep your body fed. And nowadays, there's food everywhere. No longer do we have to pack days' worth of food, rationing the last of our grub just to make it back home. If we're hungry, we can eat virtually anywhere. This means we're not going to starve, but it also means we've become less discerning about what we put into our bodies.

EATING ON THE DAY OF YOUR SPEECH

I'm one of those people who can't go without breakfast. I find that I crash at some point when I get hungry. I tend to eat first thing in the morning and then spread five or six small meals and snacks throughout the day. You may be a more traditional eater of breakfast, lunch, and supper. You may even like to fast occasionally. I'm not a nutrition expert, but I know that you have to be fueled up to be ready to speak.

On the day of a presentation make sure you're getting your regular meals. Don't make that the first day of a new diet. The timing of your meals could be important. You may find it helpful to give yourself a full hour between presentation and your most recent meal. Give yourself some time for digestion. If you're at a meeting where you're presenting after a meal, I would suggest you eat lightly.

Here are some reasons why this stuff matters for public speaking:

>> **Being hungry affects your mood.** You've heard of being *hangry* — angry or grouchy because of hunger? Hunger can negatively affect your mood, and you may not even notice. Others will, though. In no way do you want to be in any mood except "I can do this" before giving a speech or presentation.

>> **Being hungry affects your performance.** It's easy to skip breakfast or lunch. People get busy. Before I started to become more conscious of it, I tended to skip the meal directly before my speech. I was often nervous enough that I couldn't get anything down, or was working feverishly to finish preparing a speech. Feeling a little anxious about speaking can raise your adrenaline levels, which temporarily reduces hunger. You can run on adrenaline for a little while, but it can only take you so far. If your blood sugar drops too low, you may encounter the symptoms I mention earlier in the chapter: lethargy, dizziness, and muddled thinking — not exactly conducive to giving a powerful presentation.

TIP

Routine is important. Our bodies love the patterns we set for them as much as our minds do. So here's a good rule of thumb: Don't change your routine on the day you're going to speak. Try to eat the same on that day as you would on any other day.

Getting Some Exercise

When's the last time you went for a run? A bike ride? A swim? If your answer is today or yesterday, good for you. If not, you're not alone. Many people don't get enough exercise. For the vast majority of the time humans have been on the planet, that was never the problem. Quite the opposite, in fact.

Something we're built to do better than many other animals is endure the exertion of effort. We're not the strongest animals, or the tallest, fastest, or most agile. What we have, though, is the potential to outlast our prey. A hunting technique used by our ancestors was to simply chase an animal for so long that the animal got tired and couldn't go on. To put it mildly, we don't need to do that anymore, and our lives now are vastly more sedentary than they used to be.

The good news is that because such endurance has been built in to us, tapping into it and reviving it is usually not too hard, if done properly. Public speaking is an activity that can really benefit from *cardio training,* which helps tap into your natural capacity for endurance.

The key is increasing *cardiovascular activity. Cardio* is any activity that works the muscles involved in the pumping of your blood and the intake and exhaust of your breath. Weightlifting builds muscles; cardio works the whole system and helps it run more smoothly and efficiently. And that can really help your public speaking performance.

Your heart is the center of the system that pumps the blood throughout your body. Your heart is, in fact, a big muscle — and a pretty important one, as you know. There's no better way to make that muscle pump harder, faster, and longer than to make it pump hard and fast with regularity. When you train your heart, the goal is to keep your heart rate up. Your heart will become stronger if you work on it, and in turn, will allow you to go longer and harder at whatever it is you're doing. Like speaking.

WARNING

Going from a sedentary lifestyle directly to regular active cardio training like jogging can be too much of a jolt to the system. Always talk to your doctor before starting a new exercise regime.

Making your heart go thump

Lots of activities can increase the strength and endurance of your heart. Here are three of the most popular ones:

>> **Running or speedwalking:** Running is the most low-tech, natural form of cardio you're going to get. If you're built for it, you can also gain that elusive

runner's high, kicking in the body's natural endorphins that can make you feel really good. But running's not for everyone. Speedwalking can be lower impact and just as effective, depending on the distance you put in. It's also easier on the body, if you have joint problems.

TIP

It's okay (and a good idea) to start off easy. Run for five minutes. Go at your own pace, but try not to walk for those five minutes. Run from your home for five minutes and then walk home. The next day, try to run for six minutes. Increase the minutes each time until you hit 30. Then you can run for 30 minutes when you run, or increase your time a little farther.

TIP

Running *is* tough on the body, so it's important to be prepared. Don't use shoes that are completely worn out, but be cautious about breaking in new running shoes, too. Grass is soft to run on, asphalt is harder, but not as hard as concrete. Make sure you don't strand yourself without any water — water bottles on belts designed for runners are easy to obtain.

TIP

If you're going to be a walker, just like your running friends, start out slow. As you gain endurance and feel more comfortable, pick up the pace. Good footwear is important for the walker as well as the runner.

>> **Cycling:** My husband used to be a runner, but now he prefers to cycle. He's a big dude — 6 foot 2 and 220 pounds. That's a lot of weight bouncing up and down, no matter what surface he's running on. He finds cycling to be a better alternative.

For one thing, with cycling you get to do what a lot of people who don't like cardio like to do: You get to *sit.* And the leg movements in cycling are much easier on the knees and other joints. For those who don't like the slow factor of running, cycling is a little more exciting. You go fast, and it takes you much farther with the same overall effort.

>> **Swimming:** Swimming is the easiest on your body among the three exercises mentioned here. During cardio, and really during any sort of exercise, the idea is that you're *pushing against* something. With running, you're pushing against the pavement with your feet. You're also pushing against gravity. Cycling, though not as hard on your joints as running, still forces your feet and legs into one repetitive motion.

Swimming, meanwhile, is as hard as you care to make it. You're pushing against something that's all around you: water. In every direction, there is a force you have to push against to get momentum. Swimming is super easy on your joints and muscles.

Of course, there's a steep learning curve to swimming. If you weren't a swimmer as a child, swimming can be a difficult skill to master. There's the potential for real harm while swimming without the fundamentals, so make sure you have a solid grasp of the sport before you hop in the pool. For new swimmers, lessons are essential.

WARNING

Increasing your lung capacity

As I've said, the heart is a muscle, but what's it really doing, anyway? It's pumping blood to everywhere that blood needs to go. But the lungs do equally important work. Blood, after all, is an oxygen delivery system. All parts of your body need that oxygen to do whatever they do. The lungs are the blood's refueling network. With every inhale, the blood in the lungs absorbs oxygen, and with every exhale, the carbon dioxide in your blood leaves through your mouth.

TIP

With regular exercise, your lung capacity will increase. Better lung capacity helps deliver oxygen more efficiently, which can make a world of difference when it comes to public speaking.

REMEMBER

When you go through one of the exercises in this chapter, do it full on. If you've ever played an instrument, you know you should practice with the same energy you would use to perform the song. That doesn't mean that you have to push — just use the same energy.

EXERCISES: LOOSENING UP

Many kinds of exercises can help you when you're speaking. As I've suggested, if your doctor approves, engaging in cardio exercise can help in numerous ways. Here, I suggest exercises that can serve as warmups before cardio or as stand-alone activities to help you loosen up your body, release tension, find your alignment, and improve the ease with which you move. The physical release will help improve your mental well being as well:

- **Exercise 1:** Standing in alignment, let your head drop to your chest. How heavy does it feel? Keep breathing and don't let your posture collapse. Looking down at the floor, move your head gently to one side. Feel the stretch in the tendons along the opposite side of your neck. Take a few breaths and gently move your head to the other side. After taking a few breaths on that side, return your head to the center and lift it up.

- **Exercise 2:** We feel tension in our shoulders for many reasons: We may be fearful when giving a speech, it could be the way we sit at the computer or drive with our shoulders up around our ears, or it just may be a habit that we've acquired. Stand with feet shoulder width apart in an up and out position and start circling your shoulders, up and around. Move them up to your ears, forward, down, backward, and back up. Go through the cycle a few times. Then reverse and move your shoulders up, backward, down, and forward. Go through the cycle a few times. Take your time and really feel each position.

- **Exercise 3:** Shrug your shoulders up close to your ears. Hold them there for a few counts and then lightly drop them. Repeat a few times.

- **Exercise 4:** This is a great exercise to loosen your spine. Stand with your feet shoulder width apart, with a slight bend in the legs. Make sure your weight is evenly distributed between your feet. Check to make sure that your knees aren't snapping back or hyperextended. Drop your head to your chest. Imagine that your head is heavy and is slowly moving you forward down to the earth. Your arms are hanging loosely down, and your spine is curving forward. Find a position where you feel comfortable and aren't straining. Stay there for 20–30 seconds. Now using your legs, roll yourself up. Do this slowly, trying to feel one vertebra at a time. Watch that your abdomen doesn't contract and help your legs. It's your legs that are doing the work. Also, keep your chin close to your chest. When you're fully upright, you can lift your head and your chin. At that point you should be in an up and out position. Repeat a few times.

  You can do this one with a partner. As you roll up, have your partner touch each vertebra to make sure you're rolling up and stacking each vertebra on top of the one below. Get your partner to make sure you're not engaging your abdomen on the roll-up, and that your head and chin are the last to come up.

- **Exercise 5:** Stand with your feet shoulder width apart and relax your knees so they aren't locked or hyperextended. Start swinging one arm in front of you and the other in back, twisting back and forth. Allow your shoulders to move with this action, but not your neck or torso. Build momentum and let those arms really swing. Do this for a minute. Then turn from your waist and allow your whole torso and head to move with your arms. Make sure your head isn't jutting forward or moving back. Do this for about 2 minutes. This loosens the thoracic spine, ribcage, and shoulders.

- **Exercise 6:** Begin on your hands and knees. Make sure your shoulders are above your hands and your knees are above your hips. Imagine a straight line extending from the crown of your head to your tailbone. Don't drop your head; keep the neck long. On an inhale, tilt your pelvis up and feel the movement flowing through your spine as your head lifts up too. Look up to the ceiling but don't force your neck. In yoga, this exercise is sometimes called "cat-cow." On an exhale, move your pelvis forward and arch your spine, like a cat that has just noticed a dog on the property. Your navel is moving toward your spine, and your gaze is on your navel. Repeat for 5–10 rounds.

  When you're on your hands and knees, press your hands into the floor so that your shoulders are lengthening up and not crunched down into your arm sockets.

(continued)

(continued)

- **Exercise 7:** The *sacrum* is a large wedged shaped bone attached to the end of the spine. It consists of five vertebrae that are fused together above your tailbone. The sacrum supports your upper body and connects the spine with your hips. Start on your hands and knees. Press into the floor as you move your sacrum around in circles, figure eights, or even write your name. Keep breathing and have fun.

  If you have knee problems, you can do this exercise standing up, but make sure you don't hyperextend those knees.

- **Exercise 8:** This is a lovely yoga pose to end any sequence of exercises and is especially nice after you loosen up your sacrum because you're already on your hands and knees. Not only does this pose calm you, it stretches the muscles in your back, hips, ankles, thighs, shoulders, and arms. Start in a kneeling position with your thighs together. Move back toward your butt and sit on your heels. Now bow down stretching your arms out in front of you to the floor. Rest your forehead on the floor. If you can't drop your butt onto your heels, don't force it. As one of my yoga teachers once said, "Trying is the exercise!" This is called "child's pose" in yoga.

- **Exercise 9:** Don't have room in the office to get on all fours? Maybe you have knee problems? No worries. You can do this exercise sitting in a chair. Sit up straight with your feet flat on the floor. Place your hands on your knees. Take in a few slow, deep breaths. Feel your spine lengthen. On an inhale, curve your back. Tilt your pelvis back, your stomach will move forward, and your shoulders will move back. Your head will tilt toward the sky or ceiling. As you exhale, reverse the movement. Your navel moves toward your spine, shoulders round, and you look toward your navel. Repeat the entire movement for 5–10 rounds of breath.

4
Fine-Tuning Your Delivery

Prep your mind for excellence by positively visualizing success, seeing how to gain and maintain confidence, and knowing the audience wants you to succeed.

Master the ins and outs of articulation, discover and train your articulators, and tackle articulation problems like mumbling.

Discover your own body as a natural loudspeaker through an understanding of your resonators, and find out how to exercise them to enhance resonance and projection in your speech.

Chapter **11**

Prepping Your Mind for Public Speaking

Ultimately, giving a speech comes down to a mind game. Your mouth is just an instrument.

I don't have to tell you that your mind is your most important asset. Visualizing success is a great way to prepare your mind for your speech, but it's also human nature to foresee and fear catastrophic failure. If you're speaking in the role of employee or representative of your company, your speech could propel you into the ranks of executives — or not.

Negative visualization is easy, and it doesn't just happen with public speaking. Many years ago, I ran a company that offered musical theater residencies for kids in schools. A principal contacted me and asked if I'd send him a quote regarding what my company would offer in a way of mounting a production. After I faxed it (no email — this was a long time ago), he phoned and told me that I'd hear from him by the end of the week. The week went by and there was no phone call. I waited and waited. I kept reliving what I'd said on the phone. Did I say something to offend him? I imagined him getting off the phone and telling his receptionist that he'd never hire someone like me! Was my fee too high? Did he not like the musical I'd chosen? I had visions of him throwing my proposal in the garbage and offering someone else the contract. *That's* negative visualization. Of course, what I'd feared turned out to be not the case. Two weeks later I received a phone call from the principal, who apologized for not getting back to me. Turns out there was a fire in the gymnasium and he was busy dealing with insurance and other issues. And he wanted to hire me. My negative visualization had been a huge waste of time, to say the least.

TIP

With just a little tweaking, you can turn the propensity to negatively visualize into a habit of positively visualization.

Learning to Visualize Positively

You can take the power of negative visualization and turn it on its head. I'm talking about engaging in stay-in-the-shower-too-long-thinking-about-how-wonderful-your-future-can-be types of visualization. That kind is healthy, and important to success, and quite the opposite of a waste of time. But how can you switch from one type to the other?

Visualizing opportunity

The first thing you can do to visualize a positive outcome for your speech is view it as an *opportunity* rather than an obstacle. Someone has asked you to speak. This isn't an opportunity for her to ruin you. She wants to see what you've got. And that person believes you have the stuff to put it all together — otherwise she wouldn't have asked.

Your speech is your opportunity to show the world what you've got. Who knows where giving the speech could lead? Maybe a company will buy your product. Maybe it will lead to a promotion. Maybe it will lead to other speaking engagements, which could also lead to other, unknowable opportunities.

TIP

When you're working toward your goal of an excellent speech, what you're really working toward is the opportunities that will arise from it.

I worked with a client who told me at our first meeting that he was losing sleep over the thought of an upcoming presentation, even though it was months away. He had been asked to be a moderator at a conference his company was putting on. He had never been singled out like that in the past. But lately his advice on the business was being requested more often, and he was becoming involved in decision-making for his team. He began to see what the company was really asking him: Can you step into a leadership role? True, that role would have him doing the one thing that was supremely uncomfortable for him — public speaking — but he decided to prepare for it as if for a leadership role instead as a one-off speech. That focus spurred him to work harder. After I explained what he would need to ace his presentation, he always arrived at our sessions wearing a suit and tie, because that was what he was going to wear on the day. He took all my notes and practiced them in between sessions. He would practice his speech when he was doing mundane chores — he had copies of his speech in his office, home, and even his baby's diaper bag! He's now the go-to guy for this sort of thing at his work.

EXERCISE: BREAKING NEGATIVE PATTERNS

Negativity is a pattern, and we humans love patterns. One pattern is that questions breed more questions — for example, the *what-ifs*. What if my speech is boring? What if I speak too long? What if the slides don't work? The negativity starts to feel like you're in a pit. How do you climb out? Well, you have to proactively work at it a little, but it's not difficult.

Try this: Find a place where you can sit and think. This may be the very same place where you're thinking all those negative thoughts. On the couch, in the shower, waiting for the bus. Now, visualize yourself giving your speech. You've prepared for this. You've practiced out loud and you know the speech like the back of your hand. You walk up to the lectern, place your speech or index cards on it, smile, take a few breaths, and begin.

You look out to the audience and they're *with you.* They're nodding and you can see that they're completely engaged with your presentation. Your visual aids are going over well. There is laughter, and you pause, taking a sip of water — maybe you even join in the laughter. At the end, people are clapping and showing their appreciation for what you gave to them.

Don't be afraid to add detail. What does the room look like? Is there wallpaper? How big is the stage? From then on, whenever you have a quiet moment that would normally be filled with negatives, think of that room you visualized in your mind.

EXERCISE: POSITIVELY VISUALIZING THE PAST AND EVOKING EMOTIONAL MEMORY

Some of my clients feel stuck in the past. Maybe everything went wrong once, and maybe it was completely their fault. I once had a client tell me his boss once came up to the lectern to finish his speech because the boss didn't think he had given enough information. My client was totally demoralized, and it affected him every time he presented after that.

It's tough to get over such strong feelings. You may not even remember the details, or even the circumstances — but you remember that feeling.

In her book *Respect for Acting* (McMillan, 1973), the seminal acting teacher Uta Hagen created an exercise called *emotional memory* that deals with this phenomenon. In the exercise, if an actor needs to express herself in a heightened emotion on stage, she recalls a situation in her personal life when she felt that particular emotion and tries to emulate the same response onstage. For example, if she's supposed to be very sad in a scene, she might visualize the time her dog died when she was a little girl in order to summon that emotion.

We can use a similar exercise to counter the tendency to dwell on negative events in the past. Start by visualizing a time when you gave a *great* speech — even if it was "How Plants Grow" in fifth grade. How did you feel? What happened in the audience? In Rick Hanson's book *Just One Thing* (New Harbinger, 2011), he asks the reader to stick with that memory for 30 seconds. Really feel it. The longer you feel it, the more the neurons in your brain fire up. From then on, when the negative memory rears its head, switch your thoughts to your positive one.

Building Self-Confidence

Self-confidence isn't something you're born with. It's something you can develop. Sure, there are supremely confident people who seem to have been that way since they popped out of the womb. For everyone else, it's more like a muscle — you have to train it to make it strong. Some people learn to be confident quickly and easily. For others, it takes longer and it may be harder to get to the same level. But make no mistake: With proper training, self-confidence can be gained.

Becoming happier through gratitude

I remember looking down at a swirling plate of canned peas and hearing my mom say, "Be grateful!" I knew that peas were supposedly good for me and were part of a nutritious diet — but I didn't care. Now that I buy my own groceries, I'm grateful for the 18 years of free meals I received at the hands of my mother. If I didn't bother to tell my mom that I'm grateful for her meals all those years ago, what does it matter if I feel grateful in my private thoughts now?

Turns out, feeling grateful in general can make us happier. Robert A. Emmons, professor of psychology at the University of California, Davis has performed extensive studies on gratitude. He points out that because gratitude makes us happy, that happiness creates success. And don't you want your speech to be a success? Other studies have shown that gratitude reduces social comparisons. Rather than resenting people who have more money or better jobs — major factors in reduced self-esteem — grateful people are better able to appreciate other people's accomplishments.

REMEMBER

When you're happy, you see the world in a more positive frame of mind. Gratitude achieves the same thing and allows you to be humble regarding your successes and shortcomings. Being vulnerable helps people connect with you and makes them like you. When you're grateful, you're nicer, more trusting, more social, more appreciative, and more optimistic. It increases self-esteem and makes you less self-centered. And all of that helps build confidence.

EXERCISE: BEING GRATEFUL

Gratitude is about paying attention to things in your life, and not taking them for granted. So, why not take stock?

Write a list of all the things you're grateful for. They can be big things and small things. Maybe your subway stop is right next to your home and you never properly appreciated how convenient that is. Maybe your favorite coffee shop is next to work. Maybe your work schedule lines up perfectly with having to drop your kid off at school.

You might be grateful that you live in a sunny city, that the airport closest to you has lots of direct flights, that there are not many poisonous spiders in your home country. Whatever it is, big or small, write it down. Are you grateful for your friends, partner, kids, parents? Put them on the list.

Now, think about the speech you're about to give. What good things could come from it? Why are people asking you to do it? Surely there's a reason, and it's probably a good one. Rarely do judges sentence people to public speaking. It's not a chore, remember — it's an opportunity you've been given. Add it to the list!

EXERCISE: AFFIRMING YOUR FABULOUSNESS

This exercise is mostly used as a warmup. It takes a bit of confidence, but it's worth it in the end.

Go to a big room where you're free to walk around without encountering judgment. Walk around with your arms flung out wide and repeat, "I'm fabulous!" Yes, really. No one is around — why not?

This exercise is an *affirmation,* and what you're trying to do is hardwire your mind into believing what you're saying. We use this tactic all the time without knowing it — mostly with negative thoughts. Think about the time you thought, *What's the point? It's not going to work out for me.* Chances are, whatever it was probably didn't. Things we say often become a self-fulfilling prophecy.

Most of my clients are reluctant to do this exercise (maybe because I'm there, and so are several strangers! — sorry, it's my job). I usually have to pry their arms up higher than they like initially. So, count yourself lucky: You get to do it alone.

But guess what? After a while, my clients start to feel great. We really *do* believe what we tell ourselves. There's something about saying you're fabulous when you've never really thought you were fabulous before. It's a novel notion for some people.

Now say out loud, "My speech rocks, and I'm a fantastic speaker!" Say it as much as you like. How does that feel? Probably pretty good.

Engaging in positive self-talk

This section offers a collection of strategies for practicing positive self-talk:

>> **Don't let yourself off the hook.**

There's an easy way to do something and there's a hard way. The easy way is the best way *if* you can get to the result you need with less work. That's common sense. But if the easy way doesn't take you where you really want to be, then it's time to try the other way. But often we're afraid to take the step that will lead us to our goals. So, don't let yourself off the hook.

>> **Think like a winner.**

When the gun goes off and the Olympic sprinter flies out of those starting blocks, she's not doing it for second place. She's going for gold. Everybody knows only one person is getting that gold. But don't allow yourself to ever think you can't get there. Instead ask: "Why not me?"

>> **Speak to yourself as a greater version of yourself.**

Internal monologue can lead to wallowing in negative thoughts — but it can also be a great motivator. So let it be the latter. Fine-tune your inner monologue so that it's coming from a *better* version of you. It's coming from that version of you in the future, if you follow all your own advice.

>> **Don't blame others.**

The blame game is an easy habit to fall into. And, yes, sometimes other people *are* legitimately to blame. Someone t-boned your car before a presentation to the board? Yup, that's going to rattle you. The barista messed up your latte? Yeah, that's a little annoying. These things are all done by someone else, usually not on purpose, and it's fine to feel emotions about them. But when these emotions cross over and start affecting your presentation, that's *your* doing. That's on you. The person who hit your car wasn't trying to ruin your presentation, and neither was the barista. Don't blame them for something you're doing. You have to compartmentalize.

While you're at it, don't let yourself get into the habit of blaming other people for everything. It's super easy to put the blame 100 percent of the time on people that cause 80 percent of the problem. But when you're the 20 percent, you need to take some accountability. Instead, think about how you can solve 100 percent of the problem.

>> **Think of your progress as development.**

You are *developing*. Try to think of yourself as a young athlete, who looks at those in their prime and wants to be where they are, and starts imaging the pathways that can lead them there. For public speakers, the path isn't always as clear, but it does exist, and if you can do something every day to further your development, you will get there.

>> **Be uncomfortable.**

Speaking, for many, is uncomfortable. It just is. How do you get over that? Practice is a good way. Speaking publicly a lot will do it. But there's also a more incremental way: Do one *uncomfortable* thing every day. Maybe there's someone in your office you've never met. Say hi. Maybe there's a strange painting at your local coffee shop. Ask your barista what it's about. When you see a dog on the sidewalk, ask the owner if you can pet it. Doing these things routinely builds up your social confidence. The worst thing that can happen is that coworker pretends he didn't hear you, the barista doesn't know anything about the painting, and the dog owner says no. Big deal! On the other hand, you may make a new friend, discover a cool local artist, and get to pet a ton of dogs. Either way, you've made yourself more comfortable with being uncomfortable.

>> **Adapt.**

This is a tough one, but it's something to think about *before* something goes wrong. You may have to adapt and go with the flow. You may be *so* prepared. You even tried the mic days ago. You know where the washroom is, how many people will be there, exactly how the PowerPoint is going to work. But guess what? Expect things to go wrong. Maybe the place floods, and you're all forced into a church basement. Maybe the traffic is insane and you're late. You have to learn that these sorts of things can't affect your presentation. If you think about them beforehand, you won't be caught unprepared.

>> **Surround yourself with positive people.**

So you've got the positive thinking aced, but your boss is a Debby Downer. Don't let her get you down. Shrug it off. Find people in your company who think like you and sit with them for coffee and lunch.

Cutting Yourself Some Slack

I'm glad you're feeling positive, because now it's time to talk about something everyone has a problem with: mistakes. Yup, *everybody* makes mistakes in some form or another. It's not possible to go through life without messing up stuff.

Maybe there are a few really big ones in there for you. Some real tragedies. Or maybe we're talking more small-time flubs. In the world of speaking, all kinds of mistakes are waiting for you to make them. For many of my clients, the issue isn't the size of the mistake, it's the worry that *any* mistake will cost them their next shot. And in some cases, that may be true. It's sometimes harder to get a second opportunity after messing up your first.

How you react to making a mistake can make all the difference. Do you dwell on it, looking horrified and making it all the more obvious? Or do you dust yourself off and get ready for the next challenge?

REMEMBER

The way humans learn is to make mistakes and learn from them. That's not new. It's tough to make mistakes in front of peers, your boss, or an audience. But as Frank Sinatra said, "I pick myself up, dust myself off, and start all over again." It's time to learn how to give yourself a break.

Here are a few tips on how to cope with mistakes so that next time you can take the knowledge you learned and move on and do better next time:

>> **Take some time alone to think about it.**

This has to be the first step. You know you messed up, the other people at the speech know it, the audience knows it. And it doesn't matter how big the screw-up was. If you screwed up, you have to give yourself some time to just ponder it. The alone part is crucial to healing and getting over it. In the end, you're the only one who is accountable to you on this. Get your own opinion about the incident before you start to be proactive.

>> **Reflect on the whys.**

Figure out why it happened — conduct a formal investigation into the incident. Did you totally freeze for 30 seconds and become unable to go on? Why was that? Did you have a coughing attack? Find your answer, but don't feel the need to solve it just yet. Just pinpoint the reason as best you can.

Talk to someone else who has given a presentation that went awry. *Everyone* who speaks publicly regularly has had a speech go totally off the rails. It happens! I suggest finding someone who didn't watch your flub. You're looking for fraternity, not sympathy. Find out what that person did, but also what she did to get over it. Maybe she jumped back in the ring right away. Maybe she gave it some time. Bond over your shared experience.

>> **Find what worked.**

Did your entire speech suck? Probably not. Take a sheet of paper and write down three things that *worked* on the night of your speech. Even if it was a total disaster, maybe you looked especially good that evening. That's a plus. Did you make it there on time? Great. These things don't have to be huge, and they don't have to outweigh the mistake you made. You're not trying to change history here. But give yourself some props.

>> **Consider how you will improve next time.**

Take that dissection you did earlier — those whys — and do some research. If it was obviously a certain section you had trouble with, then work on that bit. You had a coughing fit and couldn't continue? You're not allergic to the stage, so maybe it was that you had no water? Or you were sick? Whatever it is, put in the time and figure out how to root that behavior out of your presentation. Check the table of contents of this book and find your problem. Work on it for the next speech.

>> **Laugh at yourself and be kind.**

You've figured it all out, and it's never going to happen again. It's a learning experience! Now it's time to let it go. When you went to that person who also made some mistake in his presentation, did he laugh about it? I bet he did. It's probably a great story now after all this time. Make *your* story, so that when you've done this a bunch, someone can come to *you* and bond. It's okay to find the funny side of it. It doesn't diminish how serious you're working to undo it. And be kind in your retelling.

>> **Do more work if necessary.**

Hopefully you've figured it out by your next presentation, but maybe you didn't. Are you cursed? Doubtful. But there may be a more persistent problem than a one-off issue. That's okay! It's common. But it's going to take more work.

>> **Forgive yourself.**

Remember, everything is temporary, even this feeling. Emotions about stuff like what happened don't last forever. So look forward to that. Then forgive yourself. I'm sure everyone else has forgiven you. Even if others haven't, make sure *you* have a benchmark for yourself so you're not feeling guilty forever. Are you doing your due diligence so this doesn't happen again? Are you jumping back into that ring? Then cut yourself some slack.

Shifting Your Focus to the Audience

The speech may be about your life — your struggles, your travels, your family, or your career. But even that speech isn't about *you.* I mean it's not *for* you. It's for your *audience.*

Sure, it's created by you, experienced by you, and delivered by you. Maybe your speech is a part of your job, or perhaps you're getting paid. Maybe you're trying to establish a greater presence in the community. There is some incentive for you to be doing this — but your incentive ends there. The *content* is the reason the audience is listening. So make sure you give them what they want.

There are three main purposes for public speaking:

>> **To inform:** A college lecture is the perfect example of this type of presentation. You're telling people — who are hopefully open to information — something they don't know, that you're an expert on.

>> **To persuade:** Political speeches are a great example. You're trying to convince someone of something. It doesn't have to be political, of course. There are plenty of persuasive speeches made in the business world and the academic world and elsewhere.

>> **To entertain:** A wedding speech is a good example. You're telling stories and getting laughs. You're sharing memories. You're trying to get the message across that the person you know is a great person, and you're trying to keep

the mood of the party intact. People have their leisure hats on, and you're following the tone of the gathering. But entertainment can also happen in different settings. Some of the best keynotes I've seen have been completely about entertaining the crowd.

TIP

But here's the key: A persuasive speech can also be entertaining, an informative speech can also be persuasive. In fact, a speech does much better if it does all three things at once.

Few people want to sit in a lecture hall and listen to scientific facts about, say, some specific animal found somewhere in the world without a little bit of spice added to the conversation. Remember these three purposes of speeches as you read on and learn how to use them to you and your audience's advantage.

Beginning with the end in mind

This idea is inspired by one of Steven Covey's habits in his book *The 7 Habits of Highly Effective People* (Free Press, 1989). Let's say you've got a message you want to get across, and you know whom you want to get it across to. That's pretty good so far. But there is a serious question still left to be asked — one that involves the audience *after* you've left the stage: What exactly do you want the audience to do with that message?

For some types of presentations, that's simple. A politician has a *stump speech* — a standard presentation touching on the issues the politician finds important, given over and over in the same way — and she wants you to vote for her. A college professor has a standard lecture he gives every semester, and he wants you to go out and study.

But it's not always so obvious. And the question of what the audience is supposed to do with your speech may get harder when you take yourself out of the equation and start asking what the audience wants.

The next few sections ask some questions to ask yourself before you face the audience.

What is the audience expecting to learn?

The audience is there waiting for you. Maybe it's a boardroom, maybe it's a parent teacher meeting, maybe it's a convocation speech at your alma mater. They are expecting something out of you, either from the description of the event or potentially from your reputation.

Are you going to give them what they expect? Now, the audience isn't always right about a speaker. Your perception of what they're looking for should not necessarily be the golden light you are walking toward. But it should guide you. If you think they're going to get something on your specialty — say, marine wildlife — there should be some talk of marine wildlife in your speech. A room full of your marine biologist peers would be disappointed in a lecture on the chemical properties of popcorn.

That doesn't mean, though, that that's *all* you have to give. Maybe you could begin with an on-land analogy. Maybe you throw some jokes in there. You can change it up with a number of devices to go from a pure, fact-based speech to a more exciting talk that gives the same message in a more persuasive and entertaining way. But you can only figure out how to do that if you have a good guess about what the audience is expecting to hear.

What are your audience's demographics?

In order to know what your audience is expecting or thinks, it's a good idea to understand who they are. You're not going to want to do a whole lecture on professional wrestling if you have elderly New York socialites sitting in front of you.

Start by supposing you're in your home country (or state, or city) and you have a pretty good understanding of the kind of people who would attend this sort of meeting (I get to foreign engagements in a moment).

The first and easiest thing to look at is age. In my experience, age is the biggest indicator of how people are going to perceive my humor, emotion, and my message in general. If you're speaking to a retirement community, and then you give the same speech on a college campus the next day, how are you going to change the speech while keeping the integrity of the message? What kind of bias does one group have that doesn't really appear in the other?

The same kinds of things can be asked about a number of different types of social groups: socioeconomic, racial, religious, education level, and others. It's so important to recognize whom you're giving the message to and how it will be best received.

WARNING

Don't outright *pander* — unless it's in a humorous way. It may be okay to throw out a few dad jokes to teens, like, "Hey, I'm old and you're young, ha ha." But walk away from that after the initial joke. People of any demographic can see right through it. It's okay that you're different from the audience. It may be why they came to see you in the first place. But don't use it as a wedge.

When you're speaking in a different country, knowing demographics is harder. It doesn't matter if you're going to another English-speaking country, the norms and traditions will be different. It's certainly best to figure those out before you get up there. Research online, find and talk to someone from that country, or better yet, have a coffee with the organizer before the event. Ask if there are any strange quirks about the audience you may not be aware of, being from a different country. If that person gives you a strange look, that's probably good. You may be in the clear.

What level of knowledge on the topic does the audience have?

You must base your presentation on the level of knowledge your audience has on the subject. You're not intending to teach graduate-level meteorology students about the ROY G. BIV method of ordering the colors of the rainbow, are you? Don't explain things to people that they already know. First, it wastes time and may insult them. The audience doesn't want to feel like you think they're dumb. If you're explaining a project you're working on to a bunch of your bosses, you probably don't need to explain the fundamentals.

The same thinking has to work in the opposite way, of course. Don't go over the audience's head. They might start to feel self-conscious, that they should already know this stuff if you've assumed they do. Or they might just get totally bored. You can't lose your audience.

How big is the audience?

This is something you should know as soon as you're asked to speak. If you're told it's just going to be a handful of colleagues, it would be quite a shock to be ushered into a large auditorium full of hundreds of people. A large audience presents a wider range of knowledge, demographics, desires, and goals.

REMEMBER

Your focus has to be much wider when speaking to a large, unknown audience. It's a lot easier to assume people know more about what you're speaking about at a small conference of your peers.

Even if the audience is large, make sure your eye contact includes the entire group. It is a great idea to break your audience into three parts: find someone in the center to speak to, then look over and find someone on the left side, and then the other side. I discuss eye contact further in Chapter 15.

Why is the topic important to the audience?

This is the big one, and that's why I've put it last. In other places in this book, I've asked you "What is the point?" of your speech. Now, if you haven't already done so, it's time to pay close attention to that question when it comes to the audience.

Why are *they* the ones who are listening? Why are *you* the one giving it to them? And what are you hoping they're going to *do* with the information? Look at your speech and be totally honest with yourself. Are they going to do what you intend them to do? If you end by asking that they throw themselves in front of whaling ships, unless you have some sort of hypnotic, cultlike powers, you're not going to get them to do that. You have to manage your expectations. If you're talking about the glorious work of blood donation, and then — surprise! — there's a place to donate blood in the lobby, that's more manageable.

Be honest with yourself about the practicality of your ask and of your ability to ask.

Going one-on-one: Addressing one person in the audience

I've had clients tell me about the techniques they've used regarding where they should look while speaking, or whom they should look at. Of course, there's the classic: *Imagine everyone in their underwear.* There's one I like to call the Pacifist: Stare right over the heads of the people in the audience. After all, it's tough to see exactly where a speaker's eyes are pointing. Even at close range, it's often hard to tell whether someone is looking at your eyes, your nose, or even your ears.

In my experience, it's good to think of your speech as having a conversation, and the best way to do that is humanize your audience as best as you can. That doesn't mean giving each audience member equal stare-into-their-eyes time. (Engaging with someone for five or six seconds is enough.) But you should act as if you know them, or are giving them a speech personally.

Here are a few tips to get you on your way to a one-on-one experience:

>> **Actually meet people in the audience.**

I've told you before to get to the event early. After you've checked everything and you're ready to go, when people start milling about, go mill about with them. They're going to want to talk to you. You're the speaker, after all.

Try to meet three of them. Get to know their names, what they do for a living, and why they're there to see you. Then, when it's time to speak, find them in the audience and speak directly to them. Give them extra attention. It's easier to talk to a friendly face.

>> **Read your audience.**

Ever hear someone say something totally inappropriate somewhere, maybe at a Christmas party, and then someone whispers, "Read the room, dude"? You don't want that to happen to you during your speech. Always understand what's going on with the audience before you put your foot in your mouth. If you think of it as a conversation, instead of you being alone up there, you should be in good shape.

>> **Don't worry if everyone isn't engaged.**

You're not going to win over everybody, so get over that idea. I know it's a bummer to look out there and see some folks looking at their phone, face lit up, texting or playing some stupid game. Don't assume they're not listening. They might just be terrific at multitasking.

Sure, you can ignore them — but you could also work a little harder to convince those people to listen. It may not work, but try speaking to the doofuses for a minute. But don't forget to appreciate everyone else who is paying attention. Those are the people you want to give your message to.

Knowing when not to apologize

Apologizing is the death of the public speaker. If you're feeling sorry, that's going to affect the audience. They're in turn going to feel sorry, or awkward, or something like that.

Everything looks bad when you apologize. You're supposed to be a strong, confident authority on your subject, yet your body language looks as if you'd rather be anywhere else. Your voice loses that timbre of someone who knows what she's talking bout. I've been to many conferences where the first thing speakers say is that they're sorry — sorry for coughing, sorry for being late, sorry for having to be the one to give you this talk, blah, blah, blah. It takes the wind out of the audience's sail.

The show must go on. When you apologize *without good reason*, you can lose credibility. It's not easy, but you need to have a good idea of what's an acceptable level for apology to an audience. How about this: Be humble. But never forget, you're the authority up there. Act like it.

Here are some examples of apologies I've heard from speakers, and how to avoid them:

>> **"I'm sorry, I'm out of time."**

The problem here is no one knows that but you and the organizer. Unless a school bell rings, if you have the audience totally rapt, finish up. Don't allow the red light coming on over their heads to become a reason to blame yourself or anyone else for it. They don't know your script. Finish up with some final thoughts and thank them. They'll be none the wiser.

>> **"I have the flu and I just found out that I was giving the speech today. I'm sorry you won't be hearing a good speech."**

Unless you've got a serious illness that will hinder your performance (sore throat, inability to stand), don't even mention it. The audience probably can't tell, and any mention of being sick may erode not only your credibility, but the credibility of the institution that threw you to the fire. And even if they can tell, they will respect you for pressing on without using it as an excuse.

>> **Apologizing at the end.**

It may sound strange, but so many people do this. And I have no idea why! "Sorry for boring you." "Sorry for keeping you so long. I know it was supposed to finish at eight." The end of your speech is not the time to apologize, so don't do it. All that great stuff you just said? All those ideas you want them to keep in your mind? You just undercut all of that, and the audience will leave remembering that you apologized for it all. Give them the old Warner Brothers treatment: *That's all, folks!*

>> **"Sorry about the projector, everyone."**

Don't be sorry about the projector. Don't be sorry about anything outside of your control. It's not your fault the back fan is really loud, or that the traffic noise is loud in the room. Just soldier on and don't mention those things.

>> **"Sorry, but I can't answer that question."**

If there's a Q&A, people are going to ask you questions you don't know. Not just in your speech, but literally everywhere. You're not a wizard. You don't know everything. People know that. They're not expecting a wizard. If you don't know something, let them know you'll get back to them. Find out the information they want afterward and let them know after the presentation.

Handling hecklers

Although hecklers are largely a phenomenon in standup comedy, every now and then someone yells something at me or a client during a presentation. It's a rattling moment. Do you engage? What can you say? Are you trying to satisfy this person, or the audience as a whole?

Here are a few tips for dealing with hecklers:

>> **Don't take it personally.**

Sometimes people just want their voice to be heard. It's very likely about the heckler, not you! Keep your emotions in check. Take a deep breath. Let them have their say. Otherwise they will keep heckling. Listen to them. But . . .

>> **Don't engage with them on their terms.**

Offer to speak with them afterwards. You can respond to their comments, but *don't* look right at the heckler. They'll think that puts them on equal footing with you and gives them permission to keep going.

>> **Never lose your temper.**

The audience may turn on you. Kill them with kindness. Then get right back onto your presentation

>> **Don't match their pitch.**

If they are speaking in a fast, high-pitched voice, speak slowly and in a low pitch. Just like dealing with kids. If they're using a pessimistic or depressing tone, try to speak in a higher pitch and sound more positive and confident.

>> **Kindly ask them to stop.**

Tell them it's great when people are so engaged with the topic, but you'd like to get on with your speech. Take a breath and carry on. You're in control.

>> **Call security if they continue.**

This should be the last resort, obviously. When you're discussing what you'll need for your presentation, ask the organizer about the venue's security policies. If your speech is divisive and may instigate heightened emotions, security should be part of your plan. If there's no security present, ask who will assume the role in case of an interruption. It shouldn't be you. Your job is to carry on with your presentation.

Chapter **12**

Mastering the ABCs of Articulation

Communication, especially when you're addressing a group of people, can become muddled by something that you may not think about much in normal life. That's articulation, the subject of this chapter.

Imagine a speaker, perfectly ready to hop on that stage and take the audience by storm. She's scoped out the venue and she's written her speech brilliantly. The breath support is there. She's confident. She's ready to command the audience. She has a smile going up the stage, totally ready to kill it. She takes the microphone from the master of ceremonies and starts speaking. But instead of that clear, crisp message she intended to give to the attentive audience, a long stream of sound comes out, punctuated only by pauses and the rare consonant. Where has she gone wrong? She's not articulating.

Although performance anxiety can cause many symptoms (including lack of articulation), articulation problems can appear out of nowhere and totally hinder an otherwise stunning performance.

Articulation is the ability of the muscles in the mouth to create meaningful sounds in such a precise manner that people can readily differentiate them from other sounds. Anyone who can speak can usually articulate enough to at least get by, but it's important to note that articulating to your friend in a coffee shop is not the same as articulating in front of 500 people.

TIP

Even if you're a confident presenter, looking at the way you articulate is always helpful to your presentation.

Meet the Articulators

The *articulators* are the muscles in your mouth that make those funny movements to form words. Have you ever said the alphabet and paid attention to what your mouth is doing with all those sounds? It's incredible what these small, strange muscles can do without your even being aware of what's going on in there.

Improving articulation is about enhancing those muscle movements, which means you have to be conscious of those movements. And the first step to doing that is learning what parts of your face are doing the work, so that's what you do in this section.

The jaw

Remember the human skeletons in science classrooms? The skull has a set of teeth fastened to it, and then, attached to a hinge that moves up and down, is the other set. You can feel it in your own mouth. Your top teeth stay put, attached to the bone dome that holds your brain, while your bottom teeth do all the chewing, gnashing, and grinding.

The top part of your jaw is called the upper jaw, and the bottom one is, you guessed it, the lower jaw, or in anatomical terms, the *mandible.* On each side of your head just in front of your ear there's a hinge called the *temporomandibular joint,* or TMJ for short. To find this joint, place your fingers on either side of your head just in front of your ears and open our mouth. The TMJ and several muscles are responsible for opening and closing your mouth. Your jaws are just there, looking great, while the TMJ and muscles move them to make beautiful sounds and convince the audience of your message.

Your TMJ is also a magnet for tension. Sometimes it may become tense because of anxiety, chewing gum, or grinding your teeth.

TIP

When you work on the exercises in this chapter, remember the proper alignment I talk about in Chapter 3: Keep your feet planted on the ground, shoulder width apart, keep your arms down by your side, and your energy reaching up toward the sky. Practice these exercises as much as you want, but when it's time to give that speech, forget about them. The whole point of exercising is to train your muscle memory. When you perform after doing these exercises enough, that muscle memory will just kick in.

EXERCISES: WORKING YOUR JAW

These exercises are intended to work and develop your jaw articulators.

- **Give your face a massage.** Massage your cheeks, nose, forehead, and chin. Using your hands and fingers, really get in there. Feels good, doesn't it? Now press your fingers right in front of your ears. Open and close your mouth. Do you feel that little bulge on either side of your cheek? That is your TMJ joint. Now release the tension in the joint and give it a gentle massage.

- **Gently open and close your jaw.** Think of your jaw as a door hinge. If you open it too wide, the door could snap. Same with the jaw. Just try to open and shut gently, massaging while you do so. Work the jaw in and up and down motion. When you move it side to side like a typewriter carriage (remember those?) it causes more tension and maybe even pain. Doing so isn't good for your TMJ joint.

- **Imagine chewing some invisible crackers.** To keep the mouth open and free, imagine you have ten crackers in your mouth. Chew them as you imagine them dissolving. Chew easily — they're just crackers.

- **Pretend you're biting into an apple.** Open your mouth wide, but not too wide that you are straining. Just enough to give your jaw a stretch.

- **Go even further with that stretch.** Give your jaw some resistance. Place your thumb under your chin. Press your thumb gently upward to create a resistance when you open your mouth. Try this ten times.

EXERCISE: BEING AWARE OF YOUR TEETH

Teeth aren't really articulators, but your bottom teeth are attached to your lower jaw, and your tongue also touches them to make sounds. To illustrate how teeth are involved in articulation, repeat the following phrases and be aware of the placement of your tongue. Once you've mastered the exercise, try it at different pitch levels.

- "The tip of the tongue, the teeth, the lips."

- "Terrible Terry took a Tootsie."

- "Theo thanked the thinkers for their thorough thoughts."

EXERCISE: GIVING YOUR TONGUE SPACE TO WORK

Ideally you should have at least a quarter of an inch of space between your upper and bottom teeth when you speak. But stress and other habits can make us lose that space, causing tension in the jaw. (This exercise is also great to strengthen the lip and jaw muscles.)

Say the months of the year as slowly and clearly as you can. Take a clean pencil and hold it horizontally across the insides of your two front teeth. Now repeat the months of the year again. Take the pencil out of your mouth and repeat the months again. You should notice that your tone is more forward in your mouth and you can move your jaw more freely. What you're trying to accomplish here is to train your jaw to gain that muscle memory to give your tongue enough space to work. Clarity always trumps volume. Also, once you can form your words clearly and pronounce the endings of the words, your projection will benefit.

Once you've mastered the pencil, move on to a wine cork. Take a wine cork and place it in your mouth between your upper and lower teeth. Be careful not to grip or clench your jaw. Say the months of the year again or part of your speech. Try to minimize the movement in your lower jaw. Now take out the cork and repeat what you said. You should feel that you're articulating better.

The tongue

The tongue is a very familiar articulator. You use it for everything that comes in or goes out: chewing, tasting, and creating speech sounds. The tongue consists of muscles covered by mucous membrane. The *extrinsic* muscles control the position of your tongue in your mouth, and the *intrinsic* muscles change the tongue's shape.

The tongue extends all the way to the back of your throat. It's way bigger than you probably think it is. With all that surface area, the tongue and muscles can hold a lot of tension, and that can impede the important work it does in shaping the sound coming out of your mouth. It's important to keep your tongue flexible, like any other muscle in your body.

This section includes a few exercises to keep that tongue toned and ready.

EXERCISE: GETTING PEANUT BUTTER OFF YOUR TONGUE

Know what it's like to have peanut butter on your tongue? Not just on top, but all around your tongue. How annoying is that? (Worse, in this exercise you're not even really eating it.) You need to get some imaginary peanut butter off your tongue in the most efficient way possible: with your teeth.

Scrape your tongue against your teeth just as you would if you had a spoonful of peanut butter gummed up in there. What this does is stretch out and work your tongue like you work your muscles in a workout. Your teeth provide resistance, giving your tongue muscle a release it deserves. Remember to breathe!

Now you deserve some real peanut butter.

The soft and hard palates

The soft palate, also known as the *velum*, is located way back along the top of your mouth, almost out of reach for your tongue, but it's pretty easy to differentiate from the hard palate. Get yourself in front of a mirror and yawn. See that part of your mouth rising? That dangling bit of flesh at the back of your mouth is your *uvula*, and it hangs at the back of your soft palate.

TIP

To find your soft palate using your trusty old tongue, raise it to the roof of your mouth and go back as far as you can go. Feel that ridge? That's the border of your hard palate and soft palate.

EXERCISES: TONING YOUR TONGUE

Another exercise that makes you feel like a kid. Move your teeth so that they're about a wine cork width apart. Place your tongue so that it is resting on your bottom lip. Now flap it in and out, keeping your jaw steady. Do this slowly. I can bet it's been awhile since you stuck out your tongue on purpose, especially like this. That's the point of this exercise. Your tongue hasn't felt those muscles move in that way for a very long time. The exercise stretches and tones the tongue muscle.

Add sound (this part of the exercise might not be a good idea at the office). This is a natural sound and you might even have felt the inclination already. Add a *Luh* sound and flap away. Do it slowly.

The hard palate is made of bone, and the soft palate is made up of muscle and connective tissue. The purpose of the soft palate is to separate your nasal cavity from your mouth for breathing, swallowing, and making speech sounds. When it's down, lots of air and vibrations pass through the nasal cavity during speech so you sound nasal. But when it's up, the air passes through your mouth and you have a richer sound.

The lips

The next articulator on our list is the lips, those two things that flap around when you speak. They're the most obvious articulator — when the lips are moving, it probably means there's sound coming out.

The lips are so fundamental to articulating that there doesn't even have to be sound coming out of them for us to understand what's being communicated. That's how lip reading works.

Lips do a heck of a lot more than help us enunciate words. They play a hand in chewing, if you're polite and don't chew with your mouth open. They cover the teeth, and they open and close the mouth.

If your face is tense, the opening to your mouth will also be tense. The lips may be tense for a variety of reasons. Lost your retainer on a trip to Europe? Maybe you're ashamed of your teeth. The phrase "stiff upper lip" has some truth to it: When we hold back feelings, we tend to tense up that top lip. We might tense our lips out of performance anxiety — we become anxious about enunciating properly.

EXERCISES: LOOSENING YOUR LIPS

You want your lips to be limber and relaxed before a performance. Here are some tips to loosen those lips:

- **Get your face moving.** Maybe you've got tense lips. Who doesn't? Sometimes it's even hard to tell whether you do or not. So try this: Move your face around as much as possible. I mean every part of your face. Make sure you hit every little tiny muscle group. Every muscle that helps you smile, every muscle that makes you frown. Scrunch and unscrunch your forehead. Blow air into your cheeks and try to move your ears. Lift both eyebrows with surprise, and then just one, skeptically. Now blow air through your lips like a tuba player. Feel relaxed yet?

- **Shake them.** Stand with your feet shoulder width apart. Now, clasp your hands together in front of you and move them to chest level. Shake your hands as hard as you can. Let your jaw go. Don't give yourself a headache, but try to shake the jaw off your face. Let your jaw relax freely and your lips with it. Your lips aren't acting as muscles in this exercise, but rather as loose tissue. Really let it fly.

- **Make horse lips.** Close your jaws, relax your lips as much as you can, and blow air through them until they flap like a horse's. If you're tense in the lips, you might have difficulty blowing the air through.

- **Pucker up.** Think back to those cartoons you used to watch on Saturday morning. When characters kiss, they pucker up super tight and then give a big old smooch. I want you to do that now. Put your lips together and then stick them out, as far as they go, like you're going to kiss someone in a cartoon.

- **Smile, why don't ya.** Not just any old smile, mind you — I want you to smile *big*. Feel your lips stretch sideways as wide as they can go. Go through a couple cycles of breathing and then release.

- **Pucker up and smile combo.** This is great to really feel those lips stretch. Pucker up for a few breaths, then smile for a few. Repeat, and remember to keep breathing.

Understanding Mumbling and Why People Do It

You know mumblers. Those who don't fully enunciate their words. Mumblers' words tend to be strung together, like one long, monotonous chant that's hard to decipher. In the movie *Dick Tracy* the character Mumbles fits the bill exactly. It may be funny when he does it, but once you're up on that stage, mumbling isn't funny — it just makes it hard to get your message across.

The lips, discussed in the previous section, are the key to your enunciation success. Not only do they work as verbal tools, people can also use them as visual aids as well. When you don't move your lips when you talk, really smacking them on those *B*s and *P*s, giving those *M*s the proper space, it reduces your intelligibility.

REMEMBER

Consonants are extremely important for speaking clearly. They break up the vowel sounds you make with your articulators. Without them, your vowels take over and it sounds like mumbling.

Mumbling is often a sign of lack of confidence. Were you ever belittled by a teacher or did something stupid and got caught? The last thing you wanted to do was speak, because you knew what was going to come out: the dreaded mumble. And when you had to say sorry or fess up to what you did, the words were as small as you could get them. It's the "please get me out of here" tone. And it really shows.

WARNING

If you mumble, you sound both unconfident and as if you don't want to be there.

EXERCISE: MAKING EYE CONTACT

What's the hallmark body position of a mumbler? Staring at the floor, like a kid being scolded, inspecting that carpet. And what is the authority figure doing the scolding saying? "Look me in the eye when I'm talking to you!" It's time to take that advice. It's hard to mumble when you're staring at someone straight in the face. People are expecting clear and concise answers.

One way to find out how big of a problem you have is to record yourself. Put your camera right in front of your face, so you're staring into the lens of your device, and speak to it for a few minutes as if speaking to someone you want to hear the message you're about to give. Now go back and listen to yourself. That's your natural speaking style.

Now do it again, but this time really exaggerate all the sounds. Make sure every consonant is punchy. Take your time, do it slowly. Then do it one more time, and this time exaggerate as much as you can — *really* bump up those consonants to eleven. Read something out loud and exaggerate each and every syllable. Focus on keeping your lips and mouth moving. You're excited because your favorite team just scored. Open up that mouth and cheer. Say hello as if to a friend who is two feet away from you. Then to a friend across the room. Then to a friend across the street.

Now watch those videos. Which one do you think is the clearest?

Mumbling as a style of speaking may come simply from habit. Sometimes families develop this style of speaking together at home. For whatever reason, be it family or it's just the way you developed your speaking style on your own, at least when public speaking, you need to break out of your mumble and enunciate fully.

Honing Your Articulation

Now that you can identify your articulators, let's look at how to use them. You'll try some important techniques that can really get the most out of them for your speech.

Twisting your tongue

We all know the classic tongue twisters. They may be cliché, but clichés started somewhere. Tongue twisters overwork your articulators. They're great to improve your articulation because the speech sounds are repeated, giving you many chances to form them correctly. At first, they may really feel as if they're twisting your tongue. But with practice, eventually your muscle memory will overcome that. Once you hit the stage and start making those sounds, it'll be a piece of cake. Plus, they're pretty fun.

TIP

Remember when working on all exercises to stand with your feet shoulder width apart and feel as if those feet are growing roots deep into the earth. Imagine there is energy growing up through your body out the crown of your head to the sky.

Voicing vowels and consonants

I'm sure this is just a refresher, but just in case: Vowels and consonants are the sounds that make up speech. *Vowels* are all the open sounds. They're formed by the tongue and lips changing the shape of the mouth, which never closes. *Consonants* are also formed by the tongue and lips but involve closing off the mouth.

Once when I was in theater school, we were rehearsing a Shakespeare play. We were given an exercise where we could only say our lines using only the vowels. What we experienced was the emotion of the scene. Next we said our lines only using consonants and guess what happened? The scene made sense.

EXERCISE: TRYING TERRIFIC TONGUE TWISTERS

In this exercise, start by saying the first sentence clearly. Make sure to pronounce the entire words, including the ends of the words. Repeat a phrase a few times at the same speed and then get slightly faster, maybe 10 percent. If you stumble on some words or a part of the phrase, do it again. Now move on to the next sentence. Use the same process.

The key is to form the words clearly, not saying them so fast that you become inaudible and out of breath. Once you're done with the whole thing, phrase by phrase, test yourself. Go through the whole thing at the speed you left off on. If you flub a word, go back to the beginning and start again.

Now it's time to try one. First, try to say it with your lips lightly together and jaw closed. Then use your lips and jaw. The third time, exaggerate your enunciation:

Peter Piper picked a peck of pickled peppers.

A peck of pickled peppers Peter Piper picked.

If Peter Piper picked a peck of pickled peppers

Where's the peck of pickled peppers Peter Piper picked?

You've mastered Peter? Try this:

What a to do to die today, at a minute or two to two

A thing distinctly hard to say, but harder still to do.

For they'll beat a tattoo, at twenty to two

A rat-tat-tat-tat-tat-tat-tat-tat-tattoo

And a dragon will come when he hears the drum,

At a minute or two to two today, at a minute or two to two.

And here's the Grand Finale:

Betty Botter bought some butter,

"But," she said, "this butter's bitter.

If I bake this bitter butter,

It will make my batter bitter.

But a bit of better butter —

That would make my batter better."

So she bought a bit of butter,

Better than her bitter butter.

And she baked it in her batter,

And the batter was not bitter.

So 'twas Betty Botter

Bought a bit of butter.

Try this in the shower: Stick your tongue out. Remember to keep breathing. Now, try those tongue twisters again. Say them with your tongue out. (Keep breathing!) Once you're done, repeat them without your tongue out. Sound clearer? It should.

You can be passionate about your speech and have great confidence in yourself, but if you don't execute *both* vowels and consonants, that passion and confidence will be useless.

Vowels

Let's name the vowels in the English language, just for fun: A, E, I, O, and U (and sometimes Y). *Diphthongs* are also classified as vowels — they consist of two vowel sounds combined.

There are two types of sounds that each vowel can represent. *Long* vowels sound like the name of their letter, but short vowels sound different. In truth, sometimes they're a bit of both. Long vowels are pretty sounding. They're the ones you'd sustain in a song, whereas short vowels are little hops you're trying to make to get to the next consonant.

Here are a couple examples of vowel sounds:

Short vowels	Long vowels	Diphthongs
Mat	Meet	My
Slept	Float	Now
Live	Loot	Near

Repeat the short vowel sounds and notice how they feel in your mouth. Then continue with the longer and diphthong vowels. This is an interesting activity because it allows you to experience different lengths of the vowels and in turn helps you create a speech that is varied in rhythm.

Consonants

Consonants can be tricky. If they're too loose and lacking in clarity it's hard to understand the person speaking. But if they're too "tight" and restricted, we may understand what the speaker is saying but may be too distracted to connect with them.

There are two kinds of consonants: voiced and voiceless. *Voiced* consonants are accompanied by your voice — the sound of your vocal folds vibrating. They're the type that you actually have to use air for. *Voiceless* consonants are generally just stopping sounds. Here are some examples:

>> **Voiced:** B, D, G, Z, V

>> **Voiceless:** P, T, K, S, F

To tell the difference, say one voice consonant and then its voiceless version right after. Say *B* and *P*. Make the sound that those two letters make side by side. The *P* sound is just a puff of air going through your lips, but the *B* sound adds your voice.

You should feel the action of muscles when you use consonants. The tip of the tongue is responsible for the sounds of *T*, *D*, *N*, and *L*, although the entire tongue is involved. When exercising, try to use as much muscular pressure as you need to give it bite and make it sail through the air.

EXERCISE: CREATING KILLER CONSONANTS

Consider where voiceless consonants occur in your mouth. For example, *P* is when you press your lips gently together. Try saying this:

Paw, paw, paw, paw, paw

T is when the tip of your tongue is behind your top front teeth.

Taw, taw, taw, taw, taw

K is the back of the tongue making contact with the soft palate.

Kaw, kaw, kaw, kaw

Now, put them together: *paw, taw, kaw.* Do you feel what your articulators are doing with each sound? Try repeating the exercise a few times, making sure to breathe when needed.

Now try with voiced consonants. Press your lips together to make a *B* sound:

Baw, baw, baw, baw

Now with *D*, a little farther behind the top of your upper teeth:

Daw, daw, daw, daw

G is a voiced *K*:

Gaw, gaw, gaw, gaw

Put them together: *baw, daw, gaw.* Repeat this a few times and take a breath when you need to.

Combine them:

Paw, taw, kaw, baw, daw, gaw

Now change vowel sounds:

Pee, tee, kee, bee, gee

Pay, tay, kay, bay, gay

Try mouthing or whispering the words. It makes you more aware of the sounds, and it makes you commit harder to the formation of consonants.

EXERCISE: SINGING SENTENCES

Pick a sentence from a favorite book. Take a breath and then sing that sentence, using any pitches you want. Give those vowels some space. Make it big. Make the vowels last as long within each syllable as your breath can sustain them. Make sure each vowel has ended completely before you go onto the next vowel or consonant. Remember to pronounce the consonant clearly. After that, try singing some nursery rhymes in the same way. How does it change when it rhymes?

Sing a sentence from your presentation. How do the vowels make you feel? What about the consonants? Immediately after you sing it, speak it. Do you sound clearer?

Singing

Singing — even if you have no musical talent — helps with articulation. When you sing, you elongate the vowels and you have to pronounce your endings clearly. Sometimes, if your articulation sounds choppy, it may be due to breathing in short bursts of air. Breathing like that almost never works in singing.

You've probably sung your entire life. Growing up, in the car, in the shower, doing karaoke. Even if you aren't trained, you're familiar with singing. As you've gotten older, you may have lost that music in your voice you had when you were a kid with less inhibitions. Try to get it back. Singing can help you articulate.

Improving Clarity for an Accent

First off, everybody has an accent, or distinctive style of pronouncing the language. Some people are self-conscious about it. Maybe new colleagues confess they can't understand them. There's a lot of "What's that?" They're asked to repeat what they say time and time again. This may cause them to hold back in meetings, even if they have a great idea to add to the discussion. That may even cause them to be passed over for promotions.

I'm from Winnipeg, Canada, which is really close to Minnesota. When I travelled to Ontario some years ago, a newly acquired friend remarked that I sounded like someone from the movie *Fargo*.

You have an accent. Do you need to lose it? *No.* You absolutely do not need to lose that accent. Accents are part of what make us human. They're audible signs of diverse backgrounds. We don't need everyone to sound the same. That would be boring.

That said, some accents are stronger than others. Mine is a bit quirky and Midwestern, but it's easily understood by other North American speakers. Accents deriving from learning English as a second language are usually stronger. Some people live in their new country for decades and never lose their accent that stems from their first language. They may often feel frustrated when they aren't properly understood.

TIP

It's always possible to retrain a foreign accent and make those English sounds a lot clearer. It's easier than you think: It starts with slowing down, emphasizing key words, pronouncing words clearly, having an "I can do it!" attitude, and finding a native speaker to practice with and listen to.

TECHNICAL
STUFF

A *dialect* is a pattern of speech that a community acquires together. It is distinctive in sounds from that particular geographical place. An *accent* is a speech pattern that is different from the primary speech pattern in a community. For example: When my husband's cousin visits us from Ireland, we hear his accent. When we go visit him, everyone there sounds like him. That is their dialect, and we are the ones with the accent.

Slowing down

The first and easiest technique you can use to help someone better understand you is to slow down. Some cultures use faster speech patterns than others. If you've been brought up in one of those cultures and start speaking English, you may be speaking too fast for native English speakers in general. Your problems stemming from your accent will be amplified. You may also speak fast because you're fearful of speaking and want to get it over with. Or it could be a mixture of both. Slowing down is the answer.

Staying positive

Easy to say, I know. We humans visualize negative thoughts all the time. But if you work on it, you can learn to visualize positive thoughts. As with anything, you need to practice. Be patient and take your time. You're not going to do it in a day, or even a week or month. It took time to acquire your speech pattern, and it will take time to find the rhythm of a new one.

TIP

Find someone you know who speaks clearly and record him. Ask him to say a few words and sentences — slowly, to give you time to repeat them slowly. Listen and watch him intently while you are recording. Why is his speech so clear? Where is his tongue and lips placed when he makes sounds?

EXERCISE: VISUALIZING RELAXED TALKING

Find a place where you can feel comfortable. It could be lying on the floor or sitting in a chair. Go to your happy place in your mind. Maybe it's a beach on a hot summer day. You hear the ocean waves, the sun is shining down on you, and you're sinking into your chair or sand. Breathe in and out. I bet you're doing it slowly and calmly.

Think about how you speak to a good friend. Maybe you're talking about the winning goal at the basketball game, what fun you had last night at a concert, or how beautiful the day is. You feel at ease and comfortable with yourself and the conversation. Now, come (gently) back to reality.

Imagine giving your presentation to your group at the monthly meeting. You're tensing up, right? Go through your body in your mind and allow yourself to release your tension.

Now get back to talking with your friend. Allow that feeling of ease to wash through your body. Try to maintain that ease when you switch to the monthly meeting again. Breathe deep into your lungs slowly and calmly, just like you do when you're with your friend.

You can also try tensing parts of your body and releasing them.

I have a client who has difficulty with the *th* sound. He pronounces *that* like *dat*. He works on finding the correct sound by placing his tongue in the front of his mouth under his top teeth. He then moves his arm in a slow underhand pitch at the same time that he pronounces the *th*. After he feels that his tongue is in the right position, he continues pronouncing the rest of the word. Moving his arm helps him feel that the sound is flowing out of his mouth into the world.

Recite the sentences your friend uttered as you do chores or other monotonous tasks. It will start to become second nature.

Chapter **13**

Good Vibrations: Resonance

esonance involves how something — in this case, your body — amplifies sound. For people, resonance starts with breathing. The first thing the human body does to produce sound is breathe. Breath is the fuel that creates your sound. Once you take that breath in, you let it out, though there are a few different ways you can do that.

One way has you breathing out soundlessly, and another has you singing a tune. What's the difference? When you breathe out without sound, the breath passes right by your vocal folds (or larynx) unencumbered. But when you want to say something, or sing something, or make some sort of noise, those vocal folds come together and vibrate.

Getting to Know Your Resonators

Your vocal folds are like a record player's needle. It's the *origin* of the sound. Have you ever put your ear up to a turntable's needle with the volume all the way down? There's a tiny, little sound there, for sure, but it needs to be amplified quite a bit before you can really hear it. That amplification comes from the stereo's amplifier and speakers. What we're talking about when we talk about *resonance* is the amplification.

Amplification comes from your *resonators.* The resonators consist of bones and cavities that the sound of your voice vibrates through. When you speak, the sound in your larynx passes through the vocal tract and then into the throat and mouth, creating sympathetic vibrations in the teeth, hard palate, nasal bone, cheekbones, sinuses, forehead, cranium, chest, lower body, and even the spine and ribcage. All these body cavities are your resonators, and together they serve to amplify these sympathetic vibrations. Using all these parts of your body together is what gives you your distinctive tone and volume.

TIP

There are two different types of resonators:

>> Your mouth

>> Your nasal cavity

Both are on the front lines of resonance. Both are ideal cavities for sound to travel through. But they're not shaped the same, and your use of them isn't the same. You might think of them as a violin and a cello. Your mouth is the cello, and your nasal cavity is the violin. Both are stringed instruments. The cello sounds bigger and deeper than the violin — it's the large, deep cavity of the cello that gives it the type of reverberating tone that the violin lacks. The violin, of course, has a pure, sweet sound that the cello can't make. Same goes for your nasal cavity and mouth: Both are important, both help produce great sound, but because of their size, they have different effects on resonance. The mouth has more effect on resonance because there's just more room to work with and it fills the space between the upper and lower resonance.

Why We Study Resonance

Here are three reasons why you should pay attention to resonance:

>> **It's the source of variety.**

Very simply, opening up your resonators gives you more variety in your sound. Try this: Give an "ah" sound out of your mouth. Without changing your breath velocity or the sound from your vocal folds, open your mouth really wide. Hear the difference? Now try it again but close your mouth a little. Sounds different, huh? This shouldn't be anything new — you do this all the time when you speak. But this should remind you that when you keep your breath constant and change how you amplify that sound, even with just your mouth shape, the results can be quite dramatic.

>> **You can learn to open it up.**

Over time, you've learned to make a variety of sounds that you use in your everyday speech. Some people use that variety better than others. Some people speak in a monotone. Others give off a bit more energy and use more variety in their tones and volumes. Either way, we all express a range of sounds that define our comfort zone when we speak normally. People who don't often speak publicly may not use the tones and volumes that work well in public speaking as part of their normal range. The good news is: They can learn to use and open up their resonators to reach those public speaking tones and volumes. Learning to consciously feel what's going on when you get louder or higher-pitched can help you get there faster.

>> **It can help you use and release tension.**

Tension in your voice can cause different problems in public speaking. When you tense resonators you won't get that clear sound full of vocal variety you hear in your head when you imagine speaking with confidence. In fact, you may be doing something harmful to your voice by increasing tension. When you present a nice, relaxed voice, you're presenting your best voice.

Putting Your Whole Body into It

Your entire body, as you by now have realized, is a gigantic resonator.

If you have a cell phone, play a song on it. Hold it in your hands and listen to the song. Now put it on the counter. Which way is louder? When it's on the counter. That's because the sound is now travelling through the wood in the countertop. The wood is now vibrating, too, which amplifies the sound waves.

The same thing happens with your body when you speak.

Knowing your resonant voice

A huge problem people face just starting out in the public speaking world is that they don't yet *know their voice.* So what do they do? They do something people in all professions do when they don't have a particular style yet: They emulate the styles of others.

There's great value in that approach for most skills, and there's certainly value for speaking. The problem arises when new speakers start trying to emulate someone else's specific tone or pitch in their speech.

In theater school, I had an acting teacher whose voice was tremendous. He spoke with such a beautiful timbre that everyone, male and female, wanted to sound like him. It was all unconscious, I'm sure, but I started to notice that many of us would sound like ourselves in class, and then, onstage in front of him, would try to emulate his deep, booming voice. Of course, very few of us had voices like his at all. Most of the men didn't even have deep voices. So, what came out of our mouths was a hollow, fake-sounding, belly voice that sounded like a kid pretending to be a TV news anchor.

We had the first part correct: We all recognized his gorgeous sound and wanted a gorgeous sound for ourselves. The problem is, that gorgeous sound needs to come from *within*. You have to start with the sound that *you* make first. What that teacher did so well was exert control over his resonators. Without that skill, he would have sounded like the rest of us.

"But wait," you say. "I'll have a microphone! There's my big powerful voice right there!" To be sure, the microphone and electronic sound systems are fantastic inventions. Sometimes you definitely need a microphone. If you're speaking to 20,000 people, I don't care how in shape your resonators are, you're not going to be able to project to everyone. But chances are, you're not booked to speak in an arena. Right? Chances are, you're speaking to a small group of people who may well be able to hear you just fine if you speak loud enough. In that case, a microphone becomes a crutch.

The microphone is not going to save you, the details of which I go into in Chapter 16. And as for resonance, a microphone essentially just messes it all up. Depending on the acoustics of the room, your resonance changes to adapt. If you're in a small, tiled room, your resonance is going to be very different than if you were in a big, carpeted room. You can adjust your voice and resonators for how you want to present. A mic and amplifier don't really allow you to do that.

WARNING

Often when people use a mic, they don't speak forward in their mouth but back in the throat. They think it sounds cool and casual, when it fact it's probably creating havoc in the back of your throat. The throat should be open and free of tension, and when you speak from the back of the throat you are making the space smaller, thus creating tension. A microphone amplifies everything, especially your mistakes.

Tension in the throat, positioning of the soft palate, the jaw, the tongue, the head, and the neck all affect resonance. The next few sections talk about helping to reduce that tension.

EXERCISE: FINDING YOUR RESONATORS

I get it — your resonators aren't too easy to picture. The mouth is easy. The throat, maybe. But everything else? It's hard to see. So here's a handy guide on how to find them.

Start with humming. I talk about humming in general a bit later in this chapter, but for now, by closing your mouth and using your vocal folds, it's really easy to feel that buzzing that normally goes on when your mouth is open. And that buzzing is the beginning of resonance.

So give this a try:

- **Hum into your head.** Imagine that your mouth is now situated at the crown of your head. Put your hand on top of your head. Do you feel the vibrations? Keep going, keep breathing. Now say a line from your speech up there. Sounds weird, but follow through.

- **Hum into your nose.** Imagine that your mouth is now in your nose. Hum. Put your hand on your nose. Keep breathing. Can you feel the vibrations in your nose?

- **Hum into your face.** Now that's where your mouth actually is, so you don't need to imagine. Place your hands on your face. Feel the vibrations?

Follow the same pattern with your throat and your chest. Really feel that vibration and notice the difference when you "move" your imaginary mouth around to your different resonators.

The throat

When children think they're not being heard, they shout. It's how we all learn to turn up the volume at first. Of course, shouting works, but what is it, really? It's just a *pushy* voice, in which the tension in your body is reflected in your throat. When your body is tense, your brain thinks you're making effort, and so closes up your larynx — which is, unfortunately, where your voice comes from.

Shouting *pushes* more air out of your body than is normal, thereby creating a louder sound. It's the fastest way to get louder in a hurry. But it's not the best way — especially in a public speaking scenario.

My son once played basketball against a team whose coach was a madman, shouting constantly at his kids and the referees. This was is in a small gym, and the kids were 12, so he probably didn't need to act that way. From across the gym, I could see his neck bulging, veins popping, face reddening as he screamed at his players to do something. It was hard to understand the guy. Our coach, meanwhile, had a strong, confident, open, and free-of-tension voice and was fully engaged with his players. He was telling his players to get into formation, without shouting, and he was perfectly clear.

While the other coach was pushing air through his body at an accelerated rate to gain volume, our coach was doing something that is vital for volume change in a public speaking setting: I call it *finding your resonance.* You need to allow your voice to find that natural resonance within you to really get it going. A good resonator to do this with is your throat.

EXERCISE: RELAXING YOUR NECK

Neck tension can be a vibration killer. I haven't talked about the neck being a resonator so much, but — surprise — it is. It's not in the same league as the mouth or nasal cavities, or even the throat (even though the neck houses the throat). The *neck* I'm talking about is the part that doesn't have any empty cavities for sound to travel through air. I mean the flesh and bone parts. But just because your neck doesn't move air doesn't mean you don't have to think about it. Tension effects resonance, and having a relaxed neck is going to help your throat, larynx, and jaw because your sound will be more freely released.

Start by standing in proper alignment (as outlined in Chapter 3). Drop your head forward onto your chest. Keep breathing and don't collapse your body. Your head is heavy, so feel the weight. An adult head weighs between 10 and 11 pounds.

Now, release your jaw and lips as best as you can. Feel the weight of your head. Drop your head to the right. Feel the tendons on the left side stretching. Keep breathing. Keep your shoulders down. Press your left hand down toward the ground and feel even more of a stretch. Your head is stretching to the right and your left arm stretching down gives you an opposite pull. Breathe a few cycles of breath. Keeping your head dropped, return it to the center. Gently lift up your head and look up in front of you.

When you move your head either right or left, your eyes should be looking straight ahead. Your earlobe should be over your shoulder.

Drop your head to the left. Keep the shoulders down. Breathe. Press your right hand down to the ground. Feel the stretch from the right side of your neck all the way down to your fingers. Breathe a few cycles of breath. Drop your head forward and gently move it to the center. Gently lift it and look in front of you. Imagine energy flowing out through your head up to the sky.

EXERCISE: ROLLING YOUR HEAD FROM SIDE TO SIDE

This is a classic stretch you probably did as a kid in gym class. Basically, you roll your head side to side. But be careful: You need to do this very slowly.

Start with your chin at your chest. Then slowly loll your head around in either direction, going for a solid stretch in every position. Remember, your neck is doing this work, not your head. Your head is just going along for the ride. Roll to the right, slowly. Roll to the back. Make sure your mouth is open. Roll to the left, and then when your head is forward, bring it up. Repeat going the other way.

Always do this slowly. Don't roll back and look at the sky — it's not great for your neck.

EXERCISE: FEELING THE LIFT OF THE SOFT PALATE

The mouth needs space to be fully resonant. That means your soft palate needs to be able to move up and down.

You know that weird thing you do with your mouth when you're tired? *Yawning* is a tremendous way to feel your soft palate moving up and helps create more space, thus giving you more capacity to resonate. Plus it feels pretty good, too.

Take a look in the mirror. Open your mouth. Right behind your upper teeth is your hard palate. Directly behind that is your soft palate (see Chapter 12 for more on the hard and soft palates). Drop your jaw and relax that tongue, and try to yawn a satisfying yawn. (I realize you can't actually yawn on command, but work with me here.) Do you see and feel that fleshy soft palate rise up? When doing this exercise, always visualize that soft palate lifting up. Visualize your throat being an open vessel, like a barrel.

Now, to work with some sound try this: Make an *NG* sound. You should feel that your soft palate is dropping as it touches the back of your tongue to make the sound. Repeat that a couple of times. Make sure your jaw is released and stays relatively still. Now imagine that you're surprised — add an *ah,* like this: *NG-AH.* Feel the soft palate rise and feel the space in your mouth.

Think of your throat as a drum, and inside it is your larynx. The cool thing about this drum is that you can shape it. When you want a big sound, you need a big drum. The bigger the drum, the bigger the sound. Simple as that. How do you make your throat big? You release the tension to create space.

When going through any of the exercises here, you can stand or sit. When standing, ensure that your feet are flat on the floor, shoulder width apart. When sitting, make sure your feet can touch the floor.

Opening up the nasal cavities

Now let's turn to one of the most unique resonators of the bunch: The *nasal cavities* are the hollow areas behind your cheekbones that you may otherwise only really notice when they fill up with fluid when you're sick. That's not all they're there for. They're pretty important resonators.

The nasal cavities often get a bad rap when it comes to resonating, though. In general, the nasal sound is not seen as overly attractive. But neither is any sound that comes from predominantly one resonator. To use nasal sounds properly, they must be used in conjunction with the rest of the resonators. To have a rich and full resonance, the mouth, head, and chest resonators must also be activated. (Chapter 4 talks more about nasality.)

EXERCISE: LEARNING ABOUT NASALITY

Place your tongue behind your bottom teeth. Say the *NG* sound. Feel the sound from the roof of your mouth to your nose.

Add the *ay, ee, eye, oh, u* sounds:

- *Ng-aaay*
- *Ng-eee*
- *Ng-iii*
- *Ng-oooh*
- *Ng-uuu*

Now you're 12 years old and teasing someone. Repeat: "Nyah, nyah, nyah." All these sounds are resonating in your nasal cavities.

Exploring oral resonance

Oral resonance begins and ends in your mouth, and your mouth on the front lines of everything to do with resonance. Not only is it the first thing your voice hits right after your larynx and throat, it's the main decider of how most sounds change. It is located in the center between your upper and lower resonators. If the space in your mouth is small, your voice will sound higher and be lacking in lower resonance.

It's very important that you have proper control of oral resonance — and know what you can use it for. When you have good oral resonance, the sound is resonating from the front of your mouth. Remember, if you sound sloppy and muffled, the sound is likely vibrating from the back of your throat.

TIP

With practice, middle resonance is clear and strong, no matter whether you're speaking loudly or softly. The sound vibrates with maximum efficiency and travels directly to its intended target. It works a little bit like the business end of a bullhorn — you can aim it like that. And with a conscious control, you can have the power of a bullhorn, too.

EXERCISE: MORE HUMMING

Start by saying, "Mmmmmmm," for as long as you can in one breath. When you stop, think about where that vibration is coming from. Try it again, this time placing your hand on your forehead. Keep humming and feel the vibrations. Eventually touch your cheeks, nose, and jaw to feel the vibrations.

Still don't feel it? Say, "Mm-hmm," with the intonation as if you're responding in the affirmative.

Now try to keep those vibrations going when you say, "Mmmmmmm," and then, "One." Keep counting, "Mmm one, mmm two, mmm three . . ." Count until you need to take a breath.

Try it with a different sentence — maybe the opening line of your speech. Say, "Mmmmmmm," and then the opening line. How does your opening line change after you say the "mmm"? Do you sound more forward in your mouth? Try recording your voice saying a line without the "mmm" and then again after saying, "mmm." Do you hear the difference?

For resonation, truly nothing is better than humming. Humming is like an internal test of your resonance. Once you open your mouth, it's harder to feel where all the vibrating is going on. This exercise is entirely portable — you can hum (almost) anywhere. In this

(continued)

(continued)

exercise, you're just looking to relax those resonators, not conduct an in-depth examination of where your resonance is coming from.

Pick any song you like, but the simpler and catchier, the better. It could be a kid's song, like "Jack and Jill." Hum it with your lips closed and your teeth slightly apart. Everything should be relaxed. Your tongue and other articulators should be resting. Relax your shoulders. Slack your jaw as much as possible. Feel the vibrations in your forehead, nose, cheeks, jaw. Humming places the sound vibrations right in the front of your face.

If you find this hard to do, try chewing while humming. Try humming in a high pitch, and then a low pitch. Don't force the hum. Enjoy it. Don't purse your lips. You want your lips to feel tension-free.

Now try this. Hum at a comfortable pitch and then move the pitch slightly lower and feel the vibrations in your chest. How does that feel? Hum in a higher pitch and feel the vibrations on your head. Open your mouth a little. Feel the vibrations in your tongue, lips, and teeth, and behind and above your mouth. Try to increase them. Repeat the whole exercise again. Remember to keep breathing.

Releasing your jaw

Although the jaw itself isn't one of your most important resonators, it does all the work to make your mouth move. When your jaw is clenched, you're not going to get that same space in your mouth you would if you released your jaw.

EXERCISE: TRILLING THE LIPS

I talk more about lip trills in Chapter 12 — for now, just know that trilling them helps relax your mouth as a resonator, too. So, relax those lips and then wake them up.

Blow air through your lips to make them flutter, like a horse. Try to give them a good blow, and really let go with it. Pretend you're a kid again and drive your toy car with sound. Feel those vibrations on the front of your face. Once you do that for a while, stop. Does your mouth feel more relaxed? How about your jaw?

Now add some sound. Pretend you're driving a motorcycle. You want to focus the sound forward in your mouth, not back. Imagine the sound flowing out of your lips.

EXERCISE: ALIGNING AND CREATING SPACE IN YOUR JAW

Open and close your jaw gently. Imagine a string attached from in front of your top teeth to just behind your bottom teeth in the front of your mouth. When you open your jaw, feel the string stretch out in a straight line from the top of the teeth to the bottom. Close your jaw gently.

Don't rush! Take your time to really feel this and see how you can change the position of your jaw. You may feel some discomfort, because you're not used to aligning your jaw. If you feel pain, it could be *temporomandibular joint disorder* (TMJ). Check with your doctor if you feel pain while aligning your jaw.

Ideally, when you speak you should have at least a quarter inch of space between your upper and lower molars. That means your teeth don't touch. When your teeth touch, that's an indication that your jaw is clenched, which leads to tension in your jaw and a lack of range of movement. Plus the space in your mouth will be smaller, so there will be fewer vibrations and your resonance won't sound as full. Your jaw shouldn't stick out or pull back. All of this makes the space in your mouth smaller so you're not resonating fully and creates unwanted tension. It even messes with posture or alignment. When your jaw is jutting out, for example, your shoulders are often moved backward, your pelvis and stomach are pushing forward, and the space in your body has shrunk. The same thing occurs when you move your jaw back in toward you and your shoulders are hunched forward. When you close your jaw, your top teeth should fit snugly behind your bottom teeth.

Opening up your chest resonance

Your chest, as you know, is the cavity that holds your lungs. Once the sympathetic vibrations travel down your larynx, they hit the chest — the cathedral of the resonators. When you figure out how to resonate from your chest, your voice will sound warmer and bigger, like a choir in that cathedral. The same choir in a truck stop washroom is not going to have the same tone. The sound when you master chest resonance is one of authority.

The biggest problem with chest resonance, as with many of the physical problems you may have with public speaking, is tension. When you tense up, you're shrinking that cathedral down to a small chapel. The sound doesn't have a chance to reverberate properly, and you lose that big, beautiful tone you get with a full, open chest. A smaller, closed chest also means smaller lung capacity, which means less air into your larynx, which then produces a smaller sound.

Stand looking out at the world in front of you, in an up and out posture, not down and in. Clasp your hands behind your back and gently pull your arms up and out, away from your body. Keep your shoulders down while you do this. Stretch your chest up and out. Take a few breaths, then release. Repeat the cycle a few times.

If you can't clasp your hands, no problem: Just bring your arms behind your back and pretend you're holding a soccer ball. Breathe, and stay in that position for a couple rounds of breath. Release, then repeat.

Now that you've opened your chest it's time to feel those vibrations. Pick a note and hum as you did before. Put a hand on your chest. Feel those vibrations? Now tap your chest gently with your fingers while chanting a *mah* sound. You can even unleash Tarzan and gently say "mahaaaa, mahaaa, mahhha" a la Lord of the Jungle style.

The tension often doesn't stop at your chest. It's a whole body problem. Your larynx itself can become tense, and then your vocal folds can't vibrate with as much efficiency, making your sound not fully resonant.

What's the key to an open chest? Posture. Bad posture makes your muscles work harder than they have to just to keep you upright. The muscles that don't need to work all that hard in proper posture end up having to bear a bigger load. Instead of being used efficiently to help you speak, they're just helping you stand.

REMEMBER

When you begin an exercise in this chapter, make sure your feet are planted shoulder width apart. Feel your energy surging through your body, growing up and out the crown of your head to the sky.

EXERCISE: FINDING YOUR UPPER RESONANCE

For men, there's often a steep jump between speaking mainly from chest resonance and using mostly high head resonance. It could be that the upper resonance reminds them of their voice as a child. After all, many men have trouble with *voice cracking* as their voice settles into that lower register during puberty.

But head resonance is vital to a healthy and varied public speaking voice. It's got that bright tone that just doesn't come out from chest resonance. You're going to have to get over it, gents, and get to know how to use it.

I use this exercise with many of my clients to help them feel that *upper* resonance. Put your hands on the top of your head. Now hum, making sure your tongue is on the roof of your mouth (this helps the sound move forward in your mouth). Hum on a slightly higher pitch. Accentuate the "mmmm" sound when you hum. Do you feel the vibrations? Now put your hands on the back of your head. Do you feel the vibrations back there? Move your hands to your forehead, cheekbones, and nose.

Using an "M" sound can help you find those vibrations. Again speaking in a slightly higher pitch, say, "Momma makes marvelous muffins on Monday," elongating the *M* sound to help you feel it more. "Mmmmammma, mmmakes, mmmarvelous mmmuffins on Mmmonday." This exercise helps you feel that upper resonance, increasing your awareness of it and giving your voice more resonant variety.

When you hum or speak in a higher-pitched range than you're used to, it feels odd. But exploring your higher notes now will help you attain them when you give a speech. You will sound more interesting and have more variety.

EXERCISE: CHANTING

This exercise was inspired by voice coach pioneer Patsy Rodenburg. *Chanting* works to elongate your vowels and gives you way more time than needed with a word to feel how full the sound can be. It also does a good job of waking up those resonators.

Pick a note that is a tad higher than you normally speak. Eventually you will drop into the optimum place for your voice. Say, "Mah, may, mee, may, mah." Keep the sound forward in front of your mouth. Take a breath after each sound. Don't rush or push. Keep your jaw free and your throat open.

When you have repeated the sequence a few times, try it on one breath. remembering to keep the jaw free and your sound forward in your mouth. Repeat it a few times. Immediately after you've tried the sequence a few times, you should go right into speaking a sentence from your speech. Do you feel more vibrations? This exercise is also excellent for improving articulation.

EXERCISE: BRINGING YOUR RESONANCE FROM UPPER TO LOWER

Is your voice too high? The problem may come from too much upper resonance. This is often caused by tension in the back of your palate and tongue, plus a lack of lower resonance. Never thought your tongue could be tense? Well, it can be, and often messes up a lot of other stuff, including that warm chest resonance.

Relax and release your tongue and soft palate to regain those rich tones. Try to release the tension in your throat and jaw as well. Give yourself a big yawn to open up the back of the throat. Do that a few times. Repeat, "Geh, geh, geh." Feel those muscles working. Now add an "ah" so it sounds like "ge-ah." Take a breath when you need it and enjoy the sound and the release from the back of your throat. Now try to speak something from your speech. Does it feel like your voice is lower, with more range?

EXERCISE: RAISING YOUR RESONANCE FROM LOWER TO HIGHER

When you make a conscious (or unconscious) decision to lower the pitch in your voice, you may be robbing yourself of your full range. You may be physically reducing the space in your body, which can hinder your resonance. A few things might be at play here. As with a "too high-pitched" voice, tension could be at work. Tension in your tongue or a depressed larynx could be a factor. (Check out Chapter 12 for more on the tongue.) Your posture could effecting things as well.

Here's something to practice. Repeat a sound like "ma" over and over. Start in a comfortable pitch and move up higher from there. Now move your pitch lower. Slide up and down in pitch until you find the note that feels most comfortable.

Now pretend you're a monk and *chant* (sing on that one note) some of your presentation. Then immediately speak it on the same note. Soon your voice will naturally adapt to the higher note.

5
Enhancing Your Speech

IN THIS PART . . .

Find out all you ever wanted to know about the top three aspects of your voice: breath, tone, and pitch.

Practice good posture and use your body language onstage, read and respond to the audience with your body, and use movement to enhance your message.

Get mentally and physically ready to perform, use the power of positive thoughts, and make your last-minute checks to be sure you haven't forgotten anything.

Chapter **14**

Breath, Tone, and Pitch

Y ou know all about breathing. It's one of the most important things your body does for you. It's the first thing you do when you are born, and it will be the last thing you do when you depart this realm.

Breath governs life in the same way that water, food, and shelter do. It's inherent that we know how to breathe — and it better be. But most of us probably take it for granted. Many go through life without really thinking about what it means to breathe properly. Right now, think about how you're breathing as you read this. Weird, right? I remember not being able to go to sleep as a child because I was thinking about my breathing patterns too much. I figured when I stopped thinking about it, I would stop breathing. But we rarely have to be conscious of our breath. And for most of us, that's fine.

But not all of us. As a public speaker, you are among those who need to have a greater understanding of how your breath works and how to put it to work. You are now a public speaker, and it's time to become conscious of your breath. You have to learn how to breathe like those who succeed at public speaking do.

Our *tone* of voice expresses our emotion. I was a bit of a hothead in my teens. Sorry, Mom! She often would ask me a question that just needed a simple answer, for example: "What are you and Cathy going to do this weekend?" Then I'd give a rude comment. She would tell me, "Don't you use that tone with me!" In public speaking, tone reveals to the audience how you feel. When you say, "Thank for you for inviting me here today," your tone had better sound like you really are thankful. If not, the audience will clue in pretty fast.

Pitch is the way the voice goes high and low as we speak. It really refers to *frequency,* or how fast the vocal folds are vibrating. Using a variety of pitches while you speak keeps the audience engaged and helps to support your meaning. A variance in pitch is the opposite of monotone, which is a good thing.

You explore breath, tone, and pitch throughout this chapter.

Breathe, Breathe, Breathe

The first thing I want you to know about breathing is the importance of the diaphragm. The *diaphragm* is the muscle attached to your ribcage located beneath your lungs. When you inhale, the diaphragm flattens, the pelvic floor muscles relax, and the ribs move up and out so the lungs can expand as full as they can go. When you exhale, it's the opposite.

Next, of course, come the lungs. Your lungs are responsible for taking in all that air so they can add oxygen to the blood that runs through them. That blood then runs throughout your body, to every part, and it brings back carbon dioxide to the lungs, which is then exhaled through the mouth. And for you now, this is key: It's that exhaled air that makes the sounds you need to speak.

It all sounds very straightforward, doesn't it? We breathe in, we breathe out. We don't even have to think about it. But it's really that lack of thought that puts us in bad habits that we can carry for the rest of our lives, and that can derail us when we get up to speak.

Supporting your breath

Breath support means using the full potential of your breath to speak as powerfully as possible in order to sustain thoughts, vary pitch, and project sound. You're not shouting. You're *adequately* filling the room with your sound. So, how are you supposed to harness everything you have, breath-wise, and put it into a powerful speaking voice? Well, we have to take a peek into the body to grasp what's going on with our respiratory system.

As other chapters mention, the sound of your voice is the result of a stream of air from your lungs, going through your vocal folds, which vibrate and make sound. What's the difference between, say, a voice projected across a large room and a soft voice reading a bedtime story? It mostly comes down to air flow. If you have low air pressure flowing through those vocal folds, it creates a softer sound. If it's soft and inconsistent, it might crackle and pop (see Chapter 4 for details on vocal fry).

EXERCISES: BREATHING "WITH YOUR BELLY"

Breathing is meditative and activates the rest and digest parasympathetic nervous system. It helps to calm you and gives you a sense of stillness. However, if your mind wanders when working on these exercise, that's okay. Just allow yourself to wander, then try to bring your focus back to breathing.

- **Breathing from the bottom up:** Stand with feet shoulder width apart. Put one hand on your upper chest and the other on your lower abs, just below your navel. Imagine your nose and mouth are situated under your hands. Breathe in and out slowly through your nose. Which hand moves first when you inhale? It should be the hand on your belly. You want to fill up your lungs from the bottom up. The hand on your upper chest should move second.

- **Dropping your breath:** This exercise is adapted from Christina Shewell's book *Voice Work* (Wiley-Blackwell, 2009). Find a chair and sit with your feet flat on the floor, shoulder width apart. Close your eyes and breathe. Focus on your breath going in and leaving your body. Imagine the word *in* when breath goes in and *out* when it goes out. Breathe for a couple of cycles. Now imagine your abdomen is a balloon. When you blow into a balloon it fills up from the bottom to the top, right? When you inhale, imagine the word *inflate*, and when you exhale, imagine the word *deflate*. Go through a couple of cycles, remembering to maintain your alignment.

- **Lying on your back:** If you can't feel that breath dropping low into your abdomen, try it while lying on your back on the floor. When you lie on the floor and allow your body to really sink into it, you allow gravity to do its thing and may stay more focused on the task at hand. When we stand, we experience a certain amount of tension — otherwise, we would fall over. When we lie down we can relieve it. Try putting a book on your lower abdomen right below your navel. Breathe in and out and feel whether it is the book that moves first when you inhale or your chest. It should be the book.

- **Changing face:** Still lying on the floor, place your hands just above your navel. Now try breathing *from* there. Breathe freely, in and out. Once you feel that the breath is dropping deep into your body, say a line of your speech. Then try the exercise standing up.

If you have a consistent stream of air going through those vocal folds at higher pressure, you get a louder and more powerful sound. When you yell, you're forcing air through those vocal folds at such a high air pressure that, although powerful, it can distort your sound.

REMEMBER

Think of a Ping-Pong ball being held up by a hair dryer pointing straight up. With too little airflow, the Ping-Pong ball isn't sustained by the air and falls. Too much and it gets fired way up into the air. But there's a sweet spot, and that's where there's just enough airflow for the ball to float. When we think of speech, we want to hit that sweet spot.

The air that holds up the Ping-Pong ball is powered by your lungs, which are squeezed by your diaphragm relaxing upward and abdominal and pelvic floor muscles engaging. It's those core muscles that push your air through your lungs, airway, vocal folds, and mouth to deliver that rich sound. If they do this weakly, they deliver a poor sound. But the breath support begins with those muscles in your gut.

TIP

One of the biggest problems people have with breath support is not using those muscles to their full capacity and instead focusing on upper regions of the breath system, like the throat and upper chest to control that support.

EXERCISE: BREATHING WITH AND WITHOUT SUPPORT

Stand a tad hunched over. Keep your arms by your side, your hips jutted out, your abdominal muscles released. Make yourself sort of look like Shaggy from *Scooby Doo*. Try to speak a few lines from your speech. How does your throat feel? What is happening to your upper chest? Are you getting tired?

Now straighten up to a position where you feel planted. Stand up straight. Head up, chest out. Feel energy coursing up through your body. Now breathe with the full power of your lower abdomen muscles. Speak the same lines but this time focus on the support. How does that feel?

Take a note of the differences. The first thing you should notice is that speaking without support sounds dull. You have little if any vocal variety, your body is slightly collapsed, you're breathing short bits of air from your upper chest, it feels like you're speaking from the back of your throat, and you're getting fatigued.

Your breath-supported voice should sound richer. Your resonators have space in which to fully vibrate, your breath feels as if it's dropped into your lower abdomen, and you feel energized. When you have a rich, powerful voice, it triggers something in the audience's mind — namely, that you have some authority. That makes them more comfortable. When you speak with support, you have more room for vocal variety and are going to sound that much more interesting to the audience.

EXERCISE: STRENGTHENING YOUR ABDOMINAL MUSCLES

Stand in alignment with your feet shoulder width apart. Now pant. Channel your inner puppy. Release your abdomen every time you breathe in. Feel your diaphragm moving up and down. Feel your abdominal muscles pulling in when you exhale. Try not to grip in your throat. When you feel a grip there, it's a sign that you're not connecting with your abdominal muscles and are relying on the larynx to do the work. Only pant for a minute, then rest. Now, add sound. Pant on a "hah, hah." Take this into a sentence and really feel the support from your abdominal muscles.

In the nearby exercises, breathe in and out through your nose as much as you can. Air pollutants are filtered and the nose is moistened that way, plus you can take deeper breaths, stay calmer, and breathe for longer. When you're speaking, you don't have the time to breathe in through your nose, so you mostly breathe from your mouth.

Adding volume for a bigger space

In the theater, whenever a director would tell me to "project" my voice, I always felt the need to "push" it out. I would end up almost yelling, which isn't what was wanted. So instead of projecting, think of just allowing your volume to increase. Doesn't that sound gentler?

Here are a few things to think about in this regard:

>> Power is not volume. *Vocal power* is the impact your sound has on your listeners. Check out Chapter 13 for more discussion of *resonance*.

>> A powerful speaker is relaxed and comfortable.

>> Big thoughts in long sentences need more energy and breath support.

>> The louder the sound, the more support you need.

>> Your jaw needs to be relaxed and moveable. Keep it open with your teeth at least a quarter inch apart. (See the exercise in Chapter 12.)

>> Your throat needs to be open and free of any tension.

>> Some speakers get halfway through a word but close off because they feel they're too loud or seem too emotional. They stop speaking with support of those abdominal and pelvic floor muscles, take short bits of breath, and begin to push from their throat.

>> Be open to the size and space and adjust accordingly.

>> Make eye contact with all the corners of the audience. Don't limit yourself to the front row.

>> Speak as if you're in an intimate conversation yet still filling the space with your breath. Just like actors need to have an intimate scene with another actor, yet still need to fill the entire theater.

>> The bigger the space, the more energy you need.

>> When you think about speaking, your energy goes to your face. Dig deeper and engage your breath.

>> Use your face to show your emotion and expression.

>> Use your lips even more than usual. This helps bring the vibrations more forward in your mouth. It also helps to shape your words for those sitting far away in the back rows.

>> Articulation needs to be really clear. The more you pronounce the endings of the words, the farther the word will sail into the air.

>> Change your pitch frequently. It helps carry your sentences across the room.

>> Slow down even more than you think you should and pause at every opportunity. This allows your words to land and the audience to register what you have just said.

Changing poor breathing habits

There are a number of things that can go wrong with your breathing, but many of my clients show the same symptoms. What follows is a list of these common symptoms and suggestions for what to do about them:

>> **Taking shallow breaths:** You know the sound. Often it's used in movies and TV shows to signify that a character is close to death. So, guess what we associate with that sound? Yeah, not great for a lively presentation. Generally, shallow breath is caused by tension, which inhibits the diaphragm and ribs from moving like they should. Instead of filling to their full potential, the lungs only draw in a portion of the breath they need. Look for a physical release of your abdominal muscles when you inhale and a release of overall tension in your body. Chapter 3 talks more about this.

>> **Running out of breath:** When you have just stopped running, at least there's an obvious reason why you're out of breath. But why does it happen when

you're speaking? The first thing to look at is your posture. Your spine is probably curved, and your shoulders are probably hunched. You're in a down and in position. Check out Chapter 3 on alignment.

- » **Not moving your ribs:** You guessed it: Your ribs should move out with your lungs on the inhale. It shows that you're trying to get that full capacity from your lungs. If your ribs aren't moving much, you are probably slumped in your upper body. You should be vertically aligned. Straighten up and lengthen your spine.

TIP

Try holding a (light) chair over your head to help you breathe deep and open the ribs. Make sure to release all your breath out of your body when you exhale so that the ribs will have to move when you inhale. Don't let your shoulders creep up to your ears.

- » **Sounding like Darth Vader:** Your breath should be pretty close to silent. When you start sounding like the masked Sith lord, things are not going as they should. It's probably due to tension in your throat. Instead of letting the air flow freely, you're sucking it like it's a nonrenewable resource. Relax your abdominal muscles and keep your throat open when you exhale. Release your exhale freely.

- » **Not fully exhaling:** This is a problem I see every once in a while with my clients. It's as if people are topping up their air, rather than exhaling it all and starting again with a new batch. Many of my clients tell me it's uncomfortable. Your breath has nowhere to go, and you're left with a squeaky sound. Say your speech and after each comma or period STOP and BREATHE. Do this slowly to really feel how much breath you need.

- » **Forgetting to breathe:** Try it now — think about how you're breathing as you're reading this. Sometimes it's kind of strange to become conscious of your breathing. You don't want to do that onstage. Remember to *slow down*. The audience wants to understand what you have to say. If you stop breathing, the audience will too.

- » **Holding your breath:** As you know, breathing brings oxygen into our lungs and releases carbon dioxide. When you hold your breath, the carbon dioxide stays in your body, and oxygen begins to be depleted in the brain. I have many clients who tell me when they hold their breath they forget what they were going to say.

TIP

Singers sometimes mark up songs with symbols for where to breathe properly during a song. You can do it too. Take your speech and a pencil, and wherever there is a comma, period, or any other place where you want to take a breath, write down a slash (/) as a reminder (see Chapter 9 for more on marking up your speech). Try some more exercises from Chapters 3, 4, 9, and 18–21. Incorporate these exercises and new ways of breathing into everyday life. How does your breath respond to what happens during your day? When do you hold it, when are you sighing?

EXERCISE: VARYING BREATH FOR VARYING SENTENCES

Breathe in and out a few times. Breathe out on an "s" sound. Try an "s" sound counting in your head to 10. Then do it again but count to 15, then again to 20. Make sure your lower abdominal muscles are doing the work, not your throat or jaw.

Now vary the intervals: Count to 5, then 20, then 15. In your speech, each sentence needs a different amount of breath and support. Say a few sentences from your speech to remind yourself that they are not all the same length. You need more breath for long sentences and less for shorter ones. Take a look at how much breath you really need.

Does breathing make you look fat?

The short answer is, of course, no. But women especially have internalized, through movies, television, and advertising that looking skinny with a flat stomach is the only way to be fashionable. Likewise, men have been told to look buff, also with a flat stomach. Many of my clients have a tough time imagining their breath dropping into their belly because of what they fear their waistline looks like. That tells me they tend not to breathe properly all the time. That's a habit that you have to break. You're limiting your lung capacity when you hold in your belly. Don't believe me? Try clenching your abdomen much as you can — really pull your abdomen toward your navel. Now try to breathe. Can you breathe as if into your belly? Probably not. You take short snippets of air through your upper chest. Try standing sideways in a mirror and breathe, letting your breath drop low into your belly. Does it really extend your belly out that far? No, it doesn't.

Just breathe

Think back to when you were a little kid and you got upset. Your world was caving in on you. Maybe you were in trouble for something. How could you ever get over it? Your mom told you to take a few breaths to calm down. Guess what? It works. Breathing slowly does help calm you down. So, when you start to feel anxious, follow your mom's advice and stop and take a few breaths. And even before anxiety sets in — preempt it:

>> Breathe when you travel to the venue where you'll be presenting.

>> Breathe when you arrive at the venue.

>> Breathe when you look for the organizer.

>> Breathe when you mingle about.

>> Breathe when you go up to the lectern.

>> Take three breaths before you start. This revs up your engine and gets you ready to go.

TIP

If you breathe, the audience will too. You will be a breath of fresh air!

Improving Your Tone

Remember when you were a child the excitement you'd get from someone telling you a story? Maybe it was at bedtime with your mom or dad, or maybe it was your teacher, or a librarian. In my kid's schools, an author or other literary person would sometimes come in and read from a book to the kids. The best readers change their voice to fit the characters. Maybe your dad was an insurance agent, but he sure didn't sound like it when he was playing Captain Hook. He took on the character head on.

There's a reason you get excited about certain tellings of stories more than others. When storytellers adjust their tone to fit the story, it's easier to imagine the story, feel emotion about it, and engage with it. In public speaking, variance of tone works the same way. We react, engage, and remember speakers better when they don't speak in a monotone. So it's important to add variance of tone to your repertoire of public speaking skills.

When working with clients on a presentation, I often have to stop them on their first sentence: "I am pleased to be speaking with you today." They don't sound like it. They are just telling us that, saying the words, not showing us how they genuinely feel.

In the late 1960s, psychology professor Albert Mehrabian studied how listeners perceive the meaning of words. His findings on communication broke it down into words (what was actually being said), tone of voice (how the word was said), and body language (which postures, facial expressions, and gestures accompanied what was being said). The findings from his study at UCLA suggested that we derive the meaning of spoken word through much more than the words themselves. Tone and body language are very important to understanding.

You work on body language in Chapter 15. It's that tone component you're going to look at in this section. As mentioned, *tone* refers to the variety of modes of your voice. Tone tells others who you are and what you're feeling at that moment. Sometimes that means raising or lowering your pitch (which you work on next), like in music. Sometimes clients are surprised when I tell them that. It seems many people believe that tone, and especially pitch, is not to be changed very much. Many of my clients believe their tone is the way it is and will always be the same, and that tone has no relation to music. I'm not going to ask you to start speaking in a major scale, but be aware that the voice rises and falls like an instrument and can be used to much the same effect.

REMEMBER

Tone is the emotional quality of your voice. It is the attitude behind your voice. Choose phrases and words that support your meaning and your tone.

Expressing meaning and emotion through tone

One of the most important things you can do through your tone is express emotion. I don't mean you should ham it up when you're talking about data points or first quarter revenue, but there is always an opportunity to use emotion to influence your audience and get them engaged in what you're saying. You might be thinking, "I'm talking about quantum computing. How can I have any emotion toward that subject?"

REMEMBER

True, sometimes it's tough. But look at it this way: If you don't have any emotion toward a subject, why is the audience even listening? So you have to ask yourself why exactly are you speaking about your topic? Should people get excited about these data points? Should they be discouraged? It there a call to action? The way you express emotion through your tone is a big part of how the audience will too.

Another issue that affects tone is, of course, tension. If you're tense because you don't know the subject well or haven't rehearsed, or you're fearful because you're speaking in general, it affects your voice. Your whole body may become tense, your throat constricts, your shoulders go up, your neck stiffens. Because the audience mirrors you, they become tense too. Listeners get an impression about how you feel through your tone.

One of my clients was working on a presentation about mental health. He began with a story about his grandfather who suffered from PTSD, and his aunt who was diagnosed with early onset Alzheimer's. These were serious subjects, yet he smiled through his entire presentation. Of course, he didn't think it was funny, but it was an odd look for a speaker on this subject to be smiling the entire time. It was as if he was making light of the subject. His tone, meanwhile, matched his facial features. He sounded happy. He had forgotten that tone should match the topic.

EXERCISE: TRYING ON DIFFERENT TONES

Practice speaking the following sentences in different tones. First say them in a firm, harsh tone, and then in a lighter, friendlier tone:

- "Thank you for taking the time to talk to me today."

- "Are there any concerns with our product?"

- "Can I speak with my supervisor and get back to you?"

- "That's very nice of you to say."

This exercise is a very basic one that shows how you can change your meaning through tone. It's not the things you say — it's how you say them — that enriches meaning.

Using a conversational tone

Yes, it's probably just you up there, but as I say elsewhere in this book, your speech is a conversation with your audience. It's best to think of it that way, and tone is one of the most important things you need to consider. We've all heard the speaker who looks out at an audience of 500, takes a big breath, and then speaks in an extremely loud or fake voice.

A speaker in that situation feels the need to fill the room with his sound. But you're looking to please the audience. Don't alienate them. Better to think of it in terms of speaking to a group of people at a cocktail party. Sure, they have to hear you. You're going to need more energy than you would when you're talking to someone one on one. But you're the only one up there, remember. You don't need to talk over anyone.

Here are a few things to remember about a conversational tone:

>> Feel the energy from the crowd and use it to feel drawn to them.

>> Live in the moment.

>> Keep the experience personal, as if you're talking to a close friend.

>> Don't work too hard and don't push it. You're already in the spotlight — you don't have to push.

>> The more natural you appear, the more the audience will believe you.

EXERCISE: INCREASING YOUR VOLUME WITHOUT TENSION

Lie on the floor, breathing in and out. Release your neck, throat, shoulders and chest. Imagine them sinking into the floor. Speak some lines of your speech, quietly, with a voiced sound (don't whisper). Gradually add volume — but try not to raise your pitch. Keep your pitch the same. You can use lots of inflection, but don't keep driving your pitch up.

Now do the same exercise while standing. Repeat the speech conversationally. You can even move around. Feel free to use plenty of inflection, but avoid going too high or low in your pitch. Speak the speech as you would to an audience. Keep your neck free. Check your shoulders. When you feel tension, stop and try to release by giving your body a good shake and think of the steps to releasing (see Chapter 3).

EXERCISES: THROWING YOUR VOICE

- **Throwing a ball:** How much energy does it take to throw something long distance? Pretend you have a ball in your hand and you're going to throw it to reach an audience member in the first row. Say a sentence of your speech while you are throwing it. Go farther back until you hit the back of the auditorium.

- **Throwing a vowel:** Pretend you have a baseball in your hand. Find a spot where you are going to throw to. Really focus. As you release the ball, chant or sing out an open vowel sound like an "ay" or "I." Watch the ball fly through the air. Continue the sound until the imaginary ball has hit your focus. Now take a word in your speech and do the same thing. Keep the sound clear the whole way.

- **Speaking to the wall:** How much breath and energy do you need to speak a foot away from you and how much do you need to speak to a room of 50 people? It's not so simple, and it's not something you want to have to find out on the fly at a speaking engagement. Find a big room. Stand in front of a wall, maybe a foot away. Say a bit of your speech. Now back up farther. Say the same sentence. Is your body aligned and upright? Are you pushing your body forward? Go farther and farther away. Each time you feel any tension in your throat or feel you are pushing things, return to the last place that you didn't feel any tension. Each distance requires a different amount of breath.

  You can also practice speaking to a friend who moves farther and farther away from you. Two feet away, six feet, all the way to the back of the hall. Ask the same questions you asked when you were talking to the wall. Get your friend to tell you things like "Can't hear you . . . look up more . . . keep breathing . . . let's hear the ends of your words."

>> Show your passion. You are excited about what you have to say.

>> If you use too much volume, your pitch goes up and your throat, shoulders, and chest become tense. Your meaning may fly out the window, and the audience may tune out.

Harnessing the Power of Pitch

Most of us use about three to five different notes of pitch in our day-to-day speech. Remember how excited you were as a kid when you reacted to a surprise? Or when you told your brother you were mad at him for losing your bike? As we get older, many of us lose that expressive musicality. Maybe we think it's silly. We want to control our voice and speak with authority. Well, pitch, and especially variety of pitch, is the key to being expressive.

Pitch is the frequency of sound waves or vibrations produced by our vocal folds. Essentially, it's the highness or lowness of your voice. Just like the notes of a musical scale go up and down, so does your voice. There's no way around it: If you want your idea to be exciting, you have to speak in a pitch that reflects that. Pitch reflects our feelings:

>> Low pitch is calming.

>> High pitch is exciting but can sound nervous.

Problems that prevent pitch changes:

>> May feel uncomfortable

>> Tension in jaw

>> Little breath support

>> Muscles that are underused

TIP

Try singing your speech. Yes, really! Singing your speech helps with finding different pitch sounds, stressing different words, and elongating word endings.

Remember resonance, discussed in Chapter 13. Your sound is vibrating forward in your mouth. Speak as high as you can without feeling any tension or pushing your voice. Start speaking some text right away in that pitch. How does it feel?

EXERCISES: PRACTICING PITCH

- **Playing with a children's story:** Take a children's story and have fun with pitch. Take words in the story and change the pitch of your voice when you say them. *Really* exaggerate your pitch changes. Pretend you're acting in a melodrama. If you haven't seen melodramatic movie in some time, you've probably watched someone in action, maybe even a coworker. "I am *sooooo* tired! I just *caaaan't* make the deadline!" Go ahead and use body language to accentuate, like putting your hand to your forehead. Anything to exaggerate the character.

- **Moving pitch changes around:** Pitch changes meaning, and so this exercise is a great method to find out which word should be emphasized in a speech. Take the sentence: "The amazing copper pot can be shipped anywhere in the world." Change the pitch on different words. Go high with your head resonance and go low in your chest. Remember to only speak in the range where you are not straining your throat — and keep breathing!

The *amazing* copper pot can be shipped anywhere in the world.

The amazing *copper pot* can be shipped anywhere in the world.

The amazing copper pot can be *shipped* anywhere in the world.

The amazing copper pot can be shipped anywhere in the *world*.

Now sing each emphasized word to elongate it and break up the rhythm pattern even more.

Now speak as low as you can (without introducing vocal fry, discussed in Chapter 4). It's okay to feel your neck muscles stretch. If you feel too much strain, give a big yawn.

TIP

You can easily change your pitch by saying, "Oh!" or the phrase, "Oh, I am happy to be here to today!"

Chapter **15**

Getting Body Language into the Act

When you're giving a speech or presentation, you're the boss, regardless of what position you hold in your organization. And when you're the boss, you should act and feel like one. We've all seen the presenter who comes onstage or into the boardroom looking sheepish. Her body is closed in, and she doesn't exude the confidence we expect from a speaker. Her movement is confusing, and we start to focus on that rather than on her message. What is her message anyway? We feel alienated because she's not looking at us and not connecting.

This chapter covers how body language can make or break your speech. It can enhance what you're saying, or take away from it. How you dress, how you move, what you do with your hands — all can have an impact on how your audience receives your message.

Becoming a Poser (in a Good Way)

My mom had a thing about posture. It was always about posture with that woman. I'd leave to catch the bus from school, and the last thing I would hear from the open window was, "Alyson June, put those shoulders back!" All these years later, I still hear her in my head every time I catch myself slouching.

And there's a problem with that. When many of the people I've worked with hear the word *posture*, they tend to do just that — pull their shoulders back as if they're about to balance a load of books on their heads. Guess what, though? That doesn't help your speaking voice. In fact, it can create tension in the throat. So let's break down the idea of posture and talk about it in the bigger sense of positioning and moving different parts of your body for effective public speaking.

Adjusting your stance

Your feet should point forward, planted shoulder width apart, for stability. As I've said before, try to feel roots growing down into the earth. Speaking with one heel tilted up or a hip jutted out to the side doesn't exude power and authority. Set your stance and then don't fiddle with it until you have a reason to move or change it.

Lowering your head with your shoulders moving toward your ears looks submissive, indicates lack of confidence, and makes you look shy. And you may have other kinds of nervous tics you're not even aware of, like shaking one hand or wringing them together, clicking a pen, touching your face, blinking, swaying side to side, or tugging on your ear.

There are exceptions, of course. Carol Burnett, for instance, tugged her ear every show. It was for her Grandma. This actually shows she *was* in control of her body — she knew very well what she was and wasn't doing. That kind of control is something beginning public speakers have to learn.

TIP

To see if you have any tics, record yourself giving a presentation in an empty room. Notice any strange movements? What are your hands doing? How about your eyebrows?

Tilting your head, on the other hand, suggests you are interested. Sticking out your chin signifies defiance.

EXERCISE: ALIGNING YOUR SHOULDERS

Get into alignment in the up and out position (see Chapter 3 if you've forgotten what this is). How does it feel? Now gently move your shoulders slightly forward. A very small movement because when your shoulders move forward so does your pelvis and then your spine collapses. Now how are you breathing? Bet you're breathing from your upper chest. Your lungs can't fill up to capacity because they're not given the room.

When you speak is the sound vibrating from the front of your mouth, or sitting in the back of your throat? Where is your focus, and what are your thoughts? When I show my clients that a simple move of their shoulders can change the way they look and feel, they are amazed.

Now let's correct that alignment and improve the posture. By simply feeling aligned and allowing the shoulders and arms to hang like clothes hangers, not moving forward or back, you can breathe more fully. Your focus is out into the world, your sound is more forward in your mouth when you speak, and you take up more space with your body. And you don't even need a gym membership.

Facial expressions

The study of facial expression has been going on for a long time. Charles Darwin, famous for his theory of evolution, studied facial expressions. He concluded that facial expressions are universal and that we can detect people's emotions by their facial expressions.

In psychologist Paul Ekman's book *Emotions Revealed* (Henry Holt, 2003), the author writes that he wanted to dispute Darwin's claim. Ekman believed that facial expressions were adopted through societal and cultural means. In 1969, he travelled to a remote area in Papua New Guinea where there was no written language, no one spoke English, and the people had never been exposed to television, books, or movies. He brought with him pictures of people showing specific facial expressions: anger, happiness, disgust, fear, surprise, and sadness. He would tell the participant a story and then afterward ask them to point to the picture that best depicted the story. With the exceptions of fear and surprise, each time the subject pointed to the correct emotion. Ekman deduced that it could be because fear and surprise often come hand in hand when it comes to emotions and facial features.

Obviously, your face is what everyone's looking at. And what it should be doing is matching and conveying the meaning of your message. Allow it to do that for you.

That doesn't mean oversell it. In stage acting, there is a rule that one must be bigger than real life. After all, the people in the cheap seats need to see what's going on. There is a little bit of that in public speaking too, but it's subtler. Don't overdo it or the audience will sense you aren't being genuine.

TIP

A good rule of thumb is to keep your facial expressions consistent with your ideas. You can have big ideas — they're only listening to you, after all. You may feel the need to keep your face neutral, which is boring, in a conversation about your ideas, but don't forget, you're the only one up there. Represent your ideas. If they're big, be big. It's easier to dial it down than ramp it up.

A few of my clients worry about their facial expressions out of concern for their appearance. For example, they may feel self-conscious about their teeth and are afraid to show them. Maybe you have a stiff upper lip. Don't worry about that stuff. People may notice at first, but it's natural for other people to want to get comfortable with a face. And they will. They want to see your ideas and what those ideas mean to you. Let them.

Another thing people forget to do (understandably) when they're stressed out is *smile*. Smiling makes it seem like you *want* to be up there. And guess what? When you smile there's an actual positive physiological response in your body.

Smiling does a few other important things that will be beneficial to your speech. When you smile, it releases those feel good chemicals dopamine, serotonin, and endorphins, which calm your nervous system. Next time you take a picture of someone and tell him to smile, think about what *your* face is doing. You're probably smiling. It's cheesy, I know, but smiling *is* actually contagious. Just by smiling you can feel better. People want to smile. When others are smiling, it's a lot easier to smile yourself.

Smiling can in fact precipitate those feel good feelings you need. Some research suggests that smiling is actually a catalyst to happiness. You've heard "fake it till you make it"? That's a good plan. A study from Penn State University found that smiling improves a person's mood and makes them more likely to be liked by others and perceived to know what they're doing.

TECHNICAL
STUFF

By the way, the *authentic* smile is called the *Duchenne smile,* after the French neurologist Guillame Duchenne who studied facial expressions in the 19th century. In an authentic smile the zygomatic muscles, which raise the corners of the mouth, are activated along with the orbicularis oculi muscle, which raises the cheeks and forms crows feet around the eyes.

The worst thing that could happen from smiling is that you look happy. Why not try it?

Making eye contact

Eyes are the windows to the soul, as they say, and it's true at least when you're speaking in public. They are definitely the windows to the soul of your message. Making eye contact with the audience is important in getting your message across. If your "windows" aren't pointed at the audience, those folks can't see in, and the potential connection can be lost.

TIP

When you're introduced and are standing on the stage, take a few seconds of silence to look at the audience. Long enough to really see them. During that time, also take three breaths to start your engine.

Here are a few things to keep in mind about eye contact:

>> It can help you feel calmer and think more clearly.

>> Look at the audience as much as you can — not at your notes. Don't cheat by looking out over everyone's head. They can tell that you're not looking at them.

>> Don't sweep around the room with your eyes. It's confusing to the audience.

>> When you don't look at the audience you seem to have less authority and less confidence, and the audience won't buy in to your message.

>> When you look at the audience they will *look at you.* When you don't, you're giving them permission to not look at you. They will be tempted to check their phones, because why not? You're not even looking.

>> Looking one person in the eye forces that person to look at you. Don't stare at one person for too long. That individual will become uncomfortable. Holding eye contact for five or six seconds is enough. Then move your gaze along to someone else.

EXERCISES: EYEING THE AUDIENCE

First, practice using those peepers. Look left and right. Look up and down. Roll them around in circles. When you do this, make sure you're only using your eyes and that your jaw and neck are free of tension.

Try this when you're ready to give your speech. Look out at the audience over their heads. How are you feeling? Are you connecting with them? Highly unlikely. The audience can tell you're not looking at them. Now try to look at everyone in the room. Make it random. Make it feel natural. Look at one side of the audience, and then the other side. Try to make eye contact with everyone in the room at some point in your speech.

Sometimes we get into the habit of not looking at the people we're talking to. Practice looking — *really* looking — at people when you talk to them. The more that becomes a habit in your daily life, the easier it will be onstage.

>> Often the audience becomes active listeners. They nod and use nonverbal signals like shaking their head yes or no, putting a hand to their faces when their thinking about what you've just said, smiling or frowning. They are in fact communicating.

Eye contact makes you look confident and self-assured.

REMEMBER

Tuning In to Audience Perception

All right, you've taken my advice and done your homework, as recommended in Chapter 11. You've taken the time to get to know who your audience will be. You've asked the event organizer about that. What are their interests? Are they for something that you rally against? Or are you preaching to the choir? You know what they're looking to get out of the speech. You know what you have to deliver.

But that's just research. When you're in front of them, it's time to execute. You walk out on that stage, or in front of the board, or into your interview — wherever it happens to be — and then what? Well, the research doesn't stop there. What is the audience feeling as you step onto the stage? What are the nonverbal messages coming from them? Are they excited about your speech? Are they worried? Can you even tell? Did some news they just got from a previous speaker spook them? Excite them? Be aware, so that when you begin your speech, you're not out of sync with the audience.

Looking and feeling genuine

During your speech or presentation, the audience wants to see you — that same person they'd be talking to if you were both tucking into a Caesar salad at lunch, one on one. Which means you need to *be yourself.* And even though that slogan is on everything from little girl's T-shirts to motivational posters, in my experience people new to public speaking find this difficult.

Some people instinctively try to be a caricature of themselves — the self that can speak like a pro. But this usually comes off as fake. Some people put on strange voices, or do weird things with their hands. Don't do that. *Be yourself.* You can be an augmented version of yourself, sure, but not a caricature.

When I started out as a professional actor, I went on many school tours putting on children's plays. Performing the same show for six months on tour is gruelling. But one thing it did for me was help familiarize myself with my performance. By the second week, I knew my character inside and out. To keep my own interest up — and, of course, that of the audience — I had to find something new every performance. I wouldn't change my performance drastically so that my fellow actors would be thrown off. The changes were subtle. Emphasizing a different word, trying a different objective. When you do it the same over and over, so that you've choreographed every move, every breath, and every word you emphasize . . . audiences see right through you. It seems like you're phoning it in. That's why being yourself can break the tyranny of over-practicing. Allow your performance to show pieces of the real you, in the moment.

As I've said, a speech is a performance, and a performance is a conversation. This is part of it. It *is* a performance, absolutely. You are performing. And therefore, it's not *exactly* you up there. You need to give some indication that the real you is in there, that your personality is driving the bus.

TIP

Be spontaneous and trust your feelings. If something goes wrong, carry on. Get in tune with the audience and gauge their response.

Here are some affirmations and some advice to help you be you while you're up there:

>> The audience trusts you and will be open to your message. They want to connect with a human being. You will be able to impact the audience.

>> Listen to the audience and be responsive to their nonverbal cues, like nodding their heads or raising their eyebrows.

>> Be open to your audience, as if they are friends. How would you give your speech to friends and loved ones? When you talk to friends, your body is relaxed, your shoulders aren't tight and hunched, and your facial expressions are easy and unforced.

>> Take a risk and allow yourself to be more real.

>> Don't stress out about recalling your speech word for word. The audience has no idea what you're going to say. They don't care about the words — they care about the meaning.

>> Make your body language match your message. If you start your speech with arms crossed over your chest and say, "I am so happy to be here today," the audience won't buy it.

>> Use pronouns like *we* and *ours* as opposed to *you* and *yours*. This makes the audience feel included. Sends the message that you're all on the same team and in it together. You are creating a relationship.

Owning the room

Yes, you're serving the audience, and yes, you're having a conversation with them. You are even in their space — or at least, you're in a public space. But your speech contains your ideas. You own those ideas and their presentation — it's time to also own the room, at least temporarily. This is *your* space for the time being.

Owning the room is all about positioning on stage. That means doing a bit of planning. Try to find out how big the stage is, and if you can, plan for that space. I have had a lot of clients who have been spooked by the size of the stage. Maybe they thought there was a lectern they could stand behind. That's easy — something solid to ground you. You don't usually even move away from one of those. Then they get there only to find no lectern, but rather a giant stage, like a TED Talk. Some see a big stage as an open ocean where they might be attacked. Just remember, there's only one fish in that sea, and that's you.

REMEMBER

Some speakers really need to stay in one spot. They just feel more comfortable that way, and that's fine with me. As long as you use eye contact and gestures, you'll be engaging.

By the way, a *podium* is what you stand on when you receive your Olympic medals. A *lectern* is a flat surface that you can put your notes on.

Are you worried that you won't be able to connect with the audience if you're behind a lectern? See how President John F. Kennedy engaged the audience in his inaugural address through eye contact and gestures behind the lectern: www.youtube.com/watch?v=PEC1C4p0k3E.

Moving with a Purpose

There is an acting exercise in which players can only enter a room for a reason and leave for a reason. They need a *reason* to move. Try to think of your movement in the same way during a speech. Resist pointless movements. If you feel you do need to move, go ahead and do it. But make sure you can justify it, because arbitrary movements can distract a viewer from your message.

REMEMBER

Remember these tenets of movement:

>> Pacing back and forth makes the audience dizzy.

>> Moving with purpose reinforces your message.

>> Walking stresses an important idea and gets the audience's attention.

>> Stepping forward reinforces that you have something important to say.

>> Stepping backward looks like you don't want to engage and get too close to the audience.

When I was working as an actor, after the first read-through of a script around a table, we got to our feet, and the director would *block* us, meaning tell us where to move. Usually the director would spend time before the rehearsal to choreograph where the actors should move. Sometimes the director would let us actors give our input. I would always ask myself, and the director, "Why?" Why would my character move to the door? Because she was ready to leave. Why does my character want to move toward the other character in the scene? Because, for instance, she wants to express love. This wasn't a criticism of the director's directions. But if I didn't understand the root causes for them, it was harder for me to act them out.

So many presenters move about the stage aimlessly back and forth, including many of my clients. When asked why they're moving, they really have no idea. Perhaps they're anxious. Walking could be a habit, or a tic. Or perhaps they feel that standing in one spot could be boring. It's fine to move, but always, always move with a purpose.

Part of moving with a purpose, and making a plan for that movement, is understanding what a standard stage looks like and how to map it out. Here are the parts of the stage in theatrical terms:

	Backstage	
Upstage Right	Upstage Center	Upstage Left
	Center Stage	
Downstage Right	Downstage Center	Downstage Left

>> *Upstage* is the back of the stage closest to the back of the set or playing space.

>> *Downstage* is closest to the audience.

>> *Center stage* is, naturally, in the center.

>> *Stage left* is the left-hand side of the stage from the point of view of someone onstage — in this case, that's you. (*House left* is left from the audience's point of view.)

>> *Stage right* (house left) is the right-hand side of the stage from the point of view of someone onstage.

TIP

Something I've found when I teach clients about the areas of a stage is that they tend to want to hit all of them equally during their talk. That's not the purpose of showing them the stage. But it's annoying when you're sitting on one side of the stage and the presenter is spending the whole time on the other side. Be aware if you're hitting one side of the stage more than another.

When should you move?

Although you should definitely do some planning, you're not going to follow a strict, choreographed movement routine. You're not dancing up there. You have a lot to memorize already without having to figure out a two-step. Plus you don't want to make it *look* like you've choreographed movements.

Here are some helpful pointers for planning, while looking somewhat spontaneous in, your movements:

>> **Use your *main points* (discussed in Chapter 6) as a jumping-off point to your movements.**

Allow your movements to punctuate your actual speech. For instance, if you have an open stage and you have three main points you want to get across, you could divide your stage into three sections, one for each point. It doesn't have to be as literal as that — small movements can accompany your piece just enough to accent what's important about your message.

>> **Never stand in front of your visual aid.**

If you have a slide show or are showing a picture, don't block it with your body. If you want the audience to be looking at something important enough that you're displaying it, for example on a screen, then your body needs to get out of the way, and your voice needs to carry the message along with the display. Feel free to jump back to center stage once it's over.

>> **Start at the very beginning.**

Chances are, the first movement you make will be going from the wings of the stage, or from your seat at the boardroom table, to the lectern or to a place in front of the group of people you're talking to. The first movement is also the first thing your audience is going to pay attention to. Don't take it lightly. Walk with a purpose to the lectern, looking confident. Smile. This is your first impression with the audience. Make it count.

>> **Move between thoughts.**

If an audience is unfamiliar with your subject matter, use your movements to help them along. It may be hard for them to figure out the structure of your arguments if this is the first time they're hearing them. If you're switching gears, give a physical indication of it using some movement.

>> **Move to act out words.**

If you're telling a story in which you were moving, act it out. If you've got an anecdote about walking into the warehouse and discovering something, act that out. Walk into that warehouse.

>> **Be front and center for the thesis.**

TIP

I don't have many rules for movements. But there is one that I strongly suggest. For your main argument or thesis, be front and center. Let the audience know that you mean business with this.

>> **Check whether there is anything in your way.**

As you choreograph your movements, pay attention to any physical obstacles that might be in your way. Where is the lectern, are there chairs on the stage for a panel discussion, a whiteboard, a flipchart, any props?

>> **Don't move without purpose.**

Remember a good deal of how we understand a speech is through body language. If you're moving, even though your feet are planted, it's distracting. If you're fidgeting, it takes away from what the audience should be getting.

EXERCISE: STANDING IN ONE SPOT

I often use this exercise the help my clients understand how much they sway or list to one side when they're speaking. You're going to need a partner for this one. Stand, as usual, with your feet shoulder width apart and imagine roots growing down to the earth from the bottom of your feet. Energy is flowing through your body past the crown of your head up to the sky.

Ask your partner to gently place his/her hands around your heels. Feel the weight and stability that brings to your body. Start to speak. Continue for about 2 minutes and then ask your partner to take her hands away. Continue speaking. How do you feel? Ask your partner if you sound different. My bet is that your voice has become lower. You probably look more confident, and the audience would be able to hear what you're saying as opposed to watch you swaying.

Sitting during a presentation

Often my clients say they want to sit while giving a presentation. This is the most natural position for most people, and it allows them to speak without leaving their comfort zone. I sympathize, but you're not going to wow anyone from behind a table. If you can stand, you should. Did your teachers ever sit while giving a lecture? If some attendees were to come late in the meeting, would they know who was presenting?

WARNING

Sitting while presenting sends a casual message to your audience that you are a contributor to the conversation, not the leader of it.

Another thing: When you sit, your body can collapse, and your energy can decrease because you're supported by your chair. Sitting can restrict your breath, and your voice lacks the potential variety it has when you're standing. However, sometimes you do need to present something behind a desk or at a conference table.

TIP

Plant those feet, even if you're sitting. I once Skyped with a client and noted that his posture was slouched a bit and he wasn't breathing to his full capacity. Turns out both of his feet weren't flat on the floor. His alignment was off.

If you can, sit on the edge of your chair on your sit-bones (those are the bones you feel when you sit erect on a hard surface). When you're on your sit-bones, your body naturally aligns itself. Check your breathing. Now sit back on your tailbone. Is there a difference? You don't have to be stiff, just be aligned with your energy surging up. Chair type makes a difference. Soft and cushy? Don't sink into it.

Here are some rules to abide by for sitting and speaking:

>> No slouching or bending forward. You can bend forward to listen and show emphasis, but don't fold into a closed in position.

>> Crossing your legs can impede your breath, especially if you're in a down and in position.

>> Playing with a pen is distracting.

>> Use your entire body in an up and open position.

>> Keep your arms in an open position — not crossed.

>> Make eye contact. Take the time to look at everyone around the table.

>> You can still use hand gestures. Don't leave them under the table.

Speaking of hands . . .

Hand Jive: Gesturing with Your Hands

This is one of people's biggest anxieties. *What are you going to do with your hands?* Hands are great for so many things. Those opposable thumbs are a marvel of evolution. Where would we be without those ten digits at the end of our arms? Yet they can cause so many problems for people when they're not doing any opening, or playing the piano, or any of the other things that they can do. Instead, they just hang there awkwardly when it feels like they should be put to work.

Be natural. Just use them.

TIP

Are you a hand talker? Ask a loved one or someone you talk to at work a lot whether you use your hands often for gesturing. It's hard to know if you don't regularly see yourself talking — which, for most of us, is never. It could give you a good indication as to whether or not your natural position is hand talker or not.

There are many ways in which you can use your hands for any number of gestures. Here are some things to keep in mind when it comes to gestures:

>> **A gesture can replace a word.**

An obvious example of this would be, for instance, a peace sign. But there are a bunch of ways you can use your hands to present an idea silently, or to augment a word, phrase, or idea you're talking about.

EXERCISE: THE "TRUTH PLANE"

In his book *Winning Body Language* (McGraw-Hill Education, 2010), Mark Bowden talks about what he calls the *truth plane* and the *grotesque plane*.

Stand still with your arms by your side. Start speaking and don't move your hands. What is happening? How is your breathing? Are you breathing deep into your lower abdomen or strictly from your upper chest? Are you breathing fast or slow? Quite possibly you're getting tired, your voice has no variety, you're speaking in a monotone, your eyes lack interest, and the listener is falling asleep. Bowden refers to this as the grotesque plane.

Now move your hands and arms and gesture on a horizontal plane 90 degrees straight out from your navel. Your voice probably changes pitch, your eyes open, and you become more engaging. Mark Bowden refers to this as the *truth plane*.

It is at the navel that we are the most balanced. That's our center of gravity. Having your hands in this area activates your calming parasympathetic nervous system and helps alleviate any anxiety. It also makes you look more authentic and genuine.

In his TED Talk on "What Makes a Good Life? Lessons from the Longest Study of Happiness," psychologist Robert Waldinger incorporates gestures easily. Check it out at www.ted.com/talks/robert_waldinger_what_makes_a_good_life_lessons_from_the_longest_study_on_happiness.

>> **You can reinforce a word with a gesture.**

For instance, you can tell the audience about a tall person. "This guy was six foot five," as you put your hand above your head to allow the audience to visualize the height difference. Gestures can also emphasize what you're saying — for example, you can shake a fist, place your hand on your heart, or point up to the sky. Gestures can underscore a compliment to the audience or a thank you to the organizer who introduced you.

>> **Gestures can help manage the audience during Q&A.**

TIP

Your gestures can signal when you want the audience to respond to a question and when you need to talk. You can direct things like a traffic cop. Stop one person who is ready to speak with a palm facing up. Gesture with the other hand for the next person to speak. You can point to the person you want to speak first. An open-handed gesture is better than pointing a finger, which may look accusatory. If a group is talking and you want to get their attention, you can put your hands out to them shoulder height with palms up. Don't put your hands up too high or back — that looks like you're surrendering.

>> **Gestures can point, describe, and enumerate.**

Angela Merkel — at the time of writing, Chancellor of Germany — moves her hands in front of her with fingertips touching, a gesture called steepling. Her arms are in the active area. She appears strong and confident. It's something she's practiced, no doubt, and she knows exactly how it looks on television.

Let's say a line in your speech is as follows: "The cost of living is higher, but your income is lower. And we're going to do something about that."

When you say, "The cost of living is higher," you could gesture to the right side of your body. When you say, "but your income is lower," you could gesture to the left side of your body. Or you could gesture to one side as before but leave your arm out there, then gesture to the other side and keep your arm out there, and then on "And we're going to do something about that," clasp your hands together.

You could raise your arm up really high on "The cost of living is higher" and then move it down low when you say, "but your income is lower." When you say, "And we're going to do something about that," you could give the OK sign. You could even pump your fist.

Many speakers use their fingers to count. They show us one finger for one, two for two. We can all count, and I just think this gesture isn't necessary. But that's my personal opinion and if you need to count to remember where you are in your speech, so be it.

There are also problem gestures that distract the audience. Watch out for these:

>> **Touching your forehead:** This indicates to the audience that you're having a tough time up there. Touching your neck, fiddling with a necklace, or touching your cheek are all referred by body language expert and former FBI agent Joe Navarro as *pacifying behaviors*. You look like you need to comfort yourself.

>> **Keeping your hands behind your back:** You don't want to look like a waiter at a fancy restaurant, or a soldier standing at attention (unless, of course, you *are* those things).

>> **Standing with one or both hands on your hips:** Unless it's for a specific effect, to illustrate a story where someone is disappointed, for instance, you don't want to do it throughout your speech.

>> **Adopting a cowboy stance:** Your thumbs are tucked into your pants or belt loops. This action frames the genitals and makes you look aggressive.

>> **Holding an arm with your other hand:** Looks like you were wounded and are cradling the injury. Unless you're just off the battlefield, don't do this.

- >> **Keeping your hands in your pockets:** It can look like you're scared, and you may just be. Or you think you're looking cool.

- >> **Clasping your hands and dropping them in front of you:** If you have kids, you know what this looks like — like you've done something wrong.

- >> **Crossing your legs or ankles is a common habit:** The body language specialists analyze this as looking like you're fearful or holding something back, or you're unsure of the situation.

TIP

Gestures need to be congruent with your message. Just like you should move with purpose, you should make gestures with purpose. Vary your gestures, but don't overdo them. They shouldn't distract the audience or detract from your speech. Give your gestures time to coordinate with the words you're saying. And remember, when you're speaking to a larger crowd, your gestures need to be bigger than usual — but not so big that they look cartoonlike.

Dressing for the Occasion

My sister went back to school after her kids were grown and completely changed her career. After graduation, while looking for a job, she'd get up every morning, put on her makeup, get dressed in business attire, and sit down at her computer to find a job. When I asked her why she couldn't do that in pajamas or sweatpants, she told me she needed to feel like she already had the job. That set the tone for her search. Her energy and professionalism came through in everything she did, and eventually she landed an interview and a job.

Dressing is an important aspect of nonverbal communication. Clothing gives the audience a clue about your personality and what they can expect from your presentation. Plus, when you dress up, you feel the part. There's a reason we play dress up as children. We can see ourselves in a new role. We feel special, instead of feeling ordinary in the regular, ordinary clothes we normally wear. And you *should* feel special when you're speaking if you don't often speak in public. I'm not saying you have to wear a tux or ball gown (unless it's mandated). But you have worked hard on your presentation, so make the effort.

Wearing appropriate clothing for your event

You are the main attraction, remember that. Nothing you wear should be more interesting than you are. Still, ask your organizer how your audience will dress. Is there a dress code? Adhere to it. If not, you should still be sure to look professional and respectful. Choose attire according to the type of audience, the event, and your message. By revealing the positive aspects of yourself through dress, you reveal confidence in your choice, and therefore confidence in your subject matter.

But what to choose? Well, if it's a business event, that'll probably make your decision for you. But there are times when the choice is not so obvious. For me, the rule of thumb is that you want to look like you've dressed up just a little more than the average attendee. You never want to be *too* dressed up, of course. If you're speaking at a barbecue commemorating the opening of a community league center, you won't be renting a tux. But if everyone's wearing jeans, wear the nicest pair you have. No rips.

When I taught oral communication and public speaking at the university level, I dressed like a professional. Universities are interesting places for that. You have students, who often wear very casual clothes, and teachers, who sometimes do the same. For me, because I am moving around coaching voice and public speaking, I can't wear a dress. I need to wear clothes that I can move in but that fit me well and look smart. I need clothes that represent the fact that I am a professional first, who happens to be teaching my trade. I dressed as my students would hopefully dress in the field.

First impressions start with what you look like. The audience judges you the minute they see you — sorry, but they do. I once was giving a morning workshop at a conference and was told that I must stay for lunch because the speaker was fabulous. The organizers had flown him in from another city, so I figured he'd be good. I was pretty excited, to be honest. The MC introduced this fella, spouted all his achievements, and then he walked onto the stage. He had long hair and seemed like an eccentric. Every time he turned to one side, which happened a lot, his hair fell into his face. His jacket was ill fitting and looked horrible, frankly. His tie clashed, and his shoes were scuffed. Every once in awhile during his speech he would scratch the side of his torso, which lifted his shirt out of his trousers. The guy was a mess. It was painful to watch. You could see it in the others' faces at this very professional conference. They weren't buying what he was selling.

I love to buy clothes and I love a good sale. But there came a time when I was buying too much (don't tell my husband) and just not wearing it. That's because I had no idea what I needed or what my style was. The "got it on sale" style wasn't working. So I found clothing stores in my community with helpful staff who took the time to work with me.

TIP

Find those stores. They're out there. And bring in some clothes from your wardrobe so that you can ask if you can pair them with new items. And find a good tailor. That jacket you bought may have fit years ago, but now you may be straining those buttons.

Suiting yourself: Clothing for men

Want to exude authority and look the part? The power suit still exists. This is the preferred order:

>> Navy blue

>> Grey

>> Black

The seams of your jacket should rest on the tops of your shoulders, not below them. Your jacket sleeve should touch the small bones in your wrist. Sleeve length of your shirt is more of a personal thing. You may have antique cufflinks that you want to show off, so you might want your shirt sleeves an inch below the jacket sleeves.

Your pants should be hemmed so they're not brushing the floor or up past your ankles like Steve Erkel.

TIP

If you're dying for that classic James Bond or *Mad Men* suit, take a picture of what you want into a reputable clothing shop and they'll find something close to that style.

These days you can have a patterned shirt, tie, and even a jacket — if it works. Trust the professionals when it comes to judging whether it does.

As for color of shirt, depending on your skin tone, you might look good in jewel tones like sapphire blue, ruby red, and emerald green. Or maybe pastels suit your complexion. Check with a stylist or a store clerk.

Men have had relatively few choices to express themselves. I know this because I raised two boys and it was difficult finding fun accessories. Things have gotten better in recent years, and men are having more fun with pocket squares, handkerchiefs, and — especially — socks. It's kind of the one thing men can go crazy with, even with a conservative suit. No longer do you have to wear matching black socks. Sure, you can if you want, but socks are colorful and fun, so go for it! The same can be said for ties. A colorful tie will add interest to any suit.

WARNING

White socks with a dark suit still don't work. It makes you seem like someone who just bought the suit and has nothing to wear but sport socks from his gym bag.

TIP

If you're color-blind, get someone to mark the labels. And put them in order in the closet. All the blues in this corner, the browns in the other.

Style and comfort: Clothing for women

Women have many more options than men. Sorry, fellas. The key to looking powerful is that your clothes fit properly. Robin Wright's character in *House of Cards* is extremely confident, and her fit is always impeccable. The clothing stylist for the show spends hours making sure her outward appearance is in sync with her confidence.

You don't have to spend hours, but you do have to spend some thought. Women come in different shapes and sizes, and designers who understand that have used spandex and stretch fabrics to account for different shapes. Wrap dresses will always be flattering because of the jersey and a V-neck.

Ideally there should always be key visual points of fit in any outfit:

>> Does it fit in the shoulder and bust?

>> Does it fit in the waist?

>> Does it fit the hip?

A flowy top should still have a seam hit right at the shoulder so you see your frame, and if you tuck it in you will showcase more hip and waist (waist being the smallest part of the frame). These visual points of your shape are how we see your frame, so you're not lost in the clothing.

Patterning the patterns

Patterns can be worn by anyone, but you should always be careful about the size of the pattern compared to your body type. If you have a petite frame, don't wear a big pattern that could overwhelm you and your audience, and vice versa. When trying patterns on, always consider where they are hitting you. Is a stripe going across the bust line in an unflattering way? Does that flower hit a funny place?

Wearing makeup

Apply your makeup to look as naturally as you can. Wear more intense lipstick and avoid too shiny, too neutral, or too light lipstick and gloss.

CLOTHING AND VIDEO CAMERAS

Be mindful of the camera. Many patterns do not look good on video. That patterned jacket that you wore for the presentation might not work when you give your interview for the media. Here are some things to avoid if cameras will be an important part of your speaking engagement:

- Don't wear all black clothing. Your head will look like it's floating.
- Don't wear anything with too much detail.
- Don't wear horizontal stripes, especially for black-and-white video.
- Polka dots, stripes, and big patterns dance and do funny things on camera.
- Don't wear anything green. TV stations often use "green screens" as background for interviews, and green clothing can interfere with that.
- Bring a change of clothes or at least a shirt in case the background is the same color as the shirt you're wearing.

Powder is your friend. If you're under intense lighting, you might sweat. Have some powder on hand to help. Men, you can use powder (after all, news anchors, male and female, wear makeup), or just have a tissue on hand to gently dab away perspiration.

Sporting tattoos

I have a couple of tattoos and I love them. But I have them where people can only see them at certain times — like when I'm wearing a bathing suit, not when I'm giving a presentation. If you have a sleeve of tattoos and choose to keep them visible during a presentation, fine. But the audience will be looking at your artwork instead of listening to your message.

If the shoe fits

I have two boys who have both graduated from school. Many of the girls they knew spent the day of graduation getting their hair and nails done for their walk across the stage, often in a brand new pair of high heels. But my boys walked across it in the same old shoes they always wore. New shoes, for men or women, probably shouldn't make their debut at a big event. Make sure you're comfortable in those shoes before walking them on stage.

I tell people to follow the rules of marathon runners: Never run the big race in new shoes. Shoes break in, as you know. The point is: If you're not comfortable in them, the audience is going to notice.

There's also the issue of how they perform. Some shoes, especially nice ones with leather soles, are very slippery. It's best to know how your feet are going to handle the shoes before stepping out in front of people to speak.

Then there's always the issue of high heels. People always ask me about them. I realize that a higher heel on a woman is more flattering and slimmer looking on the leg. But it's really hard to feel planted when you are tottering toward the audience. Plus, high heels affect your alignment and your breathing.

TIP

If you're going to wear high heels at a speech, be sure to practice in them. You can start with a lower heel, then gradually work your way up to the heel that you'll be wearing on the day.

Avoiding wardrobe malfunctions

You need to feel comfortable onstage, and that goes both for bodily comfort and mental comfort. Don't wear something you might be embarrassed to show off. A short, form-fitting dress with a low neckline may be perfect for a night of dancing, but maybe not when you're addressing the parent-teacher organization.

Meanwhile, watch what you eat and drink before you speak. You don't want to spill anything on your nicely pressed suit. Watch the coffee, or the red wine. If you're travelling out of town, bring a second outfit, just in case you do spill.

Try on and move around in your clothes beforehand to make sure they're not too tight or too loose. You don't want popped buttons or a ripped seam.

Tying back your hair

Just like in the musical *Hair*, "Give me head with hair, long beautiful hair, shining, gleaming, streaming, flaxen, waxen . . ." we all have many choices with our hair. But when you're giving a presentation, we need to see your face and expressions. If your hair is blocking your face, we stand to lose a certain portion of your message.

So, guys and gals with that long streaming hair, I envy you. You look fabulous up there. But please tie it back so it doesn't fall in your face. The audience sitting in the center may be able see your face, but the poor people on the sides won't. Hair can act like blinders on a draught horse. They'll miss what you're saying because they'll be thinking, "I need to give her a hair tie!"

Taking it easy with the jewelry

Keep it simple. Anything that makes noise when you move, like bangles or earrings, distracts from your message. Earrings can also hit the microphone of your headset. Plus, you don't want to lose an earring while giving a presentation. Don't wear necklaces that move around and make sound. That noise can be picked up if you're wearing a headset or lavalier microphone.

Doing your nails

Go out and get your nails manicured and polished if that's your thing. If you're not into that, or if you have really short nails, just keep them clean. If you wear nail polish, remove it if it starts chipping. You want to look polished, and chipped nails give the impression that you don't really care about what you look like. If you've been gardening the day before, get out a scrub brush and make those nails sparkle! Gentlemen, you're not exempt from this; if you've spent the weekend mowing and changing your oil, get a brush and wash those nails.

Chapter **16**

Ready, Set, Go!

Presenting is a performance, and a performance is a production. These facts extend well beyond public speaking.

Most Olympic athletes have a regimen that they follow before their performance. Some of it may be based on superstition, but a lot of that is about being comfortable during their whole day before they perform. They might eat the same thing, take a nap at a similar time, might listen to the same music. It's all in an effort to not upset how their body and mind are working.

Not preparing and just winging it may work sometimes, but usually it's better to be prepared. You want the audience to come away thinking that you were so *at ease* and your speech came *so easily* out of you. You want to be so prepared that you look like everything is spontaneous. You want it to seem like this is the first time you've presented your speech and it didn't take any work at all. Little do they know, right?

So why blow it after you've practiced your presentation to the nth degree just because you ate or drank the wrong thing the night before, or ran into the auditorium without knowing anything about the space? Those and other similar mistakes can really throw you off. This chapter is all about giving yourself the *best* chance to succeed on the day of your performance.

The "Four Stages of Learning Any New Skill" theory was developed at Gordon Training International by Noel Burch in the 1970s. It's now known as the "Four Stages of Competence." Here it is in a nutshell:

1. **Unconscious incompetence:** You don't even *know* what you don't know. For instance, before reading this book you likely had little idea what it took to become a successful speaker. This stage acknowledges that there are skills and concepts that you can eventually glean that you didn't even know existed.

2. **Conscious incompetence:** You become aware of what it is that you don't know. You start reading, and that familiar (if you're anything like me) sensation washes over you: *I know absolutely nothing.* Imagine you have to cram the night before the final exam for a class you never attended. That's what this step feels like.

3. **Conscious competence:** This is where you start working it. You become aware of what you do know. You're constantly thinking of everything you do. You know what you have to do, and you can do it to a certain degree, but it's not yet second nature.

4. **Unconscious competence:** This is the hallelujah moment, where everything comes together without even thinking about it. Your body is so familiarized with what you need to do, you just do it. You do it *naturally*. After all, the hockey player on a breakaway doesn't stop, line up his puck straight in front of the net, take a big breath, and score. He just shoots. What you need to do is in your muscle memory.

Completing these steps is essential to mastering anything, including public speaking. You can't think about dropping your breath when you're talking about a mortgage rate hike. You need to be in the moment and present with your audience.

But guess what? Nobody's perfect, and who wants to be anyway? You're probably not going to be at the end of these four stages any time soon. It takes *so* much work, and *so* much practice. But don't fret. Remember, the audience wants to see you, a human being. Not some robot.

In the meantime, if public speaking isn't second nature yet, you must prepare.

'Twas the Night Before . . .

TIP

You may not have the option of a nice leisurely day before you have to present. You might not have much of a day at all — maybe you're presenting your work to the board at 9 a.m. If you can spend the day settling in and letting go of tension and stress before you present, take that opportunity. This might occur more often when you're out of town giving a presentation, because the most important thing of the day is giving that presentation. But even if you can't spend the day becoming centered, or enjoying freedom the day or night before you present, it's still important to be conscious of what you do before and to maximize your potential for success.

But you may at least have the night before a presentation to yourself. Mind you, that isn't always great for people — it can actually be a killer for people with anxiety. The minute you get yourself alone, your mind may start sabotaging your self-esteem. I've been there. That a good reason to keep yourself busy preparing.

The night before, go over your presentation. No, don't write your presentation, because it's already written (right?). And don't just look at your notes while you munch $10 peanuts from the hotel bar. And don't think you can sneak in a review of your notes while you should be watching your daughter's soccer game. *Physically present it like you really will when you do it for real.*

If you're lax and just muddle through it, going through the motions, that *will* transfer in your presentation the next day.

The actors in *Mamma Mia* don't just "kind of" sing their songs in the final rehearsal before facing the audience. *They sing full out.* Treat the night before as your final rehearsal.

If you're presenting out of town, find out if you can rehearse your presentation in the space.

Practice in the clothes you're going to wear during your speech. In the theater, this is called a *dress rehearsal*. It's where you find out what fits and what doesn't. If you've practiced in rugby pants, you will feel and move differently in a suit. The tie you picked may match perfectly with your funky socks, but if you're having difficulty breathing when you speak, it will have to be loosened. Figure that out before you get onstage. I love my shoes, and since I don't always speak in flats, I have to practice in the shoes I will be wearing.

If you don't feel your best in what you're going to wear, you'd better find out in time to change it. Nothing is worse than getting onstage and realizing what you're wearing is too tight — or unfashionable. You want that kind of thing to be the least of your worries. So, dress up well before you speak. Wear what you're going to wear. Move in it, check yourself out. If you don't love it, if you feel you can't breathe or move properly, then wear something else. It's not worth it.

THE FINER POINTS OF WEARING HIGH HEELS

I mention in Chapter 15 that it's advisable to present in flat shoes because they will make it easier to find your proper alignment and feel more grounded. As your heels get higher, it becomes harder to maintain alignment. But I, for one, love to wear shoes with a heel, so I'm not going to be a hypocrite here and tell you not to.

If you want to wear heels, do it. If you think it will make you feel more comfortable, do it. But take my advice: First practice with a flat shoe and then go higher and higher until you're at your ultimate heel of choice. High heels are difficult to master. Make sure your presentation won't be about how you toddle on and off the stage. (This goes for graduation ceremonies and weddings, too, by the way.) The audience will worry for you. And if they are worried you may break an ankle, they won't be able to concentrate on your speech.

Getting Familiar with the Space

Maybe you've been to the venue before. You may have even been in the audience in the space that you're presenting in many times before. But the stage is new to you. You have never presented a speech there. Yes, you know where the lectern is placed and which side the stairs to get up there are on. But you need to *get on* that stage before your speech to "look out at the house," as they say in theater. You will get a different perspective than you do sitting in the audience. And you don't want the potential shock of that new perspective to overwhelm you just as you begin your speech.

If you know the space and it's open to you, practice on the stage as many times as you can before you give your presentation. Unfortunately, this may be a luxury you may not often get — but definitely use it if you can. Start from where you will get introduced and move to the stage the way you will on the big day. Choreograph how you will walk onto the stage. Decide where you will use eye contact. If you have a slide presentation, try to go through it.

If you can find someone willing, have a colleague come to watch and listen to you. Ask him or her to look for the following:

>> **Conversational tone:** Are you speaking as you would to a friend over lattes? (With more vocal and physical energy, of course.) Or do you sound like Mark Antony booming out "Friends, Romans, countrymen, lend me your ears"?

- >> **Body language:** Is there any aimless pacing or walking without a purpose? What about swaying side to side or back and forth? Are your arms down by your side (which can make both you and the audience tired and you seem boring)? Are you using gestures that engage you and the audience and animate your message?

- >> **Eye contact:** Really pretend like there are people there. Are you looking at certain places in the audience? Do your eyes ever drift down when you speak? Have your colleague sit in a chair and practice looking at him, not above. Do your eyes dart around?

- >> **Audibility:** Get your friend to move to various places in the audience. Can she hear you clearly from everywhere? Are you pronouncing the ends of your sentences? How is your pace? Are you pausing? Are you emphasizing words? Are you breathing? Are you shouting to make yourself heard?

Scoping out the joint

If the first time you see the space is at breakfast before the presentation, take time to suss out the place. Where is the lectern? Can you move around it?

There are many things to think about on the day you present in a room that's unknown to you, so here questions you need to answer:

- >> **Where is your contact person?**

  Find the person who originally got in touch with you. He's probably the one running in and out of the room "like a chicken with its head cut off," as my mom used to say. Introduce yourself and ask to be taken through the room. Ask questions. But that may not be possible, and you'll be on your own. Try to find the person later if you have questions.

  Introduce yourself to the technician if you're lucky enough to have one. It may be the organizer, or someone else assigned to the job. If you have a slide deck or any other audiovisuals, try to go through them.

- >> **What is the size of the room?**

  Will everyone be able to see? It may be okay to buy a ticket for, say, the hit Broadway musical *Hamilton* with a partial view. But if you're a new speaker, make sure everyone can see you. If some attendees can't, how can you fix it? If there's a huge pillar on one side of the audience, you may have to move around the stage even more than you practiced. If you practiced your speech staying in one spot, now's the time to adopt the "Yes Let's" attitude Chapter 2 promotes. Where will you stand? And how can you move so that everyone can still see you?

» Where are the electrical outlets?

Where can you plug in your computer? Do you need an extension cord? Is there an extension cord handy? These are things too many people neglect to think about until it's too late. Often, electrical outlets will be on the other side of the stage. You're going to want to know where they are if you're running a slide show or any device. If you need an extension cord, is it taped down so you don't trip over it? If not, can you choreograph your speech around it?

» What is the sound like?

Can you hear the staff in the kitchen? Or people talking in the hallway outside? Is the room divided into two spaces and will there be another speaker presenting when you are? Is it completely silent? Just be aware of this.

Warming up in the space

Sometimes you're forced to warm up in your car, your house, or your hotel room. But given the chance, and if the space that you will present in is empty beforehand, see if you can warm up there. Just don't count on it. This opportunity is a luxury that won't always be afforded to you. Often the space is occupied up until you go on.

But let's say it's your lucky day. This is a good thing. Get in there and warm yourself up. There is a reason in theater why the cast goes onstage to warm up: because that's where the play takes place. The actors want to become familiar with the acoustics and space in the room.

And you may think it doesn't matter whether you warm up in the car, in a broom closet, or wherever. But hear me out: You will present in many different rooms in your professional career, and no two rooms are alike. You need more energy for bigger rooms and less for smaller ones.

TIP

In her book *Voice and the Actor* (John Wiley & Sons, 1991), renowned vocal coach Cicely Berry talks about how to fill a space that has poor acoustics. There may be too little reverberation feedback, which would make it hard for you to project your voice. Or there may be too much reverberation so that your words don't sound clear. Think of the floor of the auditorium or room that you're presenting in as a sounding board. Find a place halfway to two-thirds the way back from the stage. Look down at the floor and hum. The sound should bounce up and fill the room. Keep humming, looking downward while moving around the room. Listening carefully, find the places in the room where your voice carries best. When you feel that you've found a good place, lift your focus to look out in front of you and say a bit of your speech. As you speak, focus on the place where your voice carried the best. Now turn your back and still focus on that spot even though you're turned away from it. When you eventually give your speech, keep that focal point in your mind.

To help fill the space, remember to articulate the *endings* of your words. That will help the words sail through the air and be heard.

Eating for Success

What do athletes eat before they compete? There was a time when athletes ate pasta to help boost energy. But as you learn in Chapter 10, pasta is a simple carb that burns through us quickly. You're not playing soccer out there. You may think that going out for a pasta dinner the night before is a good choice for a pre-presentation meal. But try something that's going to make its way through you at a slower rate.

For example, protein. Meat, fish, legumes, and nuts stick with you longer and don't leave you hungry again as quickly as simple carbs. Make sure you add some protein to it if you do have pasta.

TIP

Always eat breakfast! You've always known that breakfast was the most important meal of the day, right?

I find concentrating after lunch or dinner to be really difficult. That's because my body is spending a lot of energy digesting my food. The audience eats, too, you know. They may feel sluggish as well. Don't give in! Keep that energy up. Remember that the audience mirrors you.

I admit that I love a nice glass of red wine. And when I'm giving a presentation away from home and spending the night in a hotel, nothing is more luxurious than having a glass of wine while going over notes. (I love the spa too, but taking my notes in the steam room wouldn't work too well.)

WARNING

I don't think I need to say this, but I will because I am my mother's daughter and she always told me the obvious: Don't drink so much that your head is foggy the next morning.

Sleeping to Refresh

Before bed, go over the presentation again doing mundane chores, like raking leaves, washing the dishes, unpacking your suitcase. Going through your speech while doing something completely different helps get the speech into your body and out of your head.

Once you've gone through it once then *forget about it!* Read a book, watch a movie, and just let the speech go.

Get to bed at a decent hour, and when you go, don't worry about that presentation. Leave those negative thoughts and worry about your speech at the bedroom door. You've practiced, and you'll practice again tomorrow. Now it's time for rest.

REMEMBER

You don't have to be perfect. When you give that speech, you're doing the best you can on the day you are giving it.

What if you're tossing and turning and can't sleep? Sure, the conventional wisdom is to count sheep — use a bit of misdirection on yourself. But before you try that, try some deep breathing. Breathe in for a count of four or more and then breathe out for the same count. When you exhale, feel all your tension flow out of you. Just concentrate on your breath and nothing else. There may not be any sheep, but there sure will be breath.

Set your alarm so that you have time to warm up before the kids get up or the hotel staff kick you out to clean your room. Give yourself a nice long morning, with a little bit of breakfast, and all the necessities. Don't let yourself rush. Now, warm up for your speech. Check out the warmups in Chapter 22.

It's Show Time!

In the movie *All That Jazz*, Roy Scheider's character looks in the mirror every morning after a night of drinking, smoking, and general carousing and says, "It's show time, folks." Regardless of whether you slept for a solid eight hours or your dog was throwing up all night, it's time to be on. You can't go back now. Your mindset has to be on the performance.

Minding your mind

I've said that you think and process negative thoughts faster and hold onto them longer than you do positive thoughts. See Chapter 2 if you need a refresher. By now, I hope you know how important it is to stay positive and to think good things. You've done your work and practiced a ton — don't let those negatives undermine you!

Get those affirmations running through your head from Chapter 2:

>> "I've got this."

>> "I'm fabulous."

>> "My message rocks!"

Visualizing using imagery

Chapter 11 talks about the importance of visualization. Let's take it one step further and use a more complex version of imagery.

Just before the 2014 Olympics, the *New York Times* ran an article on how visualizing using imagery benefits athletes. Emily Cook, the U.S. Olympic freestyle aerialist, goes beyond mere visualization. She needs to feel the wind on her body and, she says, ". . . smell it, you have to hear it, you to have feel everything." Canadian bobsledder Lyndon Rush says he goes through the track in his mind many times during the day. This is echoed by U.S. Olympic team sports psychologist Nicole Detling: "The more an athlete can imagine the entire package, the better it's going to be."

There are two kinds of imagery you can use:

>> **External:** With external imagery, you see yourself doing your presentation as if you are watching a video of it.

>> **Internal:** Here you mentally and physically go through the motions from your own point of view. This is evident when you see the bobsledder before she gets ready to run the track at the Olympics. She moves her arms and body in the direction she wants her sled to go — she's visualizing it.

SETTING YOUR PERSONAL INTENTION

You've already decided on the message you're giving your audience — what you want the audience to do with what that precious information you'll be giving them (if you haven't, check out Chapter 6). Now you need to decide what you, personally, want to get out of the presentation. Sure, you want the company to buy your product, or the students to buy your idea, or the crowd to laugh at your joke about the groom. But you need to gear some of your intention toward self-growth.

Part of what you're doing is about you getting better as a presenter. Athletes and actors do this, and so should you. After all, you're reading this book, so you must want to improve every aspect of your presentation skills, correct?

So ask yourself this when visualizing your speech: If it's the objective for yourself to become better, what do you need to accomplish in order to do that? Think of it on a small, detail-oriented level. For instance, I am a fast talker, so I feel all of you fast talkers out there. My main intention when giving a workshop is to explain each point as slower and clearly as I can.

TIP

Try this visualization: Walk with purpose onto the stage. Maybe it's just you stepping up to the spot, or maybe it's you walking from one room to another. But visualize all the minutae. Is the stage smooth, like hardwood, or carpeted? Put your notes on the lectern. Hear the flipping of the pages. Find the remote for your slide show (if you're including one) and click to go to the first slide. How big is the remote? Does it fit easily in your hand? Go through all the points of the presentation. See the audience engaging with you. Hear the applause at the end of your presentation.

Breathing

You've gone through your breathing exercises in your warmup. But as you get to the room where you're going to present, you turn the corner and your breathing starts coming fast and shallow. It's that anxiety once again, stopping you from breathing as you should.

Settle yourself down. Stop in the bathroom and breathe. I know from a reliable source (me) that a bathroom stall is usually big enough to do the backward circle breathing exercise in Chapter 20.

Making the most of the microphone

To be heard, you need to breathe to your full capacity and pronounce consonants clearly at the end of your words, as I've said throughout. Generally, that's all you're going to need to do. However, if the room is really big, you may need some help. Microphones can be your friend in that case.

But watch out — mics can also be your foe. Vocal coach Patsy Rodenburg in her book *The Right to Speak* (Routledge, 1993) agrees that a microphone can help you to be heard, but points out it also "exposes your speech flaws."

REMEMBER

When using a mic, speak just as you would without a mic — in a conversational tone.

For a handheld mic, just like the name says, you hold onto it. Remember that you're speaking into it to be heard. And generally, even if the top is round, you must speak into the very tip of it to get full amplification. So, if you're pointing to the lovely garden that the sixth grade class just planted, use your other hand to point. The minute you move the mic away from your face to gesture, the audience can't hear you. The optimal distance for a microphone to be away from your mouth is about three finger widths. Any closer and you might "pop" your *P*s, and any farther, it may not pick up your voice very well.

If you have a problem keeping the mic in front of your mouth, one trick you can try is holding the mic against your chest. Then, even when you turn your head, the mic follows you.

WARNING

Don't "eat the mic." This can happen when you're speaking too close to the mic. It creates a garbled sound, and the audience won't be able to hear you clearly. Plus, it looks really dumb.

TIP

If you're at the lectern and the mic was set up for the last guy who was really tall and you're not, take the time to position the mic so that you will be heard. Never ever lean into the lectern or lean over the mic to be heard. Remember how much body language comes into play here. Always be cognizant of what your body is doing. Plus, how are you breathing if you're scrunched over?

If they give you a lavalier mic (a tiny one that's pinned to your shirt or jacket), make sure you don't have any jewelry or a lapel pin that rubs against the mic. Also, remember to turn it off when you leave the stage. I was once in a musical where an actor forgot to do that and went to the washroom. It was quite an unexpected number.

If you have a wireless headset mic, again, watch that you don't wear any jewelry that will knock against it. And make sure it's comfortable. If you haven't practiced with one, try to give it a go before your presentation.

TIP

Make sure to have a sound check prior to your presentation. Ask the technician to make adjustments during your presentation if the sound is too little or not enough.

Connecting to your audience even before you've met them

I have a dear friend who is a talented actor. Part of her preparation before a performance is to touch all the seats in the theater. Sounds strange, I know, but it works for her. Now, if the house (audience) is a large one, touching every seat is going to take a long time. So she completes one section one day, and another the next day, until she touches all the seats. It's totally weird, but her idea is that she wants to connect with the people in those seats. She wants to feel their presence. You too want to share your ideas emotionally, vocally and physically. This may not include touching the seats, but you should have the idea at least of being connected.

If you're giving a presentation out of town, get to the space the night before if you can. If the building is closed, go early the next day, even if you're presenting later. We stress ourselves with the unknown and the what-ifs. I always feel more confident after I see the space.

If you're presenting in the hotel you're staying in, sweet-talk the hotel staff into letting you go in and take a look around.

FINAL CHECKLIST

- **Eat:** Your presentation might not occur at a luncheon, so make sure to have food available to eat before a later presentation. Eat something healthy — don't fill up on junk food.

- **Warm up:** Have you warmed up? The answer is yes, of course.

- **Check your clothes:** Do they make you feel fabulous? Do they feel comfortable? Can you move in them?

- **Jewelry:** Are you wearing any jewelry that might interfere with the mic if you're using one?

- **Practice:** Go through your speech one last time.

- **Name of your contact and his or her contact info:** Sounds silly, but if you were booked a while ago to speak and you're like me and forget what you had for breakfast, remembering a name may be difficult. Bring the business card or enter it into your phone.

- **Equipment:** Did you remember your laptop, USB stick, or slide deck? Go ahead and pack a pencil with an eraser, just in case you need to add or delete any notes.

- **Your speech:** Yes, it's a good idea to bring this along. Either on a piece of paper or cue cards. Be easy on yourself and use a big font size — like, say, 18. You never know what the lighting will be like. Even if you've practiced to the nth degree, always bring your speech. You don't need to look at it, but it is nice to know that it's there. Kind of like a security blanket.

- **Water bottle:** I'm sure your venue will supply a glass or bottle of water for you. But sometimes the water is not in the room yet or the jug has to be filled, or there's some other reason that you don't have any water. You should always have water beside you when you present. No need to go through the speech with a dry mouth. If you feel anxious about your presentation or that you might drop the glass, bring the water bottle up with you.

- **Props or visuals:** If you're using these, don't forget them.

- **Toothbrush and toothpaste:** No explanation needed here.

- **Glasses:** If you sometimes wear reading glasses, bring them, even if you think you won't need them.

- **Business cards:** I know people can Google you, but having your business cards handy is good for business. Plus then you can ask for someone else's and connect with a follow-up email.

6

It's Show Time: Plying Your Trade

Ace your interview by employing your public speaking skills, divining your strengths, and selling yourself.

Engage others with witty and lively conversation, see how to avoid being a wallflower, and use manners and politeness to win anyone over.

Realize it's all in your attitude by putting "failure" in perspective, knowing that nobody wants you to fail, and discovering your creativity through improv and ad-libbing.

» Telling people about you

» Knowing when to speak and when not to

Chapter **17**

Acing the Interview

So, you've got your chance at your dream job. Or maybe it's the job that will get you to where you need to *be* to acquire your dream job. Your resume is set. It's as good as it's going to get — your whole career summed up on a page. That's it, right? They pick the best candidate, who has the best resume, the best job experience, the best references?

For some jobs, sure. Maybe they even have their mind set before they meet the candidates. But you have one final push to swing that vote your way: a real-life meeting. An interview.

An interview isn't just an opportunity to gain a competitive edge — it can also spell your downfall. People with performance anxiety can fall to those who tend to fare better at speaking in public. Employers, no matter how serious or quantitative in their analysis of candidates, can always be swayed by charisma. We are human after all.

REMEMBER

You *can* ace your interview. Becoming a better interviewee takes practice, but is well worth the effort.

Becoming an Expert on You

Before you start the process of compiling your portfolio and references and seeking an interview, I hope at some point you stop and reflect. Do you really want that job? Because if you only kind of want it, don't go through the trouble. Going for a job, especially one that is important to your career, will take a lot of effort — especially if you have to work on your interviewing skills. And it *should* take effort if it's really important to you. You should want to put the time in.

You've decided that you do indeed want that job? Great. That's the first thing you have to know about yourself that pertains to this job. Next, you want to know what the interviewer is going to ask you. What you need, besides an elevator pitch (see Chapter 18), is to build a narrative about what's brought you to this point that you can give to the interviewer. That's not necessarily a traditional story with a beginning, middle, and end. Rather, it's a narrative to augment your resume with experiences that pertain to the job. You don't have to recite it all at once, but the elements should be in place so you can bring them up at different times in the interview.

EXERCISE: CREATING THE NARRATIVE OF YOUR CAREER

So you've got your CV handy in front of you. Now get out a second piece of paper and write out all the career events that you have on your CV. They should already be isolated for those that pertain to the job you're applying for, so if you haven't done that already, do it. Now, under the headings about your other jobs, write down how having done that job will help you do this prospective job. Once you have it all figured out, memorize them in a way that you can give the interviewer a succinct reason why doing a particular job makes you uniquely capable to do the job you're interviewing for.

You should prepare this stuff because you will be asked this stuff. The interviewer has already looked at your resume. Now he or she wants to see *you*. Just like when you give a speech, the audience want to get a feeling from you. The feeling you need to exude for the interviewer consists of trust, confidence that you can do the job, and the assurance that you'll be the right fit for the team. Your narrative is the story of why you are the best person for the job.

Just like when giving a speech, you are persuading the prospective employer that you are right for the job. Prepare to answer these important questions during your interview:

» Why are you the right fit?

» What assets to you have that will be of help?

» What transferable skill do you have?

EXERCISE: TALKING ABOUT YOU AS A PERSON

Practice talking about who you are — beyond your career. Often you'll first get an open-ended question: "So, tell us a little about yourself." Remember, your resume is already on the desk. If you've done the exercise about creating your career narrative, you've got a pretty good idea about what you need to say when that sort of talk comes up. What an interviewer also wants to know is who you are. So let's do another exercise, shall we?

You already know the story of you. You add to it every day, and with every life milestone. Maybe you have a pretty good monologue ready to go when you're out with new people and they inquire. Well, this is like that. But now it should be tailored to the person and company you're trying to impress.

You don't have a lot of time. Get in and get out. Starting with, "Uh, well, I was born in, um . . ." Tick, tock! Sure, you can tell them where you were born, but get to it efficiently. You've just lost precious time with "uh" and "um." Interviewers are busy people. They have allotted only so much time for the interview.

So sketch out your background, where you were born, your mom and dad's occupations, your siblings, your favorite subjects in school, your extracurricular activities and hobbies. Whenever you can, connect your background to the job you're going for. It doesn't have to be totally applicable, but any connecting is good and may be remembered. Think of funny anecdotes about yourself. Humility and a willingness to laugh at yourself can go a long way toward endearing you to an interviewer.

Grab a piece of paper and a pen. Write down each major "plot point" in your life. This can be in whatever form you choose. Capture each stage of your life that you think you want to mention. Then go back and really personalize it using anecdotes, stories, and examples. Now go back and edit it to only contain the essence of what you want to reveal, because, as I said, you'll only have so much time.

>> Can you roll with the punches and be adaptable and flexible?

>> What are your weaknesses?

>> Do you blame your previous employer for laying you off?

>> Do you respect other workers?

>> Are you a problem solver?

>> Are you friendly and a team player?

>> Do you go on a tangent when asked a specific question, or are you clear and to the point?

Becoming an Expert on the Industry and Organization

Once you know who you are and what you're about, then it's your job to find out everything about the employer and the industry it's in. Knowledge is power, and the more you know about who they are, the better your chance to fit in. Here are some ideas on getting started:

The first thing you want to do is research the market that the company thrives in, especially if you're new to the industry. Here are a few notes you should make about the industry:

>> **What exactly does the company do?**

   This one should be easy, but sometimes it's not so cut and dried. It's not necessarily what you'll do as an employee, but what the company does in general. How does it work? What is its revenue stream, and how has it gotten there?

>> **What is the market like?**

   What has the history of the market been so far? What are some trends you note in the market? Where might the market be headed?

>> **Who are its competitors?**

   By knowing a company's competitors, you know what the company, and hopefully you, are up against. You should also note how it stacks up. Is it a little fish in a big pond? Is it a multinational with near-monopoly control?

Let's say you're applying for a job in sales for a music company. What is the main product that it sells? Is it in direct competition with a company that's offering the same product?

❯❯ What is the company's market analysis like?

Where is it trending? Is it a publicly traded company? How has it done historically? How long has it been at this? How is it doing? What is its reputation in the market?

❯❯ Is there a mission statement?

What's the company's purpose, in its own words? It's important to give the missions statement a read before stepping into an interview — in fact, memorize it if you can. The mission statement may sound jingoistic, but it can give you a good idea about a company's priorities, what it considers important, what its culture may be like, and what type of employees it's looking for.

❯❯ Do you know any people working there?

Ask them about their experience at the company.

❯❯ What's its social media presence like?

Check social media: Facebook, Twitter, Instagram, LinkedIn, and the company's own website. Can you get a sense of the company's personality? How active is it online?

Find out who's working for the company. What kind of experience do they have? You might even find out who worked in the position you applied for. How does your experience stack up?

❯❯ How are the reviews of the company and its products and services?

Use Google (www.google.com) or your favorite search engine to find out what customers are saying about the company. Search "Company Name" + "reviews" or "complaints." See if people are talking about the company on Yelp (www.yelp.com).

Take reviews with a grain of salt. Some may not be true — anybody can post anything anonymously. If there's a name attached to the review, take that more seriously. If you can, contact such reviewers.

❯❯ Has the company been in the news lately? Good or bad?

❯❯ How active is it in the community?

❯❯ Where do you see yourself fitting in?

TIP

I personally go to the company website and look for a client list and read their testimonials. These aren't necessarily the most accurate, because they will all be cherry-picked, good testimonials, but it might give you an idea of what kind of service they value. You might try contacting a few clients and seeing if they'll talk more about the company.

Take a look at perks and special events the company provides for its employees. A few companies where I've given workshops allow their employees to bring their dogs to work, for example. Some have yoga at lunch. Check to see if your values align with the company's.

Checking Out the Interviewers

You may already have been told your interviewer's name and title. If not, depending on how high up in the company you intend to be placed, you may be able to figure out who's going to interview you.

Start with the company website, where you should see descriptions of the leadership team — the CEO, VPs, office managers, and so on. There may even be pictures of the entire company.

TIP

Check out social media to find out more about the interviewers. LinkedIn, for example, is a great way to find out more about someone, including things like past education. Maybe the company just won an award, or posted something funny on Twitter. Find an opportune time in the interview to remark about it. This shows that you've done some research and are interested in the company.

Ask around. Somebody knows somebody who knows something. Try to remember a few faces so that when you meet them at your interview or walking down the hall you can greet them and use their name. Bonus points!

Using Body Language in the Interview

Don't forget the importance of body language. You could be saying all the right things, but if you're fiddling with your hair, that's what the interviewer will fixate on and — probably — remember. Sit on the edge of the chair with your feet planted on the floor. As I recommend when standing at the lectern, feel energy flow through your body up past the crown of your head.

TIP

Look the interviewer in the eyes. Here's what that does for you:

>> It helps you focus.

>> It compels the interviewer to look back at you rather than down at his phone or your resume.

>> It makes you look more confident. When we're intimidated, we look away. That's a sign of a lack of confidence.

>> Focus. You should be as interested in the interviewer every bit as much as the interviewer is interested in you. You want to find out about the company. This is your chance. Turn it around and ask *her* questions.

>> If more than one person is conducting the interview, take the time to look at everyone at some point.

Avoiding the don'ts of interviews

Here are things you should try to avoid doing as much as possible:

>> **Looking down when thinking of what to say next:** This collapses your body into the down and in pose, which, as you know, I have forbidden. Try to look up, even when you're thinking.

>> **Touching your face:** This could be perceived as nervousness or trying to soothe yourself.

>> **Tapping your foot:** It might be a nervous habit, but it signifies boredom.

>> **Crossing your arms:** This makes it look like you have something to hide or are feeling negative or defensive.

>> **Slouching:** You're not watching TV.

>> **Biting your lip:** Lip biting looks like you're nervous or you want to say something but you're holding back.

>> **Crossing your legs:** It may be an innocent habit, but it looks like you are being closed in and reserved.

>> **Locking your ankles:** This looks like you're anxious.

>> **Looking at your watch during the interview:** The interviewer is taking the time to meet with you. Make sure you've allotted plenty of time to answer all questions and never appear rushed.

>> **Touching parts of your body:** Tapping your thigh with your fingers, moving your hand up and down your arm, and fiddling with your hair all make you look like you're nervous.

Practicing the do's of interviews

Here are a few tips on what you should be doing during an interview:

>> **Adopting an up and out pose:** This makes you feel and look alert, confident, and focused.

>> **Planting your feet on the floor:** This stabilizes and balances you so you're not thinking about your balance or what to do with your legs.

>> **Sitting on the edge of your chair:** If you sit back, it looks like you're a tad too comfortable. It may also look like you don't much care. You want to look eager, but not too eager. Sitting on the edge of your chair makes you seem more engaged. If the chair is too short and your feet dangle in the air, take the time to put the chair down to your height. You want your feet planted on the ground so that you feel rooted and confident. You might even make light of it: "This always happens to me in boardroom meetings. It started in kindergarten!"

>> **Using your hands and gesturing:** If you're sitting around a boardroom table, make sure your hands are visible. You don't want the interviewer wondering what you're doing with your hands when they're under the table. That takes away from what you're saying. Move your hands in a horizontal plane from your navel. See Chapter 15 for more on this.

TIP

Use "the Merkel." The Chancellor of Germany is famous for steepling her fingers. Doing so makes you look confident. Don't do it all the time, though. Be sure to vary your hand gestures.

Public Speaking: The Interview Edition

Maybe you've just been asked a question that takes some thought. Some people tend to freak out at this. You're not always going to know the answer right away. Interviewers will wait for you if they can tell you're trying to construct a good answer.

REMEMBER

Go ahead and take a few breaths. If you stop breathing, you stop thinking.

You may be tempted to stall with something like, "That's a really good question." Of course it's a good question because the interviewer asked it. Even if it were a *lousy* question, this could be your future employer. Some of my clients say they need that time to formulate the answer. If they just took the time to breathe and think in silence, they would come up with the answer even quicker.

Getting the questions in advance

At least some of the company's standard interview questions may be available and may even be on the company website. Go look. Or contact your recruiter and ask him what the company is looking for and what the interviewers might ask (after you review your email or notes — someone may have already told you).

Even if you can't find the questions, there are some questions you should know the answers to well in advance:

» What do you know about our company?

» Why do you want this job?

» Why do you think you're right for the job?

» What are your strengths?

» What are your weaknesses?

Be humble. Tell the truth!

» Can you tell me about a challenging situation in your previous job and how you handled it?

» Do you have any questions?

You should have some. After all, you're making a change and you want to know if this company is a good fit. You're interviewing them too. Make sure you bring questions with you and take note if they haven't been addressed in the interview.

Don't be thrown by odd questions. Companies sometimes like to sneak in unexpected questions. A friend of mine is a financial advisor. When he went for his interview at a big firm, he was asked whether he had ever played sports. He was able to say he had played basketball all through school. After he got the job, he asked why that question was asked in the interview. "Because we wanted to know if you were a team player." If you were in a team sport for a single season, don't forget to mention it. If you were never into sports, though, that's okay. I wasn't either. I found my team in theater. Were you in any clubs in school? What about student council? Remember, try to always answer with a positive.

Revealing what you intend to do

For an entry-level job, you might be asked what transferable skills you have that would help the company. Be ready to make suggestions about how your skills might be applied in specific circumstances.

DON'T LIE

Please don't lie in your interview. Lying usually changes your body language and breathing patterns, and many interviewers are well aware of this. If you think I'm lying, check out ex-FBI agent Joe Navarro's book *What Every Body Is Saying* (Harper-Collins, 2008). Even if they don't detect you at the time, eventually you will get found out, and until that happens you'll be worrying about it.

The summer between my first and second year of undergrad, I went back home and looked for a job. By late spring, a lot of the jobs had been scooped up. Eventually I found a server job opening at a new restaurant. Had I ever waited on tables before? No — but I'd carried plates of food from the kitchen to the dining room for years, and I was studying acting. I decided *server* would be my new role. When I was asked in the interview how many years I'd been serving, I puffed up my body like a proud (but scared inside) peacock and replied rather loudly, "Many! Many!"

My first shift was at lunch. The restaurant was busy, and I had no idea what I was doing. The owner came up to me and snorted, "You've never been a server, have you?" Busted!

Remember that funny picture you posted on social media of you doing something with you know who? Be prepared to explain it. You've Googled the company to find info about it. Rest assured, it's done the same to you.

For a senior-level job, you might be asked what your 30-, 60-, and 90-day plans are. Here you need to tread lightly and mind your language. If you start declaring that you intend to overhaul the shipping schedule within a month, you may look overly ambitious and cocky. And who knows — the interviewer might have been the person who designed the current schedule.

You should be able to offer suggestions and a plan in order to show your capabilities. What you need to do is focus on what you can *add* to the company, not what you'll have to inevitably *subtract.*

How about this: "From looking at your delivery dates (bonus points for that since you actually took the time to research them), what *might* work smoother would be scheduling different dates for each category of product. That way there could be less confusion around the plant."

Faking it till you're making it

There is always a lot said about faking it till you make it. How do you sit when you're waiting in the reception area? Hunched over, reviewing your notes or looking at your phone? That's a down and in position — a no-no. When you're in this position your breath is impeded and your confidence is low. Social psychologist Amy Cuddy calls that a *low power pose.*

If you're seated with feet flat on the floor and feeling energy flowing up through your body past the crown of your head, on the other hand, you're more confident and you're breathing deeper "into your belly." Amy Cuddy calls that a *high power pose.* A high power pose when standing is putting your hands on your hips or your arms out in a V in over your head. In one study, she had a group of people adopt either a low or high power pose for 2 minutes. Then they went into an interview to apply for a job. The interviewers gave absolutely no responses, verbal, or nonverbal — which can be very stressful, as the interviewee is getting no feedback. The taped 5-minute interviews were given to a group of computer programmers who knew nothing about the experiment. The coders were asked whom they would pick for the job. Everyone picked the high power posers, regardless of their answers.

TIP

I recommend watching Amy Cuddy's TED Talk on body language if you're interested in learning more: www.ted.com/talks/amy_cuddy_your_body_language_shapes_who_you_are.

REMEMBER

Not only can you fake it till you make it, you can actually change the way you think and feel about yourself as well.

Needless to say, you should always be in an up and out pose during an interview — but not, however, with hands on hips or arms out in a V. Do the full-on high power pose in the comfort of your home before the interview. Adopt it even before you get there. Practice sitting at the interview. How would you normally sit? Would you be down and in? Practice sitting up and out and see how good it feels.

What should you do if the interviewer is in a down and in position? Should you match it or stick with your up and out position? I'll give you one guess. When you're in a down and in position, you're looking at the ground, breathing from your upper chest, and probably have little if anything to say. If you're both in that position, the interview will most likely go nowhere. So maintain your up and out position. You may even inspire the interviewer to look you in the eyes and adopt your pose. Test this with a colleague at work and see what happens.

Using your words positively

When our son Jack lived at home, he had a few chores around the house, including collecting the garbage before garbage day. Often I texted him a reminder. Instead of, "Don't forget that garbage day is tomorrow," I'd say, "Remember, tomorrow is garbage day." Instead of insinuating that he's a forgetful kid, I focused the subject of my concern on the garbage.

Interviewers want to know as much as they can about you, and that includes your weaknesses. They will get a sense of you from how you frame your responses. Being positive isn't just being in a state of optimism — it's also how you view everyday things. There's a range of answers, good and bad, that you can give to tough questions. For instance, if you are asked why you abruptly left your last employer, don't say, "He was a complete jerk!" Maybe he was, but do you want to really talk about him like that? You want to land the job. A kinder, gentler way might be, "He liked things a certain way and I appreciated that, but we just didn't jibe."

Looking like you already work there

Looking like you have the job is about more than just clothing. It starts with how you carry yourself. First off, adopt and up and out pose. You want to exude confidence. Act as if you're already part of the team. You're comfortable in your surroundings here, and this is a place where you would flourish.

Clothing is important too. When I would go to an audition for theater or film, I would try to dress the part. If it was for a woman who was a horse trainer and lived on the farm (and, surprisingly, a few roles were like this), I wouldn't arrive at the audition in heels, sundress, and lots of makeup. Some horse trainers, I'm sure, wear that kind of stuff, but generally people in that field don't. I was dressing more to the perception the directors had of my character, or what I thought would be their perception, anyway. I didn't want the auditioners to have to work too hard to see whether I was right for the part. So wear the clothes that you would wear if you already had the job, but also wear clothes that are going to look good. In the case of the horse trainer, I wouldn't come into the interview looking like I just came from the barn wearing jeans laden with horse manure. I would come in what they called in the olden days *my Sunday best.*

TIP

There are some exceptions to this: Obviously if you are interviewed for a job as a safety inspector in an oil field, you wouldn't come to the interview in overalls and dirty boots. Wear clothes that up the game. Maybe it would be a suit and tie.

Convincing yourself you already have the job

Olympic swimmers don't get prepped for a race by thinking, *I hope I do well!* They're thinking, *I'm going to win.* That's how you have to think about an interview. Don't allow yourself a contingency plan.

Chapter 11 talks about the power of visualization. If you *see* yourself giving a great presentation, you can tap into that feeling when you actually give the presentation. Same thing with the interview. You want this job? See yourself in it. We see ourselves and others doing negative things all the time. It's much easier than seeing positively, that's for sure. "If that neighbor blows his weeds in my yard one more time!" Give yourself a chance to visualize something positive. See the office. It doesn't have to be the actual office, because you probably haven't seen it yet. Visualize what you will offer, how you will contribute to the success of the company, how you'll connect with your colleagues.

TIP

Look back at your career narrative every time you start feeling negative. Get it in your head that you're ready to take on this job.

Competing factors

So, there's someone else you know who is going for the job. Big deal. You have the tools to be in contention, and to get that job. Maybe this person has something you don't. So what? Nobody's perfect. Don't worry about the negatives — concentrate on your positives.

You're getting the opportunity to strut your stuff. Yes, remind yourself that it's an opportunity. It's not a chore. The chore might be the job you're in now.

What happens if you know your competition personally or they have worked at the company before? This occurred in theater all the time. I'd be at the audition waiting out in the hallway with some other actors. The director would come out for a break and would see the group sitting there. In the group was a friend of his or someone who was in his play previously. "Hi, how are you? How's your baby?" This not only made the rest of us feel inadequate, it also put the director in an awkward position.

REMEMBER

Just knowing people isn't enough to grab the position. If it were, why are they holding interviews?

Note that this goes for you, too, if you think you have an in. You need to be professional and take this job interview seriously, regardless of your familiarity with your interviewer. Even if you know the CEO or have worked at the company before, don't assume you'll get the job. Imagine that this is the first time you're meeting the interviewer. Prepare every bit as hard as you would if you had never heard of the company before.

Mastering the Q&A session

The question and answer portion of an interview can be an anxious time. Just remember that the employer has asked you to the interview. Just like when you're giving a presentation, the interviewer, like the audience, wants you to succeed.

Start by remembering your breathing. And don't mutter and mumble. Instead of the dreaded "um," just breathe and think quietly of what you need to say. The interviewer will wait.

The second thing is to be prepared. I've worked with a couple of politicians, and they always have a list of common questions that they get. You may not want to be a politician, but in an interview you're doing essentially what a politician does: getting someone to like you.

Don't just think of answers. Practice saying your answers out loud. You want to sound polished and confident. You'll lose the impact if you fumble for your words. Practice them in a conversational style. You're not Winston Churchill giving a speech — you're you. That's what the employer wants to see.

WARNING

Listen intently to each question. The last thing you want to have to say is that you didn't hear what they said. It makes it sound like you aren't paying attention.

Remembering that you are the expert

Whether you're onstage giving a speech or presenting yourself at an interview, you are the boss. You have to think like it. It's the key to your confidence and the confidence the audience has in you.

When you're asked a question, go ahead and repeat it. By doing this, you make certain what you've heard is correct. It also gives you a jumping-off point to think about your answer.

Relying on interviewers too much to intervene and answer makes you look less confident and is a sure sign that they know more than you. And, of course, they do. But don't let them see this as a pattern.

Admitting you don't know the answer

For many people, the hardest thing to do in life is to admit that they don't know something that they feel they really should know. It hurts the ego. But sometimes admitting what you don't know shows good character. We are only human. We won't know everything.

I'm questioned a lot in my field, especially when I make business people in suits "brr" their lips like a horse during an exercise. I have to have my answers at the ready. For example, why do I do things this way? But sometimes a question stumps me. That's when I have to bury my ego and admit that I don't know but will find out. This is how I usually phrase it: "Wow, I never thought of that before. I'll find out and get back to you."

Being vulnerable

It is hard to reveal vulnerability in an interview. You're trying to look strong, right? You can't let your guard down. However, you're not perfect. So it's all right to show a little personality. But be careful with what you share. It has to be genuine.

WARNING

Don't get super personal, and don't share personal stories that you haven't worked through. You don't want to confide tearfully at the interview that you were the youngest in your family and your older siblings teased you out of jealousy because your parents spent a lot of time with you. Who will hire you if you're emotionally distraught?

Go ahead and tell stories about your weaknesses or dumb mistakes — just make sure there is an important lesson in there somewhere. It could involve personal or professional growth. Just telling a story for the sake of it may harm your chances.

When I applied for my second job as a server, I was asked if anything had ever gone wrong and how I dealt with it. You can bet I had plenty of stories of my time at the first restaurant that had hired me, which was called Rasputin's. Canada's national drink is the Bloody Caesar, or simply, the Caesar. It's essentially a Bloody Mary if you swap out the tomato juice for Clamato juice and serve it with a celery stick. Rasputin's was family run, and the bartender was new at his job. The recipe in the cocktail recipe book called for a stalk of celery. Not huge, just a small one. This bartender liked to put in a 10-inch celery stalk, which poked 5 inches out of the glass — really top heavy. I'll bet you can tell where this is going. A table of four ordered these drinks, and the drinks were put on a thin silver serving tray, so they wobbled as I walked. As I was passing them out, yes, one of the drinks flipped over the head of one of the guests, spilling the drink right on top of him. The funny thing was that even though the contents spilled out, the glass and the celery stalk landed right side up. "Cool," I blurted. And those who hadn't had Canada's national drink spilled on them agreed. Telling that story gave the interviewer a sneak peak into my personality. And unless I'm interviewing to be a server, it doesn't do much harm.

REMEMBER

At the end of it all, you want to leave the interview having given the employer a feeling — one of trust, authenticity, and the conviction that you would be a real asset to the company.

Chatting like a Champ: Phone Interviews

You may be of the opinion that phone interviews are easier than face-to-face ones, because all the interviewer hears is your voice. You can do whatever with your face, right? You can be in your pajamas, for all that person knows.

But that just-hearing-your-voice thing? It can be your undoing.

Once upon a time, there was *only* radio. No TV. And people gathered around and listened to radio dramas. They heard every door slam, every new character who came onto the scene, every wail or moan. And all they could do was listen and use their imagination for the rest.

The voice can reveal so much. I've heard interviews with people who I was sure had just woken up. Some can be forgiven, of course. Athletes forced to give an interview right after a competition are in that boat. But you, during a phone interview? No excuse. If you're anxious, and your voice is shaking, they'll hear it. There are no other senses to help form a better impression. Interviewers will hear it even more over the phone because that's all they're getting. They're not helped by your snazzy clothes, good posture, helpful gestures, or being looked in the eye.

Phone interview don'ts

Here are some things you'd better not do in a phone interview:

>> **Have a dog or a child in the room:** As much as I love them both, this is not the time to tell a curious toddler you can't read them a story right now, and it's definitely not the time to hear a dog barking or whining.

>> **Chew candy or gum:** This is really distracting when you're seen doing it. *Nobody* wants to hear you chomping on the phone.

>> **Interrupt:** Be in the moment and listen to what is being said before answering.

Phone interview do's

Following are tips for having a successful phone interview:

>> **Warm up your voice and your body a wee bit:** Get that blood flowing and your breath going. See the next section for ideas.

>> **Wear the clothes that make you feel great:** Sweats might make you feel great in a certain way, but that way is probably unrelated to your job or

interview. Much better to dress the part. Wear clothes that you would wear if you were attending a function for the company.

>> **Sit in an up and out position:** Sitting, that means on the edge of your chair, with your feet flat on the floor.

>> **Focus on the task at hand:** You are talking to potential employers.

>> **Set your phone so incoming calls go directly to voice mail:** Minimize distractions. You don't want the call interrupted by voice dropouts, which can sometimes happen when a call comes in.

>> **Have your resume and other documents nearby:** You want to be able to refer to dates and old employment details. If you did the exercises in this chapter, have those at the ready as well. And your list of questions.

>> **If you're near a computer, have the company's website up on your screen:** You may need to refer to something on it.

>> **Have a glass of water or water bottle nearby:** But make sure it's ice-free so it doesn't sound like cocktail hour!. Drink water if you need it.

>> **Listen to what is being said:** Concentrate and focus on the other side of the conversation.

Warming up for your interview

I know you're tired of me saying this, but you need to warm up. It doesn't have to be so arduous as in Chapter 22. You don't have to do a full warmup like you should when giving a 20-minute speech, but please do a few things.

If you have no time to do any cardio beforehand — and you should if you do have time — march around your house or office before you go to the interview. Move your arms. For added excitement, add a "fff" while you're marching. This helps drop your breath so it feels like it's going deep into your lower abdomen.

After you've caught your breath from marching and breathing, stand in one spot and try to feel your breath dropping low into your belly. Breathe in for a count of four and out for four. Breathe in through your nose and out through your nose or mouth. Breathing in through your nose helps calm you and drop the breath lower. Repeat a few rounds.

Pant a little to support your breath. When you're supported like that, your voice has more power and you sound confident.

Start humming. Humming helps open up your resonators, as explained in Chapter 13, and gives you a rich tone.

Go through a few rounds of the tongue twisters in Chapter 12. Make sure to speak them clearly and change inflection.

Visualize yourself walking through the company door, meeting the receptionist, and then going into the interview. Visualize a great conversation. Chapter 11 talks more about visualization.

Make it affirmative: Repeat a phrase that makes you feel great and gets you in the winning mindset. Does "I am a success" work for you? A little too contrived? How about "I am a rock star"? Whatever it is, find something that makes you feel great.

Don't use "I will be a success." Make it in the present. "I am a success" makes the affirmation more immediate and impactful.

Greeting the greeter

First impressions are made in the first few seconds of an interaction. The first person you see when you go for an interview won't always be the interviewer. It may be the receptionist. Your greeter will say hello in a friendly manner. Give her a greeting right back, regardless of her position in the company. Repeat her name back to them and say it's nice to meet her. Make her feel like she is important. Treating everyone in the company with respect will only help your position, especially if you get the job. Plus, you don't know what kind of power people really wield. This helps to make you feel more comfortable, and the receptionist will feel that too. If you succeed in making a good impression, the greeter may even comment about you when you're gone.

I have a friend who is a wonderful musician and actor. She often accompanies singers on the piano in auditions for musicals. When you go for an audition, you usually talk to the director for a bit, and maybe perform your monologue. Then you give your sheet music to the accompanist. My friend tells me that sometimes the actor just hands her the music without saying anything. First off, the actors should always at least tell the pianist the tempo they'd like — it's a convention. Secondly, you should just always say hello to the person who is playing for you. And at the end, a thank-you wouldn't hurt either. As may happen after you leave your interview, at the end of the day the director often asks my friend who she thought would be right for the part. If she didn't make a personal connection with the actor, she can't remember that actor.

When you're waiting in the reception area, don't look at your phone. If it is the bank manager emailing that you didn't get the approval for your mortgage, you don't want to take that feeling into the interview. Your interview is only as good as the day you give it. Try your best, and that is all you can do.

You are sitting outside of the office, the door opens and your interviewer walks out and says your name. In you go, and the game is on! If you're lucky, the interviewer will ask you if you found parking, or if you've having a good day. This is the opportunity to respond with a story. Not a long one, but not meaningless small talk either. You could explain that you went around the parking garage a couple of times and then finally found a spot right next to the elevator. Or that you just had a wonderful walk with your dog in the dog park. Just a couple of sentences will do. It will help the interviewer get to know you in a more personal way.

Winding things up

Remember to thank the interviewer for taking the time for meeting you today both at the beginning and at the end of the interview.

Shake the interviewer's firmly and say it was a pleasure to meet him or her. No one will hire someone who enters the room and gives a limp handshake (see Chapter 18). Remember to look interviewers in the eye.

TIP

Thank-you notes may seem a thing of the past, and that is one reason why you should write one. You will stand out. A written — yes, written — note of thanks has huge impact. It reveals to interviewers that you care. Regardless of whether you get the job or not, send a thank-you note. Your card will remind them of you. If you don't get the job, they will remember you and that might benefit you the next time they are hiring.

WARNING

If you talked to more than one interviewer, *don't* send a group email. That's tacky. Send it to the lead interviewer.

Chapter **18**

Engaging in Witty Repartee

I like to talk. I always have. One of my favorite things to do is to get to know people. I'm confident in my ability to do that alone. When I'm at a function or a party with my husband, we aren't glued at the hip. We wander away from each other, grabbing food or looking for someone we know at the party. Both of us are confident enough to strike up a conversation with someone we don't know, and this ability to mingle and schmooze has helped both of us immeasurably in our careers.

Yes, you can meet new clients and employers this way. But it may not be the person you were talking to who ends up giving you work. That person might just be a reference. Since I went into business for myself, I've gotten a lot of work this way. In the beginning, it felt like coincidence. People would tell me, "I have an upcoming speech, and, boy, could I use some help." Or, "There is a gal in our company who speaks so fast we can hardly hear what she has to say — I'm going to give her your card." I soon realized that I needed to treat such face-to-face networking as if it's part of my job, and actively seek out opportunities while I'm at events and parties.

REMEMBER

The art of conversation is another kind of performance, like public speaking. When you are at an event, party, or really any type of gathering and you see an opportunity to further yourself in some way, you have to be *on*. You don't need to tap dance and be phony — but you are in performance mode. You want to exude the confidence that may get you or your company hired.

When it comes to conversation, some people are naturals. I'm not sure if I was, or if I learned it somehow, but I did manage to see the development of two people first-hand and watch their interactions: my children. My boys were never shy or reserved. After all, their mother was in theater and coached public speaking, and their father was a TV and radio announcer, so our conversations were always pretty lively.

When I took my son Patrick to his first day of kindergarten, I met the kids in his class. There was one girl whom I said hello to who didn't even look my way when she replied with a meek, "Hi." Through all her years of elementary school, this girl was so quiet. She was fine with her friends, but nervous around adults. One day after she graduated from college I happened to bump into her on the bus. She initiated a conversation and was interesting, and I so enjoyed our conversation. Something happened to her in her early adulthood. She totally changed. And so can you.

You know what introductions are, of course, but let's make this really clear: When you introduce yourself to new people, you are revealing to the other person or group of people that you would like to have a relationship, even a short one. It could be a business relationship, or just a short conversation.

Here's a checklist of what you should be doing when you introduce yourself to people:

>> **Give them your name and what you do.**

You know that cliche about first impressions? Well, here it is at work. Be clear about your name and what you do. That might mean explaining what your career is, or it might mean revealing why you're at the same event they are.

TIP

After you give your name, their name should follow. If it doesn't, prompt them. It should go without saying, but you're going to want to remember it. Make a *point* of remembering it. Associate the name with something that you are familiar with, or employ a bit of alliteration. For example, if his name is Rob Adams, you could think of the Adams Family. If her name is Frances, think of Friendly Frances. It looks horrible later if you don't remember their name, so find a way.

>> **Shake their hand.**

Offer your hand for a nice, firm shake. Look them in the eye when you do this.

Minding Your Manners

So you're at a place where you don't know anyone. First thing to do is to remember the rules of engagement: manners. This section helps you brush up on the basics:

>> **Don't wait for people to approach you.**

Remember school dances? The longer you wait to go talk to someone, the harder it will be. Your heart will beat faster, and you'll end up looking down at the floor.

TIP

Think of it in terms of meeting wildlife: They're just as scared and anxious as you are. So focus on others — not yourself. Think of what can you do to make *them* more comfortable.

>> **Be friendly and polite.**

No one wants to chat with a sourpuss. Being friendly helps break the ice.

WARNING

Don't pick on other people at the event to try to gain an ally. For example, don't badmouth that guy in the corner stuffing his face with cookies. He just might be a friend or boss of the person you're speaking to.

>> **Smile.**

People judge you by looking at your face. A smile makes you look and feel authentic. When you smile at people when you pass them in the street, they usually smile back. So start your conversation by smiling, and I bet the other person will too.

>> **Do your research.**

Find out who will be there. Ask the organizer prior to the event, or a colleague who will be there. Find out as much about the company or person attending as you can beforehand, using LinkedIn or Google whatever else you can think of. It could set you apart from whomever else they're considering.

Research can avoid embarrassment too. Many years ago my husband was asked to host a sports awards dinner in a smaller city. I was not into sports at that time — I was an actor. I had no idea who would be there or what the event would be like. We met one of the keynote speakers, and I asked his name, which he told me. "Oh, what do you do?" I asked. Turns out he was the Canadian curling champion. Apparently a very big deal. So now in the car on the way to an event, I always ask my husband who will be sitting at our table. Who is receiving the award?

>> **Know what's going on in our world.**

Read the news. Keep tabs on what's been happening in your community. If you're travelling to an event, find out what's happening there. Are there any hot bands, great restaurants, problems with city government? These things can form the basis of conversations that could lead anywhere.

>> **Make a list of things you're interested in.**

You know what interests you, of course. But remind yourself before one of these events. Some people are going to share your interests, or at least be able to engage in talking about them. Talking about pets and kids is a good fallback! We all have stories. Some might even know a bit about you before you meet. On social media, some people might follow you. Now when I meet new people they often comment on my dog, Artie, because my husband and I post pictures of him constantly. And he's mentioned a lot on my husband's radio show. Artie really needs his own Twitter account, come to think of it. You can ask about the wine you're drinking, for example. Where is it from? Do you prefer red or white? Have you tried that new blend from Australia?

>> **Find out about the person you are talking to.**

Just like when giving a speech, it's not all about you. I find this to be the most fun part — I become a detective. I ask, "And what brings you here?" At a vegetarian restaurant opening, a fellow I met told me, "My wife is with the bank" (that had funded the restaurant). "She thinks I should eat healthier, so here we are!" That got the conversation rolling.

TIP

Just like in school when you saw a kid lurking in the corner, seek out the person who is alone. Remember, that person's feeling just as uncomfortable as you are.

>> **Be complimentary.**

I was downtown once on my way to a client's office. I parked my car and noticed a crowd coming from the conference center. One woman was wearing the most stunning pair of shoes. When we both stopped to wait for the green light, I exclaimed, "I love your shoes!" That got a conversation going. She asked me what I did. I told her and asked her what was happening in the conference center. We exchanged business cards, and I gained a new client that day.

Finding something you really, genuinely like about others and letting them know about it is a great way in.

>> **Include others.**

Behind the wheel, you always have a sense of what other drivers around you are doing. When people are standing outside your circle looking like they want to get into the conversation, make room for them. Step back to let them in. Then introduce yourself.

>> **Pay attention to everyone.**

Remember rushing home to tell your parents you were excited about something? Maybe you made the team or aced a term paper. You got home, but your father was immersed in his newspaper and only responded with distracted grunts instead of praise. You know that feeling? Don't inflict that on those you're speaking to.

>> **Exit stage right on a good note.**

Even if it's been the most boring conversation you've ever had, leave people feeling better that you took the time to speak with them. Be polite when you leave. Have an appropriate excuse ready, like, "If you'd excuse me, I need to talk to the organizer," or, "I've really enjoyed our conversation but now I have to get back to my colleague."

Shaking hands

A good handshake creates a strong first impression. It reveals your confidence, instills trust, and starts to build a connection between you and the other person.

Keep your right hand free so it's ready to stick out there at any time. If you wash your hands, make sure they're dry before you reenter the social fray. Nothing worse than having to awkwardly dry your hands before you shake. Everyone knows where you've been!

Here are some tips on how to properly shake hands:

>> Stand up straight, in what I call the up and out posture.

>> Look the person in the eye.

>> Slide your right hand into the other person's right hand until you feel the web between that person's thumb and index finger meet yours.

>> Shake the hand firmly and hold on for no more than six seconds. Leave your other hand by your side — not in your pocket (you look like you're not too thrilled to meet this person) or clenched (are you looking to fight or do business?).

>> Shake hands up and down. Three times is a good rule. Remember, you aren't pumping gas.

Here are a few things you *shouldn't* do when shaking hands:

>> Don't give a limp shake. A limp handshake is a terrible feeling. People who shake their hand limply really seem as if they have no confidence in themselves or their company. Don't be that person.

>> Don't crush their hand either. Don't shake hands so tightly that you actually feel bones jamming together. I really hate this one. I completely forget what that person is saying.

>> Don't hold on too long. Shake for a few seconds, then release.

>> Don't hurry. It makes it seem like you want to be somewhere else.

>> Don't look around. It appears like you're not really interested in the other person, that you're already seeking someone more important.

>> Don't put your left hand in your pocket. Visible hands make you look honest. A hand in your pocket looks like you're not really committed to engaging with that person.

>> Don't fist bump. The fist bump may be fine with people you know, or people who know you're going to fist bump. But don't leave people in an awkward lurch when they expect a handshake.

TIP

Different cultures have different ways of greeting each other. In Joe Navarro's book *What Every Body Is Saying* (William Morrow, 2008), he says, "If someone gives you a weak handshake, don't grimace. If anyone takes your arm, don't wince. If you are in the Middle East and a person wants to hold your hand, hold it. If you are a man visiting Russia, don't be surprised when your male host kisses your cheek, rather than shakes your hand." Before you travel to a foreign country, find out the proper ways of greeting.

WARNING

I am a hugger. I hug my friends hello and goodbye. Sometimes clients hug me — but they ask me first if I want a hug. If you're at a function and see your good friend talking with someone you don't know, you can hug your friend, but don't be hugging someone you've never met.

Staying Engaged in the Conversation

Conversation is a two-way street. It's not a monologue, and you're not Hamlet. Conversation is about you *and* the other person. Give and take. Speak but also listen.

The listening part is something many of my clients have had trouble with in the past. And it's usually *not* because of narcissism. They don't love hearing themselves speak. In many ways, it's the opposite. Their anxiety makes them concentrate wholly on what they're saying, and in the process, their conversational partner's speech gets lost.

Here are a few tricks to think about to really be engaged in the conversation:

>> **Maintain eye contact with the person speaking.**

   This helps you focus on what is being said. But don't burn a hole in people's pupils like a weirdo. It's all right to look away sometimes. Just make sure you're giving them your full attention.

>> **Don't interrupt people who are speaking.**

   They have the floor. Wait your turn.

>> **Acknowledge your partner.**

   Nod or smile every once in a while. A simple "uh-huh" gives speakers a clue that you are listening. You can also repeat what they have said. The phrase "What you're saying is . . ." can go a long way in both showing people you get what they're talking about and in understanding it better.

>> **As Thumper said to Bambi, "If you can't say nothin' nice, don't say nothin' at all."**

   Unless you really want to start an argument, don't fervently disagree. If there's something you don't agree with, say it. But say it nicely. "I appreciate your opinion on this." Or "That's an interesting way of thinking about that."

Remembering names

I have to confess, I'm really bad at remembering names. I really try to make a conscious effort to remember a name. It's a common problem, and there are many reasons for it: You're focused on saying your own name, you're not really in the moment of the conversation, or, let's face it, you're not really interested. You would rather talk to that guy over there, and you totally blank on the name of the person you're actually talking to.

When I taught drama to kids, we'd play a name game on the first day to help everyone remember the names in the class. It was mostly for me, but hey, now you can use it too. It went like this: Think of a word that describes you that starts with the first letter of your name. I'm Alyson, so I'm thinking *A* . . . I could be Awesome Alyson or Avocado Alyson." The first person says her name: "I'm Awesome Alyson." The next repeats it and says hers: "She's Awesome Alyson and I'm Voracious Valerie." And so on around the room.

That's a good way to burn names into your brain, but in a normal conversation things go quickly. You can do the trick in your own mind. Associate the person's name with another word that begins with the same letter. It's not so much that the other word actually means much — it's more that the very act of repeating the name and associating it with another word gets you in remembering mode and will help later when you try to recall people's names.

Here's another tip, but it requires an accomplice. When my husband and I are at a function, if we see someone coming toward my husband to say hello, and I can tell my husband is trying to figure out who this person is, I simply put out my hand and say, "Hi, I'm Alyson." The person then says his or her name, and the crisis is averted. Try this if you're with a friend or partner. Sometimes in an emergency when my husband is suddenly ambushed by someone coming out of nowhere, he'll exclaim, "What a great event!" That's code for "Help me, honey!"

What if you can't hear the name or it's from a different culture and you're not familiar with it? Blame the noise in the room. "It's so darn loud in here," you can say. They might know that their name may not be familiar to you — you're probably not the first person who hasn't caught it the first time — but at least you're making an effort.

Ask people to spell out their name and then remember to repeat it a few times in conversation.

If there's a name you find strange, and you feel the urge to comment on that fact, revert to Thumper's rule: If you don't have anything good to say, don't say anything at all. You may think a name sounds "made up," for example. Well, all names are made up. Take a breath and continue the conversation.

Another common situation is that you've been introduced to someone and then see a colleague approaching. Your heart starts beating, and your mouth goes dry — you've forgotten the person's name already. He's right beside you and you met him just seconds ago. You hope and pray that the person will introduce himself again to your colleague. Sometimes people don't, and you introduce your colleague without any response from your new acquaintance, and . . . you're out of luck. Guess what? It happens. You just have to hope that this person is a calm, humble, normal person who doesn't sweat it if you forget his name. Make light of it — then apologize, and hope he gives his name.

The best way for you to remember someone's name is to repeat the name right after you hear it. When a name comes out of your mouth, remembering it is much easier. "That's a very interesting way to think about that, Cory." In fact, repeat it a few times during the conversation. For extra emphasis, repeat it when you say goodbye.

Don't call people you have just met by a nickname, unless they've said it themselves. My name is Alyson, and only a few people in my life have called me Al — and never when I first meet them.

Adopting open body language

As with giving a speech, body language is an important part. Standing at attention with locked knees and rigid legs may be the posture you're looking for when you're in the military, but not when meeting someone for the first time at a conference. People want to see you loose. Sure, it's business, but it's also social. Plant your feet and make sure your body is in alignment. Adopt the up and out pose and high power pose from Chapter 15. That makes you look confident and may even make you start to believe it too.

Here are a few more body language tips to make it look like you're *the* person to meet:

>> **Avoid fidgeting and moving back and forth or swaying side to side.**

It's through body language that we assess people when they're across the room and you can't hear what they're saying.

>> **Stand near people.**

Standing off on your own makes you look like you're not interested in starting a conversation.

>> **Don't cross your arms.**

Crossing your arms makes you look uncomfortable and not too happy. You might look downright annoyed, and no one wants to approach someone like that. A gathering where you don't know anyone is hard enough as it is.

>> **Keep those peepers active.**

Unless you're commenting on a super cool pattern in the carpet, keep your eyes up and looking around. It makes you look interested.

>> **Turn and face people.**

When someone approaches you, turn toward that person with your whole body, not just your face. When you just turn your head and leave your body behind, you send a message that you are not interested in those people — or even that they may be interrupting you. It's the classic "What do you want?" look.

>> **Use your hands when you speak.**

You'll appear more interesting and probably *become* more interested. I do an exercise in my workshops where participants tell me what they're going to do after the workshop. But they can't use their hands — they must have their hands down at their sides without moving them. Then we do it again, but this time they can use their hands and gesture however they want. Their eyes light up, their pitch changes, they have more vocal variety, and they're more engaged.

Letting go of your fears

Everybody feels uncomfortable meeting new people. That's normal. The difference is mainly the degree to which we all feel that discomfort. Maybe you were a shy kid, or you're self-conscious of your voice, or there's something else that makes you feel inadequate or that you don't belong (check out Chapter 5's discussion of *impostor syndrome*).

This is your mantra for this chapter: The person you are approaching is probably just as nervous as you are.

Use positive self-talk. Start out by trying it alone at home. Maybe you say it when you're looking in the mirror, or maybe it's the last thing you say before bed. But when you're alone, use positive self-talk. *I am important.* Yeah, it's cheesy. But you must believe that you have something to contribute to any conversation. If you don't believe that, why should anybody else? Think of a social event as great opportunity to meet someone new, and you just might start to enjoy meeting new people.

What if you have a less-than-wonderful interaction? Don't worry if you felt you didn't click with the head of HR. It doesn't mean the interaction was a failure. If you did your best and were polite, sometimes that has to be good enough. You're not gonna win 'em all. By the way, you might be wrong. All you have to go on is your perception of how the conversation went. The other person might not have seen it that way at all.

Still fearful? Try to practice when the stakes are low. Smile at a fellow parent whom you haven't met at your kid's school. Say hi to the cashier at your gym. Ask fellow employees how they're doing — then really listen to their answers. Try these small things with small stakes. It's all about you learning to be more confident and roll with the punches.

Composing Your Elevator Pitch

Some say the *elevator pitch* came out of Hollywood when screenwriters found themselves (or conveniently placed themselves) inside an elevator with a producer and pitched their ideas for movies. Wherever it began, it is something that you need to work on. An elevator pitch, naturally, should last about as long as an elevator ride. That is, not very long.

Let's say it finally happens: You find yourself in an elevator or simply at a cocktail party with the one person who can give you your dream job. But you've only got a few seconds to tell that person who you are and create an impression that piques her interest before you reach her floor. You want to get her to notice you, exchange business cards, and if possible keep the conversation going.

It hasn't happened yet. That means you still have time to figure out what you're going to say if it ever *does* happen.

"My name is Alyson Connolly and I'm a voice and public speaking coach." That's who I am, and that's the pertinent thing about me — the whole reason I'm opening my mouth. I may be a fantastic water-skier too, but in a business situation I'm not going to lead with watersports.

After they know your job title and name, tell them what you do. For me, I say something like this: "I work with those who are good but want to be great speakers, those whose accent gets in the way of their clarity, and those who would rather die than speak in public. I listen to the clients and assess their problem and help them find ways to improve." Now, that's what I've got in my head. But I change it to sound more conversational, and less robotic, when I'm with a potential client.

Should you drop a name or two? If you're in a profession where it's ethical to name your clients, do it. If not, provide an example of people you work with. For example: "Most of my clients are business people who have to speak in public as part of their job."

Okay, fine, but, why should they care? Why shouldn't they just look up the first person who pops up on Google or LinkedIn who can do the same job you can do? Explain why you're unique. "With my experience and training, I can quickly identify people's problems and how I can be of help. Then I offer a diagnosis to the clients on what they're doing wrong and help them build a solution to their problem and implement it."

The elevator bell still hasn't chimed? Add a little pizzazz — a snappy line or two. For instance: "I can give anyone the confidence to get up in front of a crowd." Don't play it safe or be wishy-washy about it. Let them know you will do something for them if given the chance.

Chapter **19**

If at First You Don't Succeed

You've practiced your speech, have everything in place, and are as prepared as you're ever going to be. You look sharp, you sound sharp, and you ooze confidence. And then the unthinkable happens. Something you didn't plan for. Something that could derail your speech. What then?

You don't let it derail your speech, that's what.

This chapter is about preparing for the inevitable. You may be a positive person who doesn't think problems are inevitable. Well, if you do something for long enough, you see it all. And I'm telling you, if you do any sort of public speaking for long enough, *something will go wrong.* So, cheers to the inevitable. It's time to prepare.

Everyone Wants You to Succeed

The audience is there because they want to hear what you have to say. And they want to you to do well. Even if they are forced to be there, they don't want to sit through a boring speech. They want to be engaged and enthralled with what you have to say.

Watching earnest people perform and flop is difficult for an audience. People don't want to see other people fail. They are on your side. They feel empathy toward you.

Now, if you're speaking to teenagers, they may judge you the minute you walk in and may even hate you and your message. The whole empathy thing doesn't get fully formed until adulthood. They're a tough bunch — but you can win them over, too.

Let's start with a scenario. The audience has come to hear about your new business that will be hiring in town and want to find out all they can about it. We're talking jobs. They won't shoot the messenger because they want to hear the message — and maybe get employed.

These people feel your pain, to start with. Many of them who have ever had to get up and present to a group know what kind of confidence you need to muster to get up in front of a bunch of random people and speak. It's tough. Most of them are glad that it's not them. Those who haven't done it themselves still feel empathy toward you.

That's the majority of people. There are always a few in the crowd who will question you and not be in total agreement with what you have to say. They may disagree silently or may verbalize about it. If they verbalize during your speech, often the others in the audience will automatically be on your side. No one likes seeing someone shouted down. Should this happen, try to keep your message clear. Get it across to the audience. And take a look at the section in Chapter 11 about handling hecklers.

But how do you work with someone who negates your proposal, asks a ton of questions that sidetrack your presentation? How do you not get frazzled? First of all, take a breath. Then take a cue from the poster that was hung all over Britain before World War II to motivate and inspire the British people: *Keep Calm and Carry On.* You're not going to war, but that motto is wise. Defending your presentation will clarify it, even to you. A question is another opportunity to communicate your ideas.

I once worked with a new client for three hours who didn't buy into how I was helping him until 45 minutes before we ended the session! It took a lot of work for me to show him, in several different ways, how he could be a better speaker.

TIP

Chapter 15 goes through the benefits of eye contact. One good idea is to look into the audience and find someone who seems interested in what you have to say. Direct your speech to that person — but for no more than five seconds, and then find someone else.

Maybe you *will* have some flubs in your speech. The audience probably won't even notice, and if they do, they probably won't care — certainly not as much as you do. And let's face it, once they're gathering their things and heading home, they've already forgotten a lot of what you said.

TIP

The actual information you deliver isn't the only important aspect of your speech. Its overall impact is too. The audience *will* remember how you made them feel. If you made them feel comfortable when something went awry, they will remember how you pulled through.

I appreciate the fact that your presentation is important. Yes, perhaps it *will* be the deciding factor on whether you secure that contract. But if you go through the whole presentation worried about that, you won't enjoy the process. "Enjoy?" you say? Yes, *enjoy.* If you take yourself too seriously, that excessive seriousness is what will be projected. The audience mimics you and feeds off your energy.

The show must go on

Here's something that's bound to happen sooner or later if you do a lot of public speaking: You wake up the morning of your scheduled talk not feeling well. It may not be a full-blown flu or other illness. I'm talking about a sore throat or some nausea that might even be attributed to anxiety about giving the speech. Remember to release unnecessary tension through progressive relaxation or physical activity, how dropping your breath deep into your abdomen calms you, and how maintaining an up and out body position boosts your confidence — all of which are explained in Chapter 3.

REMEMBER

Hey, it's your body, and if you really feel sick, then do what you need to do. But give it some serious thought and be as detached as you can. Will this really impede your speech? If so, cancel. But if you think can power through, always, *always* do that instead.

A famous saying in show business, of course, is *the show must go on.* Recently in my city during a performance of an opera, the lead actor developed laryngitis. Another singer knew the role but didn't know the staging. So he sang in the pit with the orchestra while the original performer lip-synced on stage. Not ideal, but it worked!

No one needs to know that Google Maps messed up so you were late getting to the venue. No one cares about the fight you had with your teenager about her curfew. Leave your baggage at the door.

I love going to my physiotherapist even though he inflicts pain on me. His staff greets everyone with genuine smiles and hellos, and they make everyone feel comfortable (until they stick the IMS needles in your shoulder). He tells his staff that no matter how they feel that day or what has happened to them prior to coming to work that they have to let that go and focus on the patient. Try to compartmentalize whatever's going on and power through.

Practicing what could go wrong

I used to do some work with new recruits on our city's police force. These were brand new cops who had never worked the street before. When you call the police, you're usually not calling to tell them about a bake sale. You're calling because there is a problem, and often that problem can be life threatening. So, creating different scenarios with actors role-playing various characters can help them practice real-world responses. In these scenarios, the new cops were confronted with various problematic situations and had to find a solution. This was done in a safe place, obviously, so that the focus was on learning.

I want you to write down some things you may think are going to go wrong, and then write down a possible solution. No, you're not delving into everything-is-going-to-go-badly territory. But it's important to at least think some things through before problems occur. Along with the solutions, come up with some things to say or do.

Here are some examples of problems to get you started:

>> **What happens if the lights go out?** Whom do you ask for help? Find out. Otherwise, "and they said, let there be light, but there wasn't, so the audience waited."

>> **What if the audio system fails?** Depending on how big the room is, you may carry on — or let the audience know they should chat among themselves till things get sorted out.

>> **What if your slide show machine goes on the blink?** Have a remark ready for when your slides aren't appearing. "I worked all night on those slides, so if anyone was really counting on seeing them, I'll email them to you later — see me after this speech."

>> **What if you trip and fall onstage?** If it happened to Jennifer Lawrence when accepting her Oscar, it can happen to anybody. "I promised organizers a knockout speech, but I was hoping that would be a metaphor."

Sometimes you're ready to go with everything in place, and the power isn't working for your slide show. It may be the most common — and least likely to be your fault — kind of problem you'll encounter. Just be honest, acknowledge the problem, and tell the audience that due to technical difficulties the presentation will start in a few minutes.

When you're in the middle of your presentation and *everything* goes down — power, lights, audio — get off the stage. Don't be the center of failure. Tell the audience you'll start again when the power is back on. I always say, "While we work on fixing this problem, now's the time to talk among yourselves." They like that.

Get someone else to figure out the problem. You don't need to be in there — let the professionals or people who run the venue figure it out.

Making lemonade out of lemons

Something has gone catastrophically wrong. Maybe it was your fault, maybe it wasn't. Did your slide show get deleted mid-presentation? Did you have a sudden bout of narcolepsy and fall asleep right there onstage? Did the audience find out an executive in the company just got fired . . . right before you stepped out to do your presentation? These things happen. You can't change the fact that your computer caught fire and the CEO doused the flames with his Armani sport coat. You must confront whatever just happened head on.

Running away from your problems is probably never the best course of action, but it's especially so in this case. I would go right to the audience and talk to them. Maybe about what just happened, or maybe about the local sports team and their inability to score. This is a wonderful opportunity to find out more about the audience, and for them to find out more about you. Stay with your audience to continue that feeling of trust and authenticity.

Rolling with the Punches

It's important to navigate your troubles until you get to smoother waters. Things are going to get tough sometimes. You need to be agile in your responses and willing to make compromises.

I was once giving a workshop to a group of financial advisers. The venue was a room in a hotel. As you know, I always recommend a warmup. So, there we were, opening up our chests and pretending we were all Tarzan with long, loud bellows of "Aaaaahhhhhh!"

Chapter 16 talks about checking out the venue. Well, I didn't do that this time. If I had, I would've noticed that our room was actually half of a bigger room, separated from the other half by a folding partition. So, there we were pounding our chests and belting out ape-man calls when a woman stomped into the room and demanded, "Can you please stop all that noise?" Turns out she was running a workshop on meditation! Luckily the organizer was able to move us to a more private room.

Usually the organizer of an event will ask in advance what you need. But what if you get to the space and it's smaller than you anticipated, or there are tables everywhere that need to be cleared out? Or you asked for chairs to be set up but no chairs are to be found?

How do you react? First thing, of course: Don't have a tantrum. Blowing a gasket when the room isn't set up the way you want it to be isn't going to help anything. Remember, it's not about you — it's about your message. What kind of a impression would throwing a fit give?

TIP

Be the professional you are. Roll up your sleeves and organize the room into the configuration you want. Ask for help. Get that long table from the back and put it out front. This is also a great opportunity to meet the audience before your presentation and reveal a bit of who you are — not the presenter, but the real person.

Double booking

Here's a common situation. You have a prospective client come to your office, because it's swanky and you have a great boardroom with the most comfortable leather chairs. You thought you booked that room — only to find that it's occupied at your appointed time. You don't want to interrupt the meeting that's happening in your place. So, apologize to the client — yes, say you're sorry — and find another place. If they're all booked, go back to your office or cubicle and talk about it from there. Showing that you're a "Yes Let's" kind of person is great. Future clients want to see you flex your flexibility.

Shooting yourself in the foot

I was just at a conference on celebrating a winter city, and the emcee started with a welcome and spoke a bit about the subject. He was clear, used a bit of humor, and was to the point. He then introduced three speakers to deliver speeches on the topic. The MC was the last to speak again. He started by saying, "I was going to talk about what wonderful things you can do in a winter city, but since everyone else has touched on it so eloquently, I'm going to skip that part."

TIP

In a case like that, just skip it altogether. Don't *tell* us you're skipping something. There is no need to tell us that. We wouldn't have known.

When I hear, "I was going to . . ." it always makes me tense. He said this over and over. Then he started stumbling over the words to get to the parts that he *was* going to talk about. Poor guy. Previously he was backstage listening to the others. He could have taken a pen and crossed all of that out. When he was speaking to us, he could have just taken a breath to look down at his page and found a place to continue.

Never having to say you're sorry (when you're up there speaking)

Apologizing can be good for you. Maybe it's just a form of catharsis for you, but it can also put people at ease. From childhood, we're told to apologize when we screw up. "Tell her you're sorry" after you took a ball. "What do you say?" after you're caught doing something you shouldn't have been doing. Often, offering an apology is better than not offering it, especially if all you have to lose is pride.

REMEMBER

But there is a time and a place to apologize, and that time is not in the middle of a speech.

Yes, you are only human, and yes, we all make mistakes. And yes, apologizing makes us vulnerable, it shows we are above petty pride, it makes us human. But during the middle of a toast to the bride, you don't have to interrupt yourself to tell them you accidentally skipped the part about drinking wine at her house before a tenth grade dance. (Perhaps that was best left out anyway.)

WARNING

Here's the thing: When you say you're sorry, the audience is thrown into wondering why you feel sorry. Don't give them a reason to doubt your authority on whatever subject you're speaking about. It also distracts them away from your actual speech, which defeats the whole point of listening to you in the first place. They are not "in the moment" anymore — they're worrying about you instead. That's probably not the message you want to get across.

Chilling out: No one knows you messed up

Okay, so something bad happened. Something that was your fault. First of all, it's probably not that bad. If you did the same thing to a clerk at a store, you might not even think about it. But this is amplified, I get it. Take a second to look down at your notes, *breathe*, find your place, and start again. The audience may never know anything went wrong unless you tell them. I bet you've been to many live performances, be it plays or concerts, where someone has missed an exit or a note and no one in the audience was the wiser.

One time, I was driving my boys home from a basketball game that they had lost. I commented that they had done a great job and it looked like they played well.

"No, Mom," I was scolded. "We played terrible and couldn't pass the ball." I had no idea. To me everyone was engaged on the court and working as a team. This is often the case in public speaking.

If you do end up having to apologize for something, take it on yourself. Don't blame anybody else. No one likes a complainer, especially if that complainer is throwing others under the bus. The fact is, you have no one but yourself to blame if you're late because you forgot your slide deck, or your assistant forgot to book the room. Blaming is *negative* and puts the audience and you on edge. You are a professional, so act like one.

Owning obstacles

In the theater, when delving into a character, an actor figures out a character's objectives and how they can be attained. They also ask what are the obstacles getting in the character's way. Knowing all of this makes your character and the journey more interesting. Think of your problems as mere obstacles — not life-threatening disasters. So what if the slides are upside down? That's an obstacle, not a catastrophe. Fix it. Then you can pat yourself on the back with a "Good for me, I did it!" You had a problem, solved it, and moved on.

If your slide show fails, remember that your slides are just a jumping-off point to speak about. You can present without the slides. If you feel that you must have them, print them out beforehand so you have a copy. Then you can simply pull them out and carry on. The copies will probably be too small for you to show the audience. Just use them as a guide for you to follow.

If you lose your train of thought, what should you do? Wail? Run away? Say, "I'm so sorry, I've lost where I was"? This is a common scenario. My advice is don't sweat it. Everybody loses a train of thought sometimes. Just stop and take a breath. Remember that if we stop breathing, we stop thinking. Look down at your speech or cue cards and scan your main points. Or look at your slides — that should jiggle your memory.

You may feel that the time you take for your pause is interminable — but really it's mere seconds. Especially if you know that speech well. It's okay to be silent. A pause helps you collect your thoughts.

Another method that often works is adding a bit of humor. "I just was off in Hawaii in my mind. I seem to have forgotten what I was saying?" It doesn't have to be uproariously funny. Just something to show you're in good spirits about the whole thing. Find some way to be self-deprecating, and the audience will like you for it. You could even ask the audience what you were talking about. That'll make them sit up straight!

Getting Better at Improvising

Often we think of *improv* as a cool comedy device. But we all improv all the time. When you come home from work, look in the fridge and see broccoli, chicken, and ginger root, you improv your way into making dinner out of that.

TIP

Improv is all about thinking on your toes and trusting what's going to come out of your mouth. It doesn't have to be earth-shattering, whatever you're going to say. It just has to keep the conversation going.

The good news is that you can get better at improvising and ad libbing through practice.

Improving your improv muscles

Do you remember Mad Libs? They were created in 1953 by Leonard Stern and Roger Price. Basically they feature sentences that have blanks you need to fill in. When I worked as a drama facilitator in a stroke clinic, we used these all the time to help patients remember words they may have forgotten (and have fun doing it). The idea is to think of words that can work, or kind of work, in the sentence blanks.

You can make up your own sentences. Here's one:

I was driving to the _____ when I came across this _____. I turned around, but it was too late. That's when the _____ started _____ and _____.

EXERCISE: STORY CIRCLE

This is a fun little exercise that helps kill what's killing your improv: your inhibitions. You can do this exercise with a group, a partner, or even by yourself. It's also fun at a party. One person says a sentence and then tosses a bean bag to the next person, who has to add a line to continue the story.

> A: One day I was walking on the beach and found this beautiful rock.
> B: It was smooth and shiny.
> A: I turned it over in my hand and saw an inscription written on it.
> B: The inscription read: "To Florence, my dearest love."

Once you've mastered using one sentence, start breaking it up into half thoughts and phrases:

> A: One day (tosses bean bag)
> B: I was walking on the (tosses bean bag)
> A: beach and I found this (toss)
> B: beautiful rock

Doing this by yourself works as well. You're using your imagination and writing a story, which can be about anything. *But that's so hard to do!* you're thinking. Come on, fess up, we narrate stories all the time in our heads. "After I get the kids to bed I'm going to have a relaxing cup of tea. I think I'll have some ice cream too. I'll tiptoe quietly into the sunroom and read another chapter of my book. I'm loving this book and can't wait to get my hands on the next one." Instead of thinking it in your head, say it out loud. Couple this idea with the "taking a walk" exercise in Chapter 9, and you can practice finding how much breath you need for long and short sentences, too.

Just working on sentences like that can help exercise your brain to think on the spot and be creative. Try to fill in these blanks with the first words that pop into your head. Don't get analytical about it.

Practicing improvising about your subject

You've got your speech down pat. You've practiced a little ad libbing. It's time to try ad libbing about the subject of your speech. Kind of tough, right? Whatever your topic, you've probably done some research on it. That will come in handy. If your research was narrowly focused, take some time and widen it.

The idea here is that if you forget your place during your speech, you can spout a fun fact and then get on with your speech.

Let's say your speech is about the benefits of eating an apple a day. At one point in your presentation, a cell phone rings and you're a bit rattled by the disruption. Take a breath and know that you've got this. You've researched some cool facts about the apple — how many species of apple tree there are, where they are mostly grown, whether worms really eat apples. Have something in your back pocket. Maybe even an apple if it's big enough for everyone to see.

If you need to get folks to quiet down after a meal so that you can start, ask the MC to inform the audience (or do it yourself) that you'll begin in three minutes. After that time, if there's still some talking, try this: Ask the audience to turn to the table or person next to you and give a "shh." That takes the onus off you, and you're not the bad guy. I credit this tip to my husband. It works every time.

Adjusting your timing

Maybe you think your speech is around 20 minutes long but you didn't time it (you should have, of course). And now it really, truly has to be no longer than 20 minutes because the caterers are bringing in dinner in 20 minutes. You look up at the clock at the back of the hall and see that you have 10 minutes left but you're only a third of the way through your speech.

Don't let panic set in. Relax. You know your speech. Look down and find the stuff that's important to get your message across and weave in the important parts of your narrative to keep it cohesive. Off you go. And what are you not going to do? That's right — you're not going to apologize for adjusting your speech.

What if the opposite happens? You whip through your speech in no time and find you have time left to fill at the end? Look at it as a gift. Don't you love it when you get a little free time? The audience will too — as long as you got all your points across, engaged with them, and made an impact with your message. (Of course, if you rushed through the speech, forgetting to breathe and land your thoughts, you might take a fresh look at Chapters 4 and 14.)

7

The Part of Tens

Get over your stage fright by accepting your fear, practicing, breathing, relaxing, and using several other tricks.

Improve your delivery using a variety of tips, including analyzing and personalizing, emphasizing and breathing, recording, and enlisting others to listen, watch, and give you honest feedback.

Get ready for your speaking engagement through warmups, becoming centered, gathering what you need, and other important last-minute preparations.

Chapter **20**

Ten (or So) Tips for Stage Fright

Stage fright can afflict nearly anyone. This short chapter pulls together some tips and advice aimed at helping you overcome it.

Accept Your Fear

The first step to solving any problem is to be aware of it. Be it smoking, eating cheesy-poofs before bed, interrupting your kids and not listening to them because you know the answer — your acceptance that it's actually a problem is important. And before you work on accepting your fear, let me tell you something: It's okay to be afraid. It's natural to be afraid.

Fear of public speaking is common and widespread. As the old saying goes, many people are more afraid of public speaking than of dying. It's all right if you're in that boat. But instead of taking that information and allowing it to make you more negative, just accept it and move on.

And there's the kicker. Because how is just accepting the fear going to help you at all? By going out there and doing it, that's how. Speaking in front of people. You could be doing it every day, at work, at the parent-teacher meeting, to the check-out clerk at the grocery store. Sometimes it's as easy as that. So now, when you talk to the checkout clerk, remember what you're actually doing: You're public speaking. You don't have to be on a stage with an audience of 1,000. Start small.

And don't worry if you're nervous. If you're nervous a little a bit, that's good, because when you feel nervous that means you care about it. And the audience wants to see someone who is up there speaking about something she cares about.

If you need extra help, confide in a colleague. Talk to him about it. He might tell you his story. But *don't* confide to the audience that you're terrified. They don't need or want to know that.

Remember that it's not about you — it's about your message. You're just the vessel. Sorry about that. The more you focus on what you have to do and get across to the audience, the less you'll think about you.

Don't let nervousness turn into anxiety about the event.

Try this: Right now, wherever you are, think about that upcoming speech. Do you feel anxious about it? Remember a time when you felt this way and what happened in your body. Do you clench your stomach, is your breathing shallow, are you thinking that you have nothing to say and so why are you going up there anyway?

Now try to be as anxious as possible. Tap into the physiological responses that occur in your body. Can you do it? How hard is it? If you're upset about something and are trying *not* to cry, what happens? You cry harder than normal. That's because all the focus is giving that feeling more power as you're trying to stifle it. If you just allow yourself to cry, you might, or you might not.

Practice, Practice, Practice

Here's an all-too-common scenario: You're afraid to do that presentation, so you just leave it till the last possible second before you need to present. You don't even think about it, or at least you don't think about what you're going to say, anyway. What you *do* think about is how standing up there in front of people freaks you out. So you pull an ostrich routine. But that presentation is coming, whether you think about it or not. Maybe you think you know the content so you'll just wing it.

Don't. If you're read any other part of this book, or even have any general knowledge about how people acquire skills, you know the answer: You must practice. Not just to get better, either — to reduce the fear. The more you practice and know your speech backward and forward, the more comfortable you'll feel. It can and will become second nature.

Breathe Slowly and Deeply

When you're afraid, the "fight, flight, or freeze" response kicks into gear. You start to take short breaths from your upper chest. Or you hold your breath. Ever hear a noise in the kitchen in the middle of the night? Bet you held your breath. You can thank the "fight, flight, or freeze" response for that.

But you can combat it by breathing. Deliberately taking full breaths slowly activates the "rest and digest" parasympathetic nervous system, which calms you down.

TIP

Don't wait until you feel afraid to start breathing slowly and deeply. Instead, get into the habit of breathing like that all the time.

EXERCISE: BREATHING DEEP DOWN

Put one hand on your upper chest and the other on your lower abdomen. Your hand covering your lower abdomen should move first when you inhale. Think of dropping your breath deep down into your lower abdomen. Now breathe in on a slow breath and out the same way. Think of your lungs as a balloon. When you inhale, drop the breath deep into your lungs and fill them up like the bottom of a balloon. Make sure your shoulders don't rise up to your ears when you breathe in. Do it slowly for a slow count of four on the inhale, and then four more on the exhale.

When you inhale, try to breathe in through your nose. It's more of a cleansing breath because it filters out pollutants like dust and bacteria. Plus breathing in through your nose helps to drop your breath lower into your lungs. On an exhale, you can breathe either through your mouth or your nose. Practice this lying down so that your body is releasing into the floor and you can really feel how you breathe. When you feel anxious, visualize dropping your breath into your lower abdomen. Take the time to breathe.

EXERCISE: THE BACKWARD CIRCLE

This is a Tai Chi move adapted from voice teacher Barbara Houseman. Stand in alignment with your feet shoulder width apart. Have your feet planted and your body lengthening up to the sky. Imagine that there is a beach ball in front of you. Place your hands as if they're under the ball at hip level. When you breathe in, move your arms up in front of the beach ball toward your shoulders. On an exhale, bring your hands in toward your body and then take them down to your hips. Make sure to do this slowly.

Gently allow the breath to enter your body and then start again. Repeat at least ten times. While you are doing this, note any places in your body that feel tense. Think of letting those areas go.

This exercise is a good visual reminder to imagine dropping your breath deep into your abdomen, as that is where your hands start as they take the shape of the ball. This can help you out in the wild, too. If you get nervous or hyper and you tend to speak quickly while talking to someone, you can just move your hands in small backward circles. This will help to ground you, calm you, slow down your breath, and clear your head. The best part is, no one will know.

There are Tai Chi groups all over the world. Enter Tai Chi and your location into your favorite search engine and you're sure to find one near you. You can watch a video of someone going through Tai Chi moves at www.youtube.com/watch?v=f9BFWJsrmSY.

Remember to breathe at all times. Yeah, I know. You *are* breathing at all times. You've come this far, haven't you? But are you breathing to your full breath potential? Here are some reminders:

>> Breathe when you enter the room for your presentation.

>> Breathe when you meet and greet your contact.

>> Breathe when you gather your materials and set up.

>> Breathe when you can't find your USB stick. (Pssst, it's in your briefcase — remember you double-checked it before you left?)

>> Take three full breaths before you begin your presentation.

>> Breathe when someone asks you a question at the Q&A that you have to think about or don't know the answer to. (You may have to respond that you will find the answer and get back to that person.)

Use Progressive Relaxation

When you're afraid, you tense up your body. It's often as simple as that. It's akin to an animal being attacked. It's one of our most primitive instincts. But tension, as we know by now, is a killer for the presenter. You can't take full breaths deep into your lower abdomen, your jaw is tight, and in fact your whole body may be so tight you look like you could snap at any moment.

EXERCISE: TENSE AND RELEASE

Here's a quick exercise to get everything moving as it should. Eventually you'll be able to do this anywhere, even right at the head table before giving the speech.

Practice this one first by lying down on your back. Allow your body to sink into the floor. Let go of your jaw, and just breathe in and out. You're on a sandy beach. You're lying on a towel on the warm sand. You feel calm and there are no worries. Maybe you hear the waves of the ocean, coming in and out. The sun is shining on you, warming you up.

You're going to tense and release parts of your body, starting with your toes. Tense them for a few rounds of breathing in and out, and then release. Doesn't it feel good to release that tension? Now do the same with your feet, calves, thighs, pelvis, stomach, arms, hands, fingers, chest, neck, and all the muscles in your face.

Remember to keep breathing. At the end, for a couple of rounds, tense your entire body and release, and see how that feels.

Now that you've mastered it lying down, try it standing, and then eventually, even sitting. Make sure your body feels aligned, and you feel roots growing down to the earth from the bottom of your feet and energy growing up your body through the crown of your head.

You can do this anytime, anywhere! When you're at the breakfast meeting and feeling afraid, just tense up a body part like toes or feet, and no one will know.

Be Up and Out, Not Down and In

So much of communication comes from your body, not your words. It starts with how you pose. And that starts with getting aligned in an up and out position (head up and balanced naturally on your spine, chin not tucked or thrust forward, chest open).

Imagine your feet are planted with roots growing down from the bottom of your feet into the ground. The rest of your body is stretching with energy growing up to the crown of your head to the sky.

Your head is held up straight and your ears are aligned with your shoulders and hips. Your chest is not caved in or pushed out. It is *open* so that your breath can move freely. Shoulders are back and aligned with hips. Pelvis is aligned directly under shoulders.

When you move your body in an up and out pose, you're looking at the world with your head held high. When you're in a down and in pose, you're doing exactly the opposite: You're breathing from your upper chest in short breaths, which is what you do when you are anxious and afraid, and you don't exude confidence. When you move in an up and out pose you feel like you can take on the world, your breath drops deep into your lower abdomen, and you look confident too! And that means you speak with confidence — after all, you're the expert.

TIP

You may find yourself giving a presentation to a "down and in" group — they're looking at the floor, not at you, they're not engaged, and they look like they want to bolt for the door. Nevertheless, maintain *your* up and out position. Hopefully the group will look at you and your confidence and want to emulate you. I talk more about this in Chapter 15.

Move Your Hands

Place your hands in the horizontal plane that goes out from your navel. When you move your hands in this area, your calming "rest and digest" parasympathetic nervous system is activated. I talk about this in detail in Chapter 15.

What does that mean for your speech? The idea is to make you look and feel calmer and more genuine. And the tone of your voice will sound calmer, too. You can gesture in this *truth plane* pose, as Mark Bowden calls it, while talking to someone before the presentation, and it will calm and center you. Practice this movement when you speak to a colleague about a problem — then leave your hands down by your sides and see how that feels. You'll probably start breathing from high in your chest, feel lousy, and find little to say.

You can still feel powerful when you're sitting. When you're presenting in a board meeting in a seated position, make sure to have your feet flat on the floor and maintain the up and out position. Hands need to be above the table to help express your thoughts and ideas and help calm you down. If they're below the table, you won't seem as engaged, and the audience is wondering what's going on down there.

Get Positive — Yes Let's

Throw *I can't* out the window. You have been asked to present. Asked. So don't shoot yourself in the foot with negative thinking.

If you think your presentation will go badly because you're so darned afraid to present, it probably will. Don't prophesy against yourself. Don't be a self-saboteur. This is an opportunity to strut your stuff and tell the world what you know. Lucky you, right?

» **Say, "Yes, let's."** I talk about this drama game in Chapter 2. Say *yes* to everything, both in your head and to others. Yes, I'm excited. Yes, I'm scared. Yes, I know my stuff. Yes, I can adapt my presentation without slides if necessary.

» **Smile.** Smiling makes you look more approachable. Plus it makes you feel good, and others often smile back. The audience often mimics you — if they see a scared face up on that stage, that might not bode well for their perception.

» **Be grateful.** You should be so lucky. You should feel fortunate that you've been asked to present. And you should appreciate the fact that the organizer thinks you're the one to do it.

Make that list of what you have to be grateful for: coffee in the morning, your suit fits perfectly, your boss thinks you're the right person to present because you know what you're talking about.

» **Be positive in your self-talk.** Something good will come out of this. Someone thinks you've got something to say or she wouldn't have asked you. The audience wants to hear what you have to say.

» **Surround yourself with positive people.** Bypass Negative Ned at the reception desk and seek out your pal in the office three floors below who always thinks positive.

>> **Visualize yourself on the day giving your presentation.** You're looking and feeling confident up there at the lectern. You're speaking clearly and slowly. The audience is listening intently and is thoroughly engaged. You're enjoying yourself!

Roll with Mistakes

As much as you want to be perfect, you don't want to be the robot speaker who does everything correct and plays it safe. That's boring. Plus, striving to be *perfect* is a recipe for failure. Instead, strive for *excellence*. Doesn't that make you feel better? At the end of the day, you're doing the best you can.

Don't worry if your slide show isn't working. Your whole speech is not ruined. If you forgot your USB stick at work and can't get back there to retrieve it, you should know that speech so well that you can give it without the need for slides.

REMEMBER

Whatever it is, roll with it.

Repeat an Affirmation in Your Head

You are your own worst enemy. No, that's not the affirmation. It means we are ultimately the hardest on ourselves. If you repeat negative thoughts in your head all the time, guess what? Sooner or later, you're going to believe them.

Switch it. Instead of thinking "I'm a terrible at this," go for "I love presenting!" Or, okay, maybe take baby steps: "I *like* presenting."

"I'm a great presenter. My message rocks!" Notice how I'm using the present tense. You need to think in the present. You aren't convincing yourself that you will be a great presenter someday. You *are* — right at this moment.

Focus on an Engaged Audience Member

There will be many engaged viewers in the audience, and they're here because they want to hear what you have to say. The majority of them are probably thinking, "I'm glad it's you and not me up there!" Well, they haven't read this book.

Find a compadre in the audience who is giving you nonverbal cues like nodding or otherwise looks really engaged. He's your *friend,* and we know our friends make us feel better. Give your speech *to him* for a few seconds, and then find someone else. Take in the entire audience and find others. Find people who will nonverbally boost you up and make you feel good. After all, they want you to succeed and want to hear what you have to say.

Slow Down

When we're fearful, we speed up. Could be because our heart is beating faster and we just want to get the speech over with and sit down. Maybe you already have a habit of speaking quickly, and it gets even quicker when you're afraid.

Remember that you have a fabulous presentation, and the audience wants to hear you and your message. When you're done, don't rush off the stage.

When we speak slowly, we slow down our breathing, which helps calm us. Practice taking a breath — a good one — after each sentence. Speak to the end of the sentence.

Chapter **21**

Ten Ways to Improve Your Delivery

Here are ten ways to improve your delivery in your speech or presentation, culled from all over the book and collected and summarized here in one handy place.

Analyze Your Script

So you feel like you need to work on your delivery. But maybe it's not all in *how* you're saying it. It may be *what* you're saying.

Many of my clients seem to believe that their speeches are set in stone once they feel they're done writing them. But you can't think of them that way. A speech is a living document. You should always be able to go back and improve it.

In analyzing your script, first answer these questions:

» **What is your main point?** Can you sum up the main point in one sentence?

» **Why are you speaking to the audience?** What makes *you* the expert?

>> **What do you want to say?** You're giving a speech to preteens about the benefits of staying in school. Are you giving a good presentation of your message?

>> **Is it relevant to your audience?** You believe that what you have to say is important for the audience to hear — but is it important from their perspective?

>> **What does the audience need to hear?** How will the audience be better off having heard what you say?

>> **What is their call to action?** What do you want the audience to with your information? You want them to stay in school? How do you do that? You let them know that they can talk to school counselors and find support if they're having difficulty with their courses or attending school.

>> **Do you have a hook?** For example: Ask, "Have you ever thought of dropping out of school?" The audience doesn't have to answer. The question just arouses their curiosity. The audience can just think about it and answer the question in their own heads.

>> **Do you have a powerful quote?** Use a quotation by someone you and the audience admire.

>> **Do you have a visual?** Bringing out a visual will arouse curiosity. It also unites you with the audience when you glance briefly up at it.

>> **Do you have an interesting fact or statistic?** This can grab the audience's attention.

>> **Can you compliment the audience?** You might start with "It is an honor . . ." Or after you've watched them listen to the previous speaker, "Wow, you really are an attentive audience."

>> **Can you add some local flavor?** Talk about the local baseball team winning the championship. Just stay away from anything controversial that may be going on locally.

>> **Can you tell a relevant story?** Start with one that relates to the topic.

>> **Could you use sound effects?** For example: The sounds of kids talking and having fun could start your speech about staying in school.

>> **Can you tell a joke?** People love good jokes. Just don't use jokes that are off-color or that pit one group against the other.

>> **Does your ending create impact?** This is even more important than the hook. It's the last thing the audience will hear from you.

I'll throw in one last bonus question: Does your speech have all the essential components of a good speech? Remember PIE (from Chapter 6):

>> **Point:** State your point near the beginning of your speech.

>> **Illustrations:** Give examples for why you think your point is correct or important.

>> **Explanations:** How do your examples relate to and develop your point?

>> **Conclusion:** Return to the main point and write a conclusion with impact so the audience will remember you and your message.

Personalize Your Speech

Who's speaking in front of the crowd? Guess what. It's you. So by all means, go ahead and personalize it. Even a professor used to writing extremely impersonal papers can show some flair in the lecture hall. Everyone loves a story. Talking about yourself gives the audience a glimpse into your life. If you're trying to convince a bunch of kids to stay in school, tell them about a family member who dropped out. What happened to that family member?

TIP

Your inflection has to be personable as well. When you practice it out loud — you are doing that, right? — be sure you sound like yourself. Do you sound like you would when speaking to a friend? Are you connected to the topic or somebody who is just saying a bunch of words?

Emphasize Key Words

When your speech is still just on the page, all the words generally look the same, right? Some are longer, some are shorter. It's not immediately obvious what's really important in all that text. You have to emphasize the words or phrases that your audience really needs to listen to.

What are the words that you want to lift off the page — that you want the audience to really hear and be impacted by? Use a highlighter or pencil to make them stand out.

What words would you want to emphasize in the following line?

Staying in school is important in securing a good job.

You can find your own way of marking up your speeches. Here's mine: If you want to emphasize using volume, write the words you want louder in CAPITAL letters and put in parentheses ( ) when you want words to be quieter.

REMEMBER

There's more to do than adding emphasis. You may need to adjust the words or phrases themselves, depending on the room. If you're speaking to a group of pre-teens, telling them their school is among the "preeminent" schools in the district, that word may fly right over their heads and forget your point while they try to figure out what that word means in their heads. Better to use a word like "important," which is more common and part of their vernacular.

Change Up Your Pitch, Tone, and Word Duration

When you listen to music, you don't want to hear the same note over and over. That would be terribly boring. The same goes for your speech. Yeah, I know you're not singing, but variety in your pitch — raising and lowering the frequency ("note") of your tone — helps your audience hold on better. Varying your pitch makes your speech more interesting and helps add spice to your presentation. You don't want to give a monotonous speech that drones on.

So what's the prescription for varying your tone? Well, that's something you have to figure out for yourself. You can definitely play around with pitch, tone, and word *duration* (how long you say or draw out the pronunciation of words) and find what combinations work for you. For example:

>> **Pitch:** "Staying in school is important to securing good jobs." You might raise the pitch when you say *school* and *jobs*. Make a notation where you want to raise and lower your pitch — I use a swoop, like a Nike swoosh.

>> **Tone:** How do you express your emotions and what you really mean through your words? Tone can change meaning. Does your tone match what you are saying? Are you *warning* the audience about the perils of dropping out of school or are you *encouraging* them?

>> **Word duration:** Play with how you pronounce or draw out words. You might say, "Staying in *schoooool* is important to securing a good job," or "Staying in school is important to securing a good *jooooob*."

Breathe!

Everything about speaking really comes back to breath. Breathing is the driving force in literally everything we do — but *especially* speech. Most chapters in this book have a section on breath, and that's for a good reason. Your speech is coming from that breath. So it is a huge advantage to know how to use your breath properly, with as much efficiency as possible.

First, don't rush things. Take the time to breathe — doing so also gives the audience time to register the last thing you said.

REMEMBER

You always need to have enough breath to last to the end of each sentence.

When you breathe in, visualize your breath dropping deep into your lower abdomen. Your lungs are expanding like a balloon, and if you watch a balloon inflate, it inflates from the bottom. On an exhale, your abdominal muscles are contracting and pressing toward your spine.

Say the first sentence in your speech. Take the time at the end of the sentence to breathe in fully. Don't rush it. Go through a good chunk of your speech like this. I know it may seem tedious, but this kind of focus on breathing really helps. You'll notice that each sentence is different in length and you may have breath left over. That's okay. Exhale it and inhale again for the next sentence.

Repeat the speech in real time, and soon you'll learn to take as much breath as you need for each sentence. Remember to visualize the breath dropping low.

Other breathings tips:

>> Don't hold your breath. The audience will too!

>> You can mark your breaths on your page with a slash (/). I have clients who mark up their speeches with *BREATHE* scrawled all over them.

>> Take a breath after a period or a comma. This is how we speak in real life.

Slow Down Your Pace

You may be a fast talker in real life, and that might work just fine for you. But a speech isn't real life. As I say throughout this book, a speech is a performance. You're in the public speaking world now. The audience won't understand or register what you're saying if you're just barreling along. Plus, audiences get tense when people speak fast. They may even stop listening because it's too much work to try to follow.

Antidote? Pretty simple. Try this when practicing: Pronounce each word clearly and deliberately. Form each vowel and consonant in all the words. This will slow you down. But that isn't how we speak normally. We don't give each word the same weight. Now imagine you're speaking to your friend. Increase your pace but make sure all your words are clearly pronounced and that your pace isn't so fast that your friend can't understand you.

Land Your Thoughts

Here's a scenario: You've practiced and know your speech very well — so well, in fact, that you forget that the *audience* hasn't. They've never heard it before. So give them time to register what you've said before you go on to the next thought.

TIP

Think of the audience as newcomers to your country, and English is their second language. It's very new to them. They can only understand you if you speak slowly and with clarity. (Don't get me wrong — you should trust their intelligence, but not that they can follow you if you mumble.)

To practice, you could try moving your arms to emphasize:

"I have constantly hit my quota, and I have hit it again this year."

You might gesture with your right arm out to the right when you say, "I have constantly hit my quota" and then gesture with your left arm when you say, "and I have hit it again this year."

Note: You don't have to gesture like this when you actually give your presentation. This physical gesture gives you the time to slow down when you practice.

Another way to make each thought clear is to move — physically move to a different spot on the floor. For example:

"I have constantly hit my quota, and thanks to a large order from overseas I have hit it again this year."

You might move to the right on "I have constantly hit my quota," move to the left on "and thanks to a large order from overseas," and move to center stage on "I have hit it again this year."

REMEMBER

Again, you don't need to actually move when you give this speech. It might make the audience dizzy. The point is to practice so that moving helps to make each thought clearer in your mind, and that will transfer to the audience.

Use the Power of the Pause

Pauses allow you time to take a breath and gather what to say next. So use them liberally!

Pauses also build suspense. "You want a good job? (pause) . . . then stay in school."

Try the following:

>> Pause after a comma.

>> Pause after a sentence.

>> Pause before a new paragraph.

>> Pause when you show a visual.

>> Pause for laughter.

>> Pause after a rhetorical question.

WARNING

Avoid fillers! When you pause, there is no need to say anything — especially "um" or "uh." Really, just stop talking. It's all you have to do. The pause will only take a few seconds. The audience will wait. Filler words don't give the audience time to register your last sentence. Plus, it's annoying.

Record Your Presentation

As I say elsewhere in this book, I don't advocate standing in front of the mirror when you practice your speech. We look in mirrors to check ourselves out, sure. But when you practice in front of the mirror, you're still checking yourself out. You can't help it. And that takes the focus off your speech.

Video yourself

You can play it back and really see you the way the audience will see you. See the next entry for questions you can ask a colleague if you have someone watch you.

Record your voice

Of course, your voice is the most important part, not that great tie that works with your shirt. Recording audio of your practices makes it easy to find those voice habits that might be detrimental to your impact without getting distracted by the visuals.

Listen for vocal habits and patterns. For example, listen for *upspeak*, which sounds like you're turning your sentences into questions.

> "Staying in school is important in securing a good job."

That's a statement. When you upspeak it into a question, it sounds like you're not sure, as if you're saying, "Is that okay for me to say?"

Listen for times when you drop the ends of sentences:

> "Staying in school is important in securing a good . . ."

What? We can't hear that last word. The energy drops and falls, splat, like pancake batter on a griddle. *Dropping* often happens when you run out of breath. Make sure to grab enough breath to last you till the end of the sentence.

Listen for filler words. Saying "so," "like," "you know," and "right" too many times. You may be surprised how these words can creep into your speech. When you feel a filler word coming on, stifle it.

Ask a Friend or Colleague to Watch and Listen

Give this person specific things to watch and listen for, too. He or she might just say you did "great," which really doesn't help you. And even if you were *great*, even the most polished presenter can always improve.

Here are some things to have that person pay specific attention to:

>> Do you address the audience at the beginning without looking down at your notes when you say your name?

>> Are your points concisely strewn together?

>> Does your hook catch the audience's attention?

>> Are you rushing? Can your helper understand everything you have to say?

>> Can your helper hear you from different areas of the room?

>> Are you emphasizing key words or do they all sound the same?

>> Are you speaking your speech in the same (monotonous) pitch or are you using vocal variety?

>> Does your tone reflect your meaning?

>> Are you ending your presentation with a bang?

Chapter **22**

Ten Tips for Preparing to Speak

So, you have a speech coming up? This short chapter is designed to help you prepare for it.

Warm Up Your Body and Your Voice

You know who warms up? Pretty much everyone. Your favorite athletes, your yoga instructor — anyone who uses his or her body for some sort of performance warms up. And guess what? Public speaking counts as using your body.

You know when you see speakers up there, talking your ear off, not doing all that much moving around, and they're sweaty? Like dripping with sweat? Yeah, they may be nervous, but chances are their body is working a lot harder than you think. So, if you're not working hard up there, you're not doing your job. And if you don't warm up, you can't work hard.

The rest of this section offers sample warmups from some of the exercises throughout this book, but you can have fun and create your own.

Get physical

You can go for a run, practice some yoga — heck, walk up some stairs. Try the Elaine dance from *Seinfeld.* Anything that gets your cardio going.

Get aligned

Place your feet shoulder width apart. Imagine roots growing from your feet ten yards down into the earth. There is energy growing up past your head. Your shins are stretching up to your thighs. Your pelvis is set straight, where it should be; you aren't sticking your stomach in or out. Imagine your vertebrae stacked neatly on top of each other. Your neck is released. Your head is loose like a bobble head. The energy is stretching from your feet up through the crown of your head out to the sky.

TIP

When you go through a warmup, do it full on. If you ever played piano, you have to practice your scales with the same energy that you perform the song. That doesn't mean you have to *push*, just use the same energy. Have a certain intensity. Here are some things you can do to warm up:

>> **Hum.** Make humming sounds, moving from a high-pitched hum to low and back to high.

>> **Make horse lips.** *Brrr* like a horse. Add some sound and go high and low. Have some vocal variety.

>> **Be Tarzan.** Pound your chest on an "Aaaa-aaa-aaah!"

>> **Be fabulous.** Put your arms up and walk around the room repeating, "I'm fabulous." You might just feel it!

>> **Wake up your face muscles.** Lightly tap all over your face.

>> **Give your face a massage.** Make sure to release your lower jaw.

>> **Be a cat.** If you're alone (or not self-conscious), try meowing. Exaggerate your jaw opening.

>> **Work your jaw.** Pretend you're chewing a mouthful of crackers; count to ten while chewing. Keep breathing!

>> **Work your lips.** Pucker up, then smile. Repeat a few times.

>> **Work your tongue.** Stick your tongue out. Draw circles with your tongue one way, then the other. Keep breathing!

>> **Try some tongue twisters.** She sells seashells down by the seashore. How much wood could a woodchuck chuck if a woodchuck could chuck wood?

>> **Pant like a dog.** Just a little. Now add a "Ha." Move up and down in pitch.

Breathe

Visualize dropping your breath deep into your lungs down into your lower abs. Breathe in through your nose for a count of four, and then out for the same. Increase your counts when you feel comfortable. Keep your body aligned with energy reaching up to the sky.

Breath of joy

Try this, inspired by yoga expert Amy Weintraub's book *Yoga Skills for Therapists* (W. W. Norton, 2012). Breathe in a third of your breath capacity while stretching your arms out in front. Then breathe another third with arms out in a *T*. Then inhale the final third of your breath with your arms up high above your head. On an exhale, open your mouth, say, "Ha," and bring your arms down while bending your knees to a standing squat. Swing the arms behind you with your palms facing up. Make sure your arms are stretched to the fullest. When they're above your head, try not to lift the shoulders up as well. Repeat this up to nine times and you should begin to feel joyful. At the very least, you'll be warmed up. When you're done, close your eyes and take note of how you feel.

WARNING

You may want to avoid this pose if you have untreated high blood pressure, head or eye injury, migraines, or glaucoma. Many of my clients feel light-headed when they do this exercise. If that happens to you, stop the exercise.

You can also try the following inspired by Patsy Rodenburg in her book Right to Speak (Routledge, 1993): Stand in alignment. As you breathe in, move your arms up into a T. Make sure your shoulders don't creep up to your ears. Allow your arms to drop down by their sides when you breathe out. Repeat this a few times. Now do it again, and when you drop your arms and breathe out, say, "Ssss," "Ffff," or, "Hmmm." Allow all the breath to exit your body with that sound. Try not to collapse your spine or create any tension when you do so. Feel the need to take a breath and then breathe in. Repeat up to five times.

Adopt a Power Pose for at Least Two Minutes

When Amy Cuddy discusses the power pose in her TED Talk, "Your Body Language Shapes Who You Are" (www.ted.com/talks/amy_cuddy_your_body_language_shapes_who_you_are), she states that adopting the pose for only two minutes can change the way you think and feel about yourself. In other words, all you have to do is look powerful, and you might start to *feel* powerful. We humans are pretty smart — sometimes we can even outsmart ourselves to our advantage. This is one of those times. With the Power Pose, you're more confident and have greater self-esteem.

How does it look? In a Power Pose, either extend your arms over your head in a *V* shape or rest your hands on your hips like Superman or Wonder Woman. It's as simple as that. Stand still and maintain that position for two minutes to really get the full effects.

TIP

If your arms are over your head, make sure your shoulders don't creep up to your ears.

You probably can't walk into the board meeting with your arms up in the air. Or maybe you can. What you definitely can do is maintain an up and out position (head atop the spine, chin up, not hunched over) *at all times,* which is also a power pose in my book.

Practice Your Speech While Doing an Unrelated Task

You want to get this speech down? You need to know it as well as you possibly can. And unless you're a billionaire, you probably have some monotonous tasks you have to do with nothing to entertain yourself while doing them.

Try this: Recite your speech while doing chores. Take out the garbage, clean the coffee machine, put those files back in their folders. Practicing this way helps you get the speech out of your head and "into" your body, so that it becomes second nature. Think muscle memory — for you brain.

Eat Healthy, Drink Water

This is overlooked so much it isn't even funny. I'd say most of my clients have okay diets. It's one of the first things I ask them about themselves: "What do you eat?" But for some reason they rarely concern themselves with their health on the day they have a presentation. One of my clients even told me he treats himself to junk food before a presentation, as a reward.

WARNING

That's a no-go. Here's the golden rule: Don't deviate from your normal eating routine, don't *not* eat, and don't get "hangry." *If* you're going to deviate, do it in a healthy way.

Protein maintains you and gives you the fuel you need.

>> Have a meal with protein and some carbs: good, complex ones like beans, lentils, or brown rice. Let that energy take its time.

>> Don't stuff yourself so that you feel like you'll have to roll onto the stage. You can eat later — for now have something small and eat smart.

>> Drink water. You don't need to drink eight glasses. Just drink enough so that you don't feel thirsty and you're well hydrated.

>> Don't drink that can of pop. It has loads of sugar, plus you'll be full of burps. You'll feel great for awhile, then you'll crash and burn.

>> Drinking milk can be iffy. It may feel like you have mucous in your throat, but really it's the texture and thickness of the milk that can cause you to clear your throat to get rid of it.

Visualize a Successful Presentation

Have you ever seen race car drivers before a race? You might see them sitting in a chair, full race gear on, visualizing every last corner they're about to zip through. These guys know everything about the course and what they can expect from the conditions. They always win in their minds. Why not take the same advice?

Before you've dressed up to speak, find a place where you can have silence and be still. Not when the kids are running around getting ready for school or when your colleagues are discussing the party last night. Find a quiet place where you can be alone.

You can sit on the floor, on a chair, on the couch. You might try some external imagery, such as watching a video of yourself. Allow your mind to think about your upcoming presentation. Think about what you're wearing. Whatever it is, it should make you feel good. Really see it on you. The shirt, jacket, pants, tie, dress, shirt, shoes. You'll feel powerful and ready to go.

The MC is reading your bio. And you know what? You've achieved a lot in your field. You're sitting and waiting while he discusses your successes.

It's time to walk up to the front of the room. You walk with purpose. You're taking slow, deep breaths. You put your speech on the lectern, take three slow breaths, and begin.

You look at the audience. You find someone who is engaged and direct your message to her for five seconds of your speech. Then you move onto someone else. You see the audience nodding in agreement and listening to what you have to say. Your slides roll easily from one to the other. Any props are well received. You're enjoying yourself!

You have ended the speech and there is applause. In the words of Sally Field when she won her Oscar, you think, "You like me, you really like me!"

The presentation has been a success and you feel great!

You can also actually go through some of the motions, mentally and physically. Walk with purpose onto the stage — maybe this is just you walking in place, maybe you're walking from one room to another. Visualize all the minutae. Is the stage smooth or is it carpeted? Put your notes on the lectern. Hear the flipping of the pages. Find the remote for the PowerPoint and click on the first slide. How big is the remote? Does it fit easily in your hand? Go through all the points of the presentation. See the audience engaging with you. Hear the applause at the end of your presentation.

Recite Your Speech Dressed in Your Presentation Clothes

You want to look good, right? Of course you do. But there's more to dressing up than just looking the part. You also have to make sure nothing you wear is inhibiting your speech.

Ask yourself some questions:

>> Do your clothes fit?

>> Can you move your arms?

>> Is your hem too high when you walk onstage?

>> Does that necklace hinder your breathing?

>> Does your tie need to be loosened?

>> Are you feeling grounded with your high heels? If not, practice with low heels, then gradually move to the ones you want to wear.

Practicing in your clothes also helps you feel more professional and ups your game.

Arrange Your Notes and Visuals

Before you step up to that lectern, you need to have everything in order. And that includes, of course, what you're going to be referring to in your whole speech. Have you ever seen speakers fumbling with their notes? Don't be one of them.

Get organized. Number the pages of your cue cards or speech and organize them in order. You really don't want to lose your place up there! Get your USB stick, or computer, for your slide show in order. Any other visuals or props should be prepared and ready.

Don't forget to put everything you need in your bag or briefcase.

Bring Water

You may be presenting at a hotel where you know it has that water jug. You ever hear of Murphy's law? What if all the water jugs need to be refilled, and that won't happen until after your presentation?

TIP

Being hydrated is the easiest and most often overlooked way to get your body into equilibrium. You *will* need water. You don't want to take a glass and go to the bathroom to fill it with water, or ask the hotel staff for some when you only have minutes to present. Pull out that handy water bottle you brought from home. You don't have to use the expensive brand name bottled water. Nowadays you can buy sleek water bottles that look really snazzy and fill them up yourself.

Arrive Early

You want to get to the venue in plenty of time to be able to check out the place and make sure everything's as it should be — and if it's not, you'll need time to fix that.

Here is your early bird checklist:

>> Introduce yourself to the organizer.

>> Were you planning to use a lectern? Is there one? Do you need to move it?

>> Are the chairs organized so that everyone can see you?

>> Is there a screen to project your visuals?

>> Is there a microphone, and will you need it? Is there a technician to help you? Who will help you if there isn't a technician?

>> Go ahead and walk on the stage if no one is using it.

>> Move to where you'll be starting your speech, and to the other areas as well. If you're really early and no one is there, go ahead and practice your presentation. The more practice you get on the stage, the more comfortable you'll feel.

Introduce Yourself

Be the early bird, as I say. But you won't be the only one. There are always a few people who feel they have come early. I have a confession: I am one of them. Even if I'm not the speaker, I like to find a decent place to park, find the venue, get a good seat. I really hate being late for anything, and being early is that antidote.

If you see a few people coming into the space early, don't despair that now you can't be alone to check out your space. You've taken my advice and got there with time to spare, and these people are doing the same. Maybe they also feel uncomfortable with the venue and wanted to give themselves tons of time to figure it out. Maybe it's a new topic or there's a speaker they're excited about. Maybe they've been there all day and come in yacking with the friends they met, or with old friends they haven't seen in a while. Either way, go over and say hi. Maybe they'll recognize you from your bio picture (unless you used the one from 20 years and 20 pounds ago — in that case, shame on you, get a new one).

The more people you connect with and establish a relationship with early on, the more comfortable you'll feel. And they'll feel a connection with you, too. Be pleasant and polite — don't complain about the technician or lack of one. They don't care and don't know. The technician may have been on a well-deserved break for all you know.

Ask them about themselves. Why are they here, what did they like about the morning session, how was the lunch? If you're from another city, ask them where you should go for dinner or what you should see while visiting. Compliment them on the flowers around City Hall or the clean streets.

REMEMBER

The more comfortable you become before your speech, the more comfortable you'll be during it.

Index

A

abdominal muscles, 65, 225, 226, 227

accents, 20, 204–206

achievements, accepting, 79–80

acoustics, 264–265

acting out stories, 132, 247

ad libbing, 315–317

adaptability, 180. *See also* improv; problems, during speech

adrenaline, 10, 34–35

affirmations, 11, 178, 267, 292, 328

age, audience, 184

air flow, role in voice, 224–226

alcohol consumption, 162, 265

Alexander Technique, 54

alignment. *See also* posture

  kinesthetic lightness, 46

  overview, 13

  relieving tension through proper, 12

  of shoulders, 239

  tension, relieving, 44–46

  warming up with, 342

aloud, practicing speech, 140–145

amplification, 207–208. *See also* resonance

analyzing script, 331–333

Anderson, Chris, 64

animating slides, 120

anxiety. *See also* performance anxiety, overcoming; stage fright, overcoming; tension

  calming through breathing, 230–231

  effect of caffeine on, 163

  fight, flight, or freeze response, 10–11, 34–37, 53–55

  related to slide use, 107

  symptoms of fear, 30

  voice, effect on, 50–53

aphorisms, 62

apologies, avoiding, 26, 187–188, 313

argumenting to support point, 90–93

arriving early, for speech, 347–348

articulation

  accents, improving clarity for, 204–206

  articulators, 192–197

  defined, 191

  honing, 199–204

  mumbling, 197–199

  overview, 20–21, 191–192

  singing, 204

  tongue twisters, 199, 200–201

  voicing vowels and consonants, 199, 201–203

  when filling space with voice, 265

  when increasing volume, 228

asking question, as hook, 88

athletes, tension in, 44

attention

  grabbing, 87–90

  role in art of conversation, 299

attire. *See* dressing for public speaking

audibility, checking before speech, 263

audience

  addressing one person in, 186–187

  apologizing to, 26, 187–188, 313

  connecting to, 270

  considering when choosing point, 87

  dealing with, 23–24

  demographics of, 184–185

  engaged member, focusing on, 328–329

  engagement, 19, 135, 187

  expectations of, 183–184

  explaining business to, 101

  flip charts, engaging with, 121

  focusing on, 182–188

  goals regarding, 183

  hecklers, dealing with, 24, 189

  honing speech for, 332

  hooking, 87–90, 332

  humor, tailoring to, 126, 128, 133

  importance of topic to, 186

  level of knowledge of, 185

  looking at, to correct devoicing, 64

reacting to problems with, 314

rule of three, 129

self-deprecating, 131–132

as serious business, 124

tension, reducing with, 137

tips for using, 124–125, 128–129

writing stories and jokes, 125–128

hunger, effects of, 165

hydration, 162–163, 345

hypernasality, 66

hyponasality, 66

I

"I," using in speech, 100

iceberg theory, 99

icons, explained, 4

illness, on day of speech, 309

illustration step, PIE method, 92, 333

imagery, visualizing using, 267–268

Imes, Suzanne, 74

impostor syndrome

being yourself, 79–81

criticism, reacting to, 75

diagnosing yourself with, 74

overview, 39, 73–74

progress, recognizing, 76

reasons for, 76–79

improv, 38, 86, 315–317

improvement, acknowledging need for, 75

in and down position, 13, 53–55, 64, 154, 285

incompetence, stages of, 260

industry, researching, 278–280

inflection, marking up speech for, 149

information overload, 75

informing, as purpose of speeches, 19, 182

inhaling, 65

intensity, marking up speech for, 148

intention, setting personal, 268

interests, in art of conversation, 298

internal visualization, 11–12, 267

interviews

body language during, 280–282

checking out interviewers, 280

competition for job, 287

dressing for, 286

faking it till you're making it, 284–285

getting questions in advance, 283

greeting greeter, 292–293

looking like you already work there, 286

lying in, reasons to avoid, 284

narrative for, building, 276–278

overview, 275

by phone, 290–291

positive use of words during, 285–286

posture during, 285

public speaking techniques for, 282–289

question and answer portion, 288–289

research before, 278–280

showing what you add to company, 283–284

talking about yourself, practicing, 277

tips for, 24–25

visualization for, 286–287

vulnerability, revealing, 289

warming up for, 291–292

winding up, 293

intonation, correcting, 60–62

intrinsic muscles, 194

introductions

personal, 296, 348

to speech, 19

Isaacson, Walter, 108

italics, 105

J

Jacobson, Edmond, 12

jaw

aligning and creating space in, 217

articulators, 192–193

releasing, for resonance, 216–217

jewelry, 258, 271

job interviews. *See* interviews

Jobs, Steve, 108

jokes. *See also* humor

avoiding telling audience about, 129

comedy notebook, keeping, 128

commitment to telling, 124–125

cringe-inducing, avoiding, 134–135

honing delivery, 332

R

rate of speech, marking up speech for, 149

reading
  audience, 187, 242–245
  lists, 151
  out loud, when composing speech, 97–98
  slides, 114, 115
  speech, avoiding, 154–156

recording speech
  to beat impostor syndrome, 78
  to check for filler words, 154
  commanding crowd exercise, 63
  delivery, honing, 337–338
  dressing for camera, 256
  humor, honing, 136
  to measure progress, 76
  when practicing, 145–147

refined sugar consumption, 160–161

rehearsing. *See* practicing speech; preparation for speech

relaxation. *See also* tension
  progressive, 12, 325
  versus releasing tension, 48

relaxed talking, visualizing, 206

releasing tension, 47–49

Remember icon, explained, 4

reprogramming brain. *See* brain, reprogramming

resonance
  chanting exercise, 219
  chest, 217–218, 220
  finding, 212
  humming exercises, 211, 215–216
  jaw, releasing, 216–217
  knowing your voice, 209–210
  lip trills, 216
  nasal cavities, 214
  oral, 215
  overview, 21, 207
  pitch, relation to, 235
  reasons to study, 208–209
  relaxing neck, 212–213
  resonators, 207–208, 211, 214–215
  soft palate exercise, 213
  throat, 211–212, 214
  upper, 218–219, 220

resting, before speech, 266

rhetorical questions, 105, 153

ribs, moving when breathing, 229

Rivers, Joan, 128

Rodenburg, Patsy, 46, 219, 269

rule of three, for humor, 129

running, as cardio exercise, 166–167

running out of breath, 228–229

Rush, Lyndon, 267

rush, resisting urge to, 151

S

sacrum, exercise for, 170

Schumer, Amy, 89

script. *See* speeches

security, calling over hecklers, 189

self-confidence, building
  gratitude, 176–177
  overview, 176
  positive self-talk, 178–180

self-deprecating humor, 127, 131–132

self-doubt. *See* impostor syndrome

self-talk, positive, 38–39, 178–180, 267, 304, 327

sense of humor, figuring out, 127–128. *See also* humor

sentences
  filling in blanks in, 315–316
  pausing after, 152
  singing, 204
  stating point in, 87
  varying breath for, 230
  walking, 157

Shakespeare, William, 130

shaky voice, 51

shallow breathing, 50, 228

Shewell, Christina, 225

shoes, 256–257, 262

short vowels, 201–202

shortening speech, 150

shoulders
  aligning, 239
  exercises for tension in, 168–169

shouting, 211–212

show, don't tell technique, 98–99, 110

show must go on attitude, 309–310

show time, tips for, 266–270

About the Author

Alyson Connolly, BFA, MFA, is a voice and public speaking coach and an expert in helping people overcome the anxiety of public presentations. She has built her career consulting with some of the top executives in Canada as well as up-and-coming business people trying to build their brand.

She received a master's degree in theater voice pedagogy from the University of Alberta in Canada. Her thesis was "Alleviating Performance Anxiety in Public Presenters." She offers her Painless Public Speaking Workshops and Elite Presentation Skills Master Classes to organizations and also coaches individuals one-on-one. She works with speakers who are good but want to be great, those whose accents get in the way of their clarity, and those who would rather die than speak in public.

Alyson began her career as a professional actor on the stages of Western Canada after earning her BFA in acting at the University of Alberta. She brings to her work 30 years of experience teaching drama, directing plays and musicals, and performing onstage. She is also a keynote speaker herself, presenting the story of her life through a difficult childhood to overcoming her fear onstage, as well as speaking about public speaking.

Her website is www.alysonconnolly.com. On Twitter she's @alysonjconnolly, and on Facebook she's Alyson Connolly Voice and Public Speaking Coach.

Author's Acknowledgments

When I first received an email from Tracy Boggier, I actually thought it was spam. I was a vocal coach from Canada. Why the heck would anyone from the Dummies group want to contact me? The only thing I'd written up to that point was a thesis, some business proposals, and blogs.

Tracy, thanks for the opportunity. I enjoyed the process. It made surviving the cold winter in Canada go by quickly.

Thanks to the following people, because without their help this book wouldn't be what it is:

My husband Mark, who with his Yes Let's and "You can do it!" attitude encouraged me all the way.

My sons: Patrick, who often cast a critical and welcome eye on my manuscript, and Jack, who supported my mental health on the days when I needed a break from writing. "Mom, want a coffee?"

Beth Dunbar, my first speech teacher, who instilled in me a passion for speech.

Professors Betty Moulton and David Ley, whose wealth of knowledge guided me through my master's degree.

Dr. Derek Truscott, for his positive suggestions regarding my thesis.

Dawn Sadoway, technical editor, and my fellow voice pedagogue who asked a lot of tough questions.

Corbin Collins, editor extraordinaire, for keeping me on task in a kind, gentle way.

Tracy Boggier, senior acquisitions editor, for giving me the opportunity to write this book.

Others who made big contributions:

Dr. Robyn Fowler

Margot Ross-Graham

Valerie Planche

Elaine Dunbar

Chelaine Kerr

Glenn McEown

All of my clients, who teach me every time I work with them and challenge me to become a better coach.

Thank you all!

Publisher's Acknowledgments

Senior Acquisitions Editor: Tracy Boggier

Editor: Corbin Collins

Technical Editor: Dawn Sadoway

Production Editor: Magesh Elangovan

Cover Photo: © Caiaimage/Agnieszka Olek/ Getty Images

PERSONAL ENRICHMENT

Staying Sharp dummies
9781119187790
USA $26.00
CAN $31.99
UK £19.99

Facebook dummies
Carolyn Abram
9781119179030
USA $21.99
CAN $25.99
UK £16.99

Guitar dummies
Mark Phillips
Jon Chappell
9781119293354
USA $24.99
CAN $29.99
UK £17.99

Investing dummies
Eric Tyson, MBA
9781119293347
USA $22.99
CAN $27.99
UK £16.99

Beekeeping dummies
Howland Blackiston
9781119310068
USA $22.99
CAN $27.99
UK £16.99

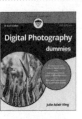

Digital Photography dummies
Julie Adair King
9781119235606
USA $24.99
CAN $29.99
UK £17.99

Meditation dummies
Stephan Bodian
9781119251163
USA $24.99
CAN $29.99
UK £17.99

Pregnancy ALL-IN-ONE dummies
9781119235491
USA $26.99
CAN $31.99
UK £19.99

Samsung Galaxy S7 dummies
Bill Hughes
9781119279952
USA $24.99
CAN $29.99
UK £17.99

iPhone dummies
Edward C. Baig
Bob "Dr. Mac" LeVitus
9781119283133
USA $24.99
CAN $29.99
UK £17.99

Crocheting dummies
Karen Manthey
Susan Brittain
9781119287117
USA $24.99
CAN $29.99
UK £16.99

Nutrition dummies
Carol Ann Rinzler
9781119130246
USA $22.99
CAN $27.99
UK £16.99

PROFESSIONAL DEVELOPMENT

Windows 10 dummies
Andy Rathbone
9781119311041
USA $24.99
CAN $29.99
UK £17.99

AutoCAD dummies
Bill Fane
9781119255796
USA $39.99
CAN $47.99
UK £27.99

Excel 2016 dummies
Greg Harvey, PhD
9781119293439
USA $26.99
CAN $31.99
UK £19.99

QuickBooks 2017 dummies
Stephen L. Nelson, MBA, CPA, MS in Taxation
9781119281467
USA $26.99
CAN $31.99
UK £19.99

macOS Sierra dummies
Bob "Dr. Mac" LeVitus
9781119280651
USA $29.99
CAN $35.99
UK £21.99

LinkedIn dummies
Joel Elad, MBA
9781119251132
USA $24.99
CAN $29.99
UK £17.99

Windows 10 ALL-IN-ONE dummies
Woody Leonhard
9781119310563
USA $34.00
CAN $41.99
UK £24.99

SharePoint 2016 dummies
Rosemarie Withee
Ken Withee
9781119181705
USA $29.99
CAN $35.99
UK £21.99

Fundamental Analysis dummies
Matt Krantz
9781119263593
USA $26.99
CAN $31.99
UK £19.99

Networking dummies
Doug Lowe
9781119257769
USA $29.99
CAN $35.99
UK £21.99

Office 2016 dummies
Wallace Wang
9781119293477
USA $26.99
CAN $31.99
UK £19.99

Office 365 dummies
Rosemarie Withee
Ken Withee
Jennifer Reed
9781119265313
USA $24.99
CAN $29.99
UK £17.99

Salesforce.com dummies
Liz Kao
Jon Paz
9781119239314
USA $29.99
CAN $35.99
UK £21.99

Coding dummies
Nikhil Abraham
9781119293323
USA $29.99
CAN $35.99
UK £21.99